Dubai: Behind an Urban Spectacle

Planning, History and Environment Series

Published titles

Selling Places: The marketing and promotion of towns and cities, 1850–2000 by Stephen V. Ward

Changing Suburbs: Foundation, form and function edited by Richard Harris and Peter Larkham

The Australian Metropolis: A planning history edited by Stephen Hamnett and Robert Freestone

Utopian England: Community experiments 1900–1945 by Dennis Hardy

Urban Planning in a Changing World: The twentieth century experience edited by Robert Freestone

Twentieth-Century Suburbs: A morphological approach by J.W.R. Whitehand and C.M.H. Carr

Council Housing and Culture: The history of a social experiment by Alison Ravetz

Planning Latin America's Capital Cities, 1850–1950 edited by Arturo Almandoz

Exporting American Architecture, 1870–2000 by Jeffrey W. Cody

Planning by Consent: The origins and nature of British development control by Philip Booth

The Making and Selling of Post-Mao Beijing by Anne-Marie Broudehoux

Planning Middle Eastern Cities: An urban kaleidoscope in a globalizing world edited by Yasser Elsheshtawy

Globalizing Taipei: The political economy of spatial development edited by Reginald Yin-Wang Kwok

New Urbanism and American Planning: The conflict of cultures by Emily Talen

Remaking Chinese Urban Form: Modernity, scarcity and space, 1949–2005 by Duanfang Lu

Planning Twentieth Century Capital Cities edited by David L.A. Gordon

Olympic Cities: City agendas, planning, and the world's games, 1896–2012 edited by John R. Gold and Margaret M. Gold

Planning the Megacity: Jakarta in the twentieth century by Christopher Silver

Designing Australia's Cities: Culture, commerce and the city beautiful, 1900–1930 by Robert Freestone

Titles published 2008

Ordinary Places, Extraordinary Events: Citizenship, democracy and urban space in Latin America edited by Clara Irazábal

The Evolving Arab City: Tradition, modernity and urban development edited by Yasser Elsheshtawy

Titles published 2009

Stockholm: The making of a metropolis by Thomas Hall

Dubai: Behind an urban spectacle by Yasser Elsheshtawy

DUBAI
Behind an Urban Spectacle

Yasser Elsheshtawy

Routledge
Taylor & Francis Group

LONDON AND NEW YORK

First published in 2010
by Routledge
2 Park Square, Milton Park, Abingdon, Oxfordshire OX14 4RN

Simultaneously published in the US and Canada
by Routledge
270 Madison Avenue, New York, NY 10016

Routledge is an imprint of the Taylor & Francis Group, an informa business

Typeset in Aldine and Swiss by PNR Design, Didcot
Printed and bound in Great Britain by TJ International Ltd, Padstow, Cornwall

This book was commissioned and edited by Alexandrine Press, Marcham, Oxfordshire

British Library Cataloguing in Publication Data
A catalogue record of this book is available from the British Library

Library of Congress Cataloging in Publication Data
Dubai : behind an urban spectacle / Yasser Elsheshtawy.
p. cm. — (Planning, history and environment)
Includes bibliographical references and index.
1. Dubayy (United Arab Emirates : Emirate)—History. 2. Dubayy (United Arab Emirates :
Emirate)—Economic conditions. 3. Urbanization—United Arab Emirates—Dubayy
(Emirate)—History. 4. Economic development projects—United Arab Emirates—Dubayy
(Emirate)—History. 5. City planning—United Arab Emirates—Dubayy (Emirate) 6. Dubayy
(United Arab Emirates : Emirate)—Pictorial works. I. Title.
DS247.D78E57 2010
953.57--dc22
2009013196

ISBN10: 0–415–44461–6 (hbk)
ISBN10: 0–203–86970–2 (ebk)

ISBN13: 978–0–415–44461–3 (hbk)
ISBN13: 978–0–203–86970–3 (ebk)

Contents

Preface

The first inkling for an international interest in Dubai as an urban phenomenon, worthy of serious scholarly attention, came during the 2003 workshop organized by Harvard's Graduate School of Design, dubbed 'Dubai Conglomerated: The urban planning and design challenges of building a city of many cities'. Invitees included a multitude of 'stakeholders' who had a vested interest in discussing the city: political scientists, government officials, hoteliers, anthropologists and, of course, architects and planners. I was assigned the task of presenting an architectural overview. Rather than merely introducing a picturesque portrayal of the city's buildings – which I did – I also began to contextualize its buildings which in turn opened an area of investigation which led me to examine the city's 'hidden urban spaces'[1] and to go beyond/behind its spectacular architecture. The outcome is this book which was preceded by many years of painstaking research and fieldwork supported in large part by a 2003 research grant from the UAE University Research Council who deserve a special recognition as do my colleagues at the Department of Architecture, headed by Ramy El Diasty. His encouragement throughout these years was always helpful. I also would like to acknowledge the *International Journal of Urban and Regional Research* and *Architectural Theory Review* which published earlier and much shorter versions of Chapters 7 and 8 (see, Elsheshtawy, 2008c and 2008d).

There were many individuals and institutions whose help has been invaluable not only in sharpening my inquiry but also in broadening my research questions and enabling me to share my research and observations with a wider audience. They include: the Holcim Research Foundation from Switzerland and particularly Mark Angelil; Hashim Sarkis at the Graduate School of Design, Harvard University; the United Nation's Economic and Social Commission of Western Asia (UN-ESCWA); Notre Dame University in Lebanon, especially Jean Pierre Al-Asmar; Martina Rieker at the American University in Cairo; the Virginia Commonwealth University in Doha; Maysa Sabah and Rachelle Levitt from the Urban Land Institute, Washington DC; and especially Nezar AlSayyad and the International Association for the Study of Traditional Environments (IASTE), at the University of California, Berkeley and the Aga Khan Award for Architecture, directed by Farrokh Derakhshani.

In Dubai, I would like to thank Dubai Municipality for sharing their information and for the discussions held with various officials, in particular

Rashad Bukhash, Head of the Department for Historical Buildings and Iman Al Assi, Conservation Expert. My special thanks go also to Mohsen Abou El Naga, founder of the Emirates Green Building Council and currently advisor to the Office of the UAE Prime Minister. I also would like to thank some of my former students. In particular, Khaled Al Awadi, who introduced me to the traditional neighborhood of Satwa, and allowed me to gain a local perspective and Marei Al Zouabi whose drawings appear in this book.

I should also mention Jill and Mark Harris for allowing me to access some of the historical records of John Harris, who developed Dubai's first master plan and is architect of its first iconic building – the World Trade Center. Their stories and memories of Dubai provided a much needed grounding of the city – and showed me that it is not simply an overnight phenomena. I also would like to thank Ann Rudkin for her painstaking editing, for sorting and organizing my references, and especially her patience while receiving my various drafts and constantly shifting deadlines were admirable!

There were many journalists, artists, and writers whose interest in the city led to various insightful meetings and discussions: Peter Waldenberger from ORF (Austrian public radio); Beate Anspach and Silke Wagner from the Heidelberg Kunstverein; Jason Fulford and Hernan Diaz writing for *Harper's*; and Can Altay and Philippe Missellewitz organizers of the 'refuge city' exhibition at the International Architectural Biennale in Rotterdam (2009). In addition the following (some formerly) PhD students should be mentioned: Nadine Scharfenort, Universty of Vienna; Elizabeth Schein, Technical University-Munich; Behzad Sarmadi, University of Toronto; Ahmed Kanna, Stephen Ramos and Gareth Doherty from Harvard University.

Lastly I would like to thank the wonderful, multi-cultural folks at Starbucks, Jumeirah (Dubai) for allowing me to spend countless hours in their shop, writing, reading, consuming endless amounts of coffee, meeting people – and turning the place into a virtual office!

Note

1. Further information about my investigation into Dubai's hidden spaces, and a complement of sorts to the book, can be found at: www.sheshtawy.org/hidden.htm.

Yasser Elsheshtawy
Al-Ain, UAE
June, 2009

At times all I need is a brief glimpse, an opening in the midst of an incongruous landscape, a glint of light in the fog, the dialogue of two passersby meeting in the crowd, and I think that, setting out from there, I will put together, piece by piece, **the perfect city, made of fragments mixed with the rest, of instants separated by intervals***, of signals one sends out, not knowing who receives them. If I tell you that the city toward which my journey tends is discontinuous in space and time, now scattered, now more condensed,* **you must not believe the search for it can stop***. Perhaps while we speak, it is rising, scattered, within the confines of your empire.*

The inferno of the living is not something that will be; if there is one, it is what is already here, the inferno where we live every day, that we form by being together. There are two ways to escape suffering it. The first is easy for many: accept the inferno and become such a part of it that you can no longer see it. The second is risky and demands constant vigilance and apprehension: **seek and learn to recognize who and what, in the midst of the inferno, are not inferno, then make them endure, give them space***.*

Marco Polo talking to Kublai Khan (my emphasis)
Italo Calvino, *Invisible Cities*, pp. 164–165

Chapter 1

The Emerging Urbanity of Dubai

*'... In that Empire, the craft of Cartography attained such Perfection that the Map of
a Single province covered the space of an entire City, and the Map of the Empire itself
an entire Province. In the course of Time, these Extensive maps were found somehow
wanting, and so the College of Cartographers evolved a Map of the Empire that was of the
same Scale as the Empire and that coincided with it point for point. Less attentive to the
Study of Cartography, succeeding Generations came to judge a map of such Magnitude
cumbersome, and, not without Irreverence, they abandoned it to the Rigours of sun
and Rain. In the western Deserts, tattered Fragments of the Map are still to be found,
Sheltering an occasional Beast or beggar; in the whole Nation, no other relic is left of the
Discipline of Geography.'*

'Of Exactitude in Science' from *Travels of Praiseworthy Men* (1658)
by J.A. Suarez Miranda (Borges, 1975)

The above fantasy tale is cited when making a case that the representation takes on
the dimensions of reality to the point of replacing it. French theorist Jean Baudrillard
(1995) uses the story as a metaphor for his notion of the simulacrum; he suggests
that it is the map that people live in, the simulation of reality, and it is reality that
is crumbling away from disuse. One could argue that the city of Dubai is perhaps
the ultimate realization of this vision. Our perception of the city is to a large degree
shaped by representations in the media. Opinions are formed based on what is
presented to us. Thus, Dubai is a city of islands shaped like palm trees, a sail-like
hotel, Pharaonic temples used as shopping malls, and the list goes on (figure 1.1).
This representation becomes in the mind of many a Borgesian reality – this is the
true Dubai. Actual visits are merely used to confirm such views.[1] But if one were
to look beyond this seemingly naïve view of the city, a different picture emerges.
Dubai is not merely composed of megaprojects; it certainly is not a fake or artificial
city – observing its everyday life shows a place full of aspirations, struggles, and
encounters taking place in all sorts of settings. It is also a unique, unprecedented
urban experiment. No other city houses more than 200 nationalities, nor is there
one whose native population represents less than 10 per cent of its residents. Such
a situation has created a unique urban condition which cannot be explored by
looking only at its spectacular projects and urban developments; one must move
into its lesser known spaces, hidden in the alleyways and streets of Deira and

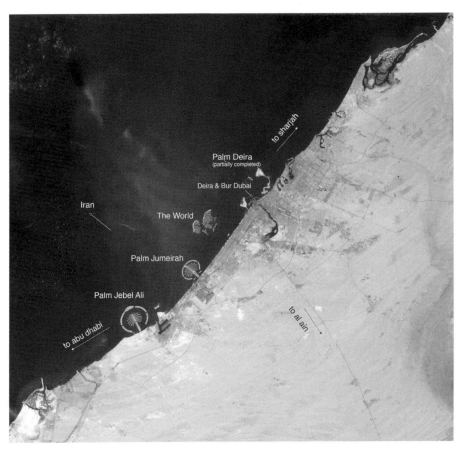

1.1. Satellite view of Dubai in 2006. (By courtesy of NASA)

1.2. The teeming alleyways of Meena Bazaar.

Bur Dubai – its 'traditional' neighbourhoods from where the city originated and grew (figure 1.2). Here the true Dubai emerges which is not a representation or a fake reality. My aim in this book is to uncover and reveal these spaces, which I believe constitute the essence of the city and where its unique urban experiment is expressed spatially.

Aside from uncovering the real city, why should we be concerned with Dubai in the first place? It is not a great city – not in the sense that London, New York or Paris are great cities. These constitute our urban imaginary, the model that all those seeking global stature must aspire to. Their symbols of urbanity are a source of emulation all over the world – gleaming high-rises, quaint or ethnic neighbour-hoods, and fancy restaurants. So, what lessons could possibly be learned from Dubai? To wit, the reasons – usually cited in this context – could be summarized as follows: it is an Arab success story, an example of successful urbanization that has eluded other parts of the region; it is also a good model for transnational urbanism, i.e. the degree to which, seemingly, it has been able to integrate various ethnic groups in a multi-cultural setting (labour camps notwithstanding). And it also has become a source of great influence in the region – to the extent that the so-called Dubai model became an actual term, connoting the exportability of its particular mode of development. I discuss these characteristics throughout the course of the book. They are debatable of course – some may not even be true – but they do constitute the reasons why there is such a fascination with the city.

One particularly potent argument is that there is, among many observers, a strong belief that the centre of power has shifted to the East. Moving away from the crumbling, perhaps even decaying, urban centres of the West, new centres are emerging. These can be found not only in China's burgeoning urban conglomerates such as Shanghai, Shenzhen or Beijing, but also in Singapore, Hong Kong, Kuala Lumpur, Mumbai and, of course, Dubai.[2] A passing visit through any of their newly-built airports shows a dramatic contrast to their European counterparts. Their newly-built city centres are shining examples of societies in transformation. Dubai is positioning itself as a gateway between these newly emerging centres of the East and the West, a 'crucial staging post in the shift in economic power from the west to emerging Asia'.[3] Its mode of urbanism is a response to this positioning. All of this illustrates the importance of examining developments taking place in Dubai, particularly in the light of the recent economic slowdown and the extent to which it has affected the city. This has shown the degree to which Dubai has become integrated in the global economic system – more than anywhere else in the region.

In this introductory chapter, I present the book's scope and provide a summary of its chapters. I conclude by discussing the global financial crisis and its impact on the city of Dubai – leading some observers in the media, but also in academic circles,[4] to proclaim the city's demise. But, to parody Mark Twain, reports about Dubai's death have been greatly exaggerated. In fact such views are expressed because the city is exclusively viewed through a Borgesian lens. Thus, this book is not just about the city's megaprojects. I am going behind them – as implied in the title – digging deeper, uncovering Dubai's multiple layers, in the process hoping to reveal a *real* city, whose urbanity has the potential to be a viable model for urbanism in the twenty-first century.

The Scope of the Book

It could be argued that Dubai's transformation is unprecedented in the history of urban development – perhaps rivalled only by China. Its megaprojects have become a source of debate, argument and, most importantly, an influence throughout the region and the world. Dubai is a city attempting to become a global player, competing with cities in the Southeast Asian region, for example. Here comparisons are made with Hong Kong and Singapore among others. Conventional modes of discourse attempt to understand the 'Dubai phenomenon' by critiquing its fragmentation, polarization and quartering of urban space. Analogies are drawn to other world cities where such issues have been widely debated and cited as evidence for the drawbacks of globalization and its impact on urban form. Yet Dubai is quite unique in that it does not have a conventional historical core, or a conventional population make-up. Situated in the desert it is, seemingly, a *tabula rasa* allowing it to become a laboratory where various urban experiments are being carried out. Moreover its transient population, drawn from all over the world, has created a unique mix where the boundaries between local, Arab, and expatriate have been challenged. Its cultural landscape has seemingly blurred the distinctions of East/West, orient/occident, colonial/post-colonial, etc. Yet a closer examination reveals a movement towards segregation and fragmentation, a 'post-urban' centre resulting in a unique mix of urban spaces. All of this is accelerated and heightened by a perceived absence of a historical burden.

As noted, I am arguing that a new form of urbanity is emerging in Dubai. Fuelled by a unique adaptation of neoliberal economic policies, a series of urban spaces are created which cater for a wide range of social groups. In that same vein, its 'traditional' centres are transformed to cater for the forces of capital flow. Its urban form is moving away from the old concentric city model and is constituted as a series of decentralized neighbourhoods or fragments. My examination of the city's urban development, which stretches back to the turn of the last century, is admittedly an ambitious task. I began this investigation with the following preliminary questions:

♦   What are the economic factors/policies driving this urban growth? To what extent do these policies relate to the globalization of the world economy, and the flow of capital?

♦   To what extent do these policies relate to the megaprojects and free zones spread throughout the city? How do these projects relate to global developments?

◆   Where is Dubai situated within the global network of cities?

◆   What are the various forms of urbanity emerging in the city? Are conventional notions of place, identity, history and heritage challenged and re-constituted to respond to local as well as global conditions?

◆   Aside from the city's much cited mega-developments are there are any other settings that may offer lessons for urban growth and development?

In addressing these questions the book is grounded in a historical discourse, exploring the city's origin from a small fishing village to its current state. Relying on historical narratives, travel writing, and archival media accounts, I attempt to visualize the city's development, moving it from what is typically a factual and remote depiction. By looking, for example, at the descriptions of travellers, a subjective dimension can be added which will be a closer approximation of the city's character and the extent to which changes have affected its citizens. In that same vein, I include my own personal experiences and encounters in the city to add another subjective reading – or layer – to the narrative.

Further, I draw on urban theory to understand the extent to which the city is an approximation of, or a deviation from, contemporary theoretical constructs. The global city construct is usually taken for granted as a starting point in assessing the city's development. Yet it has been subjected to criticism on a historical basis (e.g. Abu-Lughod, 1995); others have argued that the notion of a global city may not be a very useful concept for all cities and that we need to establish differences rather than similarities between cities (e.g. Peter Smith, 2002; Ley, 2004). To understand the parameters of this debate, I provide a critical review of the literature starting with the origination of the global (or world) city concept, the notion of 'space of flows' – an abstract space through which global cities supposedly interact – and the outcome of a 'splintered' urban form (Friedmann and Wolff, 1982; Friedmann, 1986; Sassen, 2001; Castells, 2000; Graham and Marvin, 2001). The work of Michael Peter Smith, David Ley and others, who have subjected the 'Global City' construct to serious criticism, is reviewed and their approach employed as a basis for a critical examination of Dubai. I also use the writings of Guy Debord and his notion of the urban spectacle as being symptomatic of modern life, and Marc Augé's argument that super-modern cities are characterized by non-places, to see whether these characterizations could be applied to Dubai (Debord, 1967, 1995; Augé, 1995). It is through such an analysis that I hope to overcome both the 'hype' of Dubai's success and the 'myth' of its artificiality.

Existing Literature

While there is an overabundance of journalistic accounts, there is a dearth of academic studies dealing with the city's urban development. Exceptions exist and they range from the mildly ironic – a piece titled 'Let's build a palm island' by Mattias Jumeno (2004), to the descriptive – Roland Marchal's (2005) examination of Dubai as a global city – and the critical, exemplified by the work of anthropologist Ahmed Kanna (2005), who looked at the *utopian* image of Dubai. The last is admittedly a rarity. There are some scholarly articles dealing with Dubai in the context of other world cities, for example Benton-Short's *et al.* (2005) article on migrant cities. My chapter on Dubai in a book on Middle Eastern cities, provides a general overview of the city's development, with a particular focus on two projects – the Palm Island and the Burj Al-Arab hotel. I have also written two chapters examining Dubai's influence in the region (Elsheshtawy, 2006, 2009) and have examined the city's retail landscape and its hidden spaces in two papers (Elsheshtawy, 2008*a*, 2008*b*).

There are no books on the city's urban development with the exception of an excellent geographical analysis by Erhard Gabriel from the Ahrensburg Institute of Applied Economic Geography. Published in 1987 the book is of 'historical' value, given that since that time the city has changed rapidly. Other books on Dubai deal with it from an historical (Wilson, 1999; Kazim, 2000), political (Davidson, 2005, 2008), or economic perspective (Sampler and Eigner, 2003). A recently published book by political scientist Waleed Hazbun (2008) sheds light on the role of tourism in the region, Dubai included, and the extent to which it is promoting both economic globalization and political authoritarianism. One curious book is an edited collection by well known urbanist Mike Davis and Daniel Bertrand Monk, portraying Dubai as an 'evil paradise' (Davis and Monk, 2008). Davis's chapter in the book relies to a large degree on rumour and is based on a previously published article (Davis, 2005). It plays on the author's thesis about neoliberal developments and simply repeats various accusations hurled at the city while failing to uncover the complex factors at work.

This dearth of academic works, particularly any that examine the city's urban development, plays into a common stereotype that cities such as Dubai are not worthy of serious academic study – except perhaps to make a point about artificiality or outlandish spending. In this view the city is conceived as an artificial creation and that it will somehow disappear after the oil dries up (which partially explains some commentators glee at the city's struggles due to the current world financial crisis). Yet while academics are still trying to catch up with the city's developments, the popular press and various serious articles are pointing out that these developments are worthy of study and need to be carefully examined.

The Structure of the Book

In structuring the book I wanted to offer the reader, at the outset, both a theoretical introduction and a visual overview of the city, setting the stage for the discussions that follow. Thus, Chapter 2 is a theoretical review where I situate Dubai within the current discussion about globalization, in the process examining and defining theoretical constructs which I use throughout the book. It sets the tone for the discussions that follow. The visual overview is provided in Chapter 3. Chapters 4 to 8 discuss the case of Dubai in detail by presenting a brief historical overview, a discussion of its urban development and the role of its iconic projects in this regard. A series of case studies illustrates some of the constructs developed in the theoretical framework, setting them within the context of the city's urban development. In a process of contextualizing the focus will shift from a macro to a micro view – the main locus of the book – by studying the city's low-income areas, home to its migrant community. I conclude by discussing the influence of Dubai on the wider Middle East, where I will debate the merit, or lack thereof, of the Dubai model. A brief summary of each chapter is provided below.

As I noted, Chapters 2 and 3 set the stage for understanding the Dubai phenomenon. In Chapter 2 (Arab Cities and Globalization) I situate the city within the wider debate about globalization by examining the term and identifying its various dimensions, focusing in particular on its social and cultural aspects. The ramifications of these globalizing processes as they relate to the Arab city are also discussed. This theoretical prelude is used as a framework for critiquing the Dubai project. Chapter 3 (The Other Dubai: A Photo Essay) provides the reader with a general overview of the city, focusing not so much on its widely circulated images but on some of its hidden spaces and buildings. In that way an attempt is made to move away from a touristic view of the city, and to offer through these images a critical narrative of transience and resistance. The focus is on the interaction between the built environment, exemplified by buildings and urban spaces, and the people using these settings, showing how they both influence and are a backdrop for human activity. In that way the city is humanized and the stage is set for a more thorough examination.

In Chapter 4 (The Illusive History of Dubai) I place the city within its historical context, focusing in particular on its urban development. This is an historical and political narrative, examining the city's origin and the extent to which its growth was strongly tied to political developments in the region and covers roughly the timeframe of its first appearance as a settlement (1822) to its transformation into a modern city as a result of the discovery of oil in the mid 1960s. Personal narratives and travel accounts form the third and fourth part with the aim of offering a history and an account of the city's urban life, and the extent to which it was transformed from a small fishing village to a modern metropolis. Here the accounts rely on personal biographies, historical photographs, and turn-of-the century travel accounts. Other archival sources are also included.

Chapter 5 (The Transformation of Dubai or Towards the Age of Mega-structures) focuses on the transformation of the city which occurred between 1960 and the present day, providing a general macro view. The first two parts discuss the city's urban development and its Masterplan, establishing main zones of growth, which was subsequently replaced by a Structural Plan giving the authorities more freedom in locating megaprojects. Recognizing Dubai's unique social make-up, the third part provides a survey of the city's social zones, through a social-geography analysis – trying to show the extent to which development is guided by a seemingly segregatory policy – poor vs. rich, local vs. expatriate etc. I also look at the city's morphology and the resulting urban form. I conclude this chapter by focusing on real estate and architectural strategies and the extent to which they are playing a major role in establishing Dubai as a global city.

I review the much discussed megaprojects in Chapter 6 (Spectacular Architecture and Urbanism). My focus is on three projects: the Burj Al Arab hotel, the Jumeirah Palm Island and the Burj Dubai. My aim is to show that the city is trying, through such iconic developments to establish significance and in turn be recognized as a major global centre. The discussion of these cases is preceded by a review of the theory of spectacle and the extent to which the use of iconic buildings and projects has become a defining feature of world cities. The relevance and sustainability of such undertakings is discussed to provide a critical assessment.

Chapter 7 (The Spectacular and the Everyday: Dubai's Retail Landscape) focuses on the city's retail landscape. Dubai is a city primarily defined by its commercial character, as can be seen in the proliferation of various kinds of themed shopping malls and the staging of 'spectacular' events such as the Dubai Shopping Festival. Yet alternative spaces of consumption do exist, slipping between the cracks of the carefully maintained image of the city. I uncover these hidden spaces of consumption and contrast them with the city's spectacular retail spaces. My critique is based on a problematization of the Debordian spectacle construct – discussed in the preceding chapter – and its applicability within a modern metropolis. The increased emphasis on exclusive developments within Dubai suggests the potential danger of such spectacular modes of urbanism.

Seeking to uncover a hidden side of Dubai, Chapter 8 (Transient City: Dubai's Forgotten Urban Spaces) investigates the city's forgotten urban spaces. This is in response to a shift in global city research, emphasizing the everyday, as well as transnational connections in which both the local and the global are closely intertwined. I argue that such processes can be observed in these 'forgotten' settings used by Dubai's low-income migrant community for the exchange of information as well as being a major gathering point. Through an analysis of users, their activities as well as the morphology of these spaces, I situate them within the overall development of Dubai. A key construct developed in this chapter, and used as a unit of analysis, is the notion of transitory sites, viewed as a key element in understanding migrant cities.

Among Middle Eastern cities Dubai – for better or worse – has become a prime source for emulation, to the extent that words such as 'the Dubai model' and 'Dubaization' are entering scholarly discourse. At a more popular level, the word Dubai is synonymous with unabashed consumerism. In the final chapter (Global Dubai or *Dubaization*), I focus specifically on Dubai's influence. To understand the notion of influence, I discuss projects underway in the Arab world's traditional centres which are a direct response to, and an imitation of, projects in Dubai. The focus then shifts to Cairo – the traditional centre of the Arab world – to show how it is attempting to catch-up with Dubai. The chapter concludes with an assessment of the viability of the *Dubai Model*.

Concluding Thoughts: Returning to the Original Vision

'We do not wait for events but we make them happen.'

Sheikh Mohamed bin Rashid Al Maktoum.

A billboard placed at the World Trade Center Roundabout, in February 2009 (figure 1.3)

1.3. A billboard placed near the World Trade Center.

Perhaps no other project captures the excesses, exaggerations and ultimately the awakening to reality than 'Jumeirah Gardens'. It was meant to replace the traditional, low-income neighbourhood of Satwa, located behind the über-luxurious Sheikh Zayed Road. The district is home to some of the oldest buildings in Dubai where, over the years, its residents have cobbled together homes with gardens, outdoor seating areas and graffiti. Following two years of rumours about the district's demise, Jumeirah Gardens was unveiled at the Dubai Cityscape exhibition in October 2008 (figure 1.4). A scale model of the entire development, occupying a large double height room, showed what developers had in store: numerous skyscrapers shaped in an indescribable manner, a canal snaking its way through the development, and a variety of mixed-use and residential buildings. All, of course, geared, to the luxurious sector of the market. Prior to this unveiling, residents of Satwa, mostly labourers from South Asia, Arabs, and *bidoon* (stateless Arabs), had been issued with eviction notices and buildings had been marked with green numbers, indicating their dreaded fate. Promptly, newspapers and film-makers began lamenting the district's destruction. Portraying it as Dubai's version

1.4. A scale model of Jumeirah Gardens in the Cityscape 2008 exhibition in Dubai.

of Greenwich Village, these reactions underscored the thirst for, and lack of, an authentic and vibrant urban living in the city. In many ways the district did capture these qualities, but it was also perceived as home to illegals and to have a high crime rate. Many local residents would never dare venture into Satwa. Decision-makers used this exaggerated threat to justify their plans (see Chapter 8 for a more detailed discussion).

The Cityscape exhibition had already begun to feel the impact of the global financial downturn. While well attended no sales were forthcoming. The Jumeirah Gardens project was viewed with a mixture of curiosity, awe at its sheer scale, and a creeping realization that it simply could not get off the ground. A few weeks after this event, news about layoffs, the collapse of financial markets and a halt to many projects leaked out. By November, it became clear that Dubai's boom was nearing its end. The Jumeirah Gardens project was put on hold. Consequently evicted tenants began to return to their 'homes'.[5] All that is left of this fantasy are fences which were used to mark houses slated for demolition and a lonely sign heralding the construction site lying on the street – a reminder of the results of excess, greed and unbridled ambition (figure 1.5). Satwa, it seems, has received a new lease of life.

Yet, given the global financial downturn, should Dubai be written off? Is it merely a footnote in the annals of urbanism? A curiosity that simply cannot compete with the real cities of the world? Certainly reading news headlines, one gets the sense that developments have come to a grinding halt. Such a 'respected' publication as the *New York Times* even goes so far as to declare that parts of Dubai have begun to resemble a 'ghost town'.[6] That same publication had only a few years earlier promoted Dubai as 'the Oz' of the Middle East.[7] Clearly both positions are an exaggeration – the city was hyped beyond what was real and its troubles are exaggerated. And one cannot discount a sense of *Schadenfreude* in all of this – no doubt encouraged by some of the arrogant attitudes displayed by players

1.5. A sign marking the construction site of Jumeirah Gardens.

in the Dubai scene – developers, academics and journalists. One went so far as to declare that this is Dubai's moment in history, replacing Cairo, Baghdad, and Beirut (discussed in Chapter 9). It may for all practical purposes have been a very brief moment indeed.

But, going beyond some of the media hype and trying to provide a more realistic picture of current developments may prove difficult. Events were still unfolding at the time of writing (Spring 2009), however it is clear that the financial crisis is having a substantial impact on the city's ambitious plans. The extent and the degree of this remains to be seen. But this much is known: 50 per cent of all projects have either been postponed, re-assessed, or cancelled; property prices have declined by as much as 50 per cent; layoffs will lead to a 5–8 per cent decline in population.[8] Anecdotal evidence suggests that the effects of this slowdown can already be seen in the city's streets and public spaces – a decline in traffic and numbers of people. In spite of this gloomy picture, one must also consider that some of the more significant projects are still on track: the Burj Dubai, tallest building in the world, is set to open in September 2009; the Metro project, a magnificent engineering feat, is continuing and its first line will also open in September 2009 (figure 1.6). The Business Bay project is well under way and portions of Sheikh Zayed Road are about to be closed to facilitate the Creek's extension to the Gulf, thus turning Bur Dubai into an island. Other projects are continuing as well – a simple drive through the city shows construction activity on numerous sites.[9]

The Economist in an article titled 'The Beauty of Bubbles' offers an interesting historical perspective enabling us to situate the Dubai phenomenon.[10] Miami in the 1920s underwent a similar real estate boom, speculators descended on the city and property exchanged hands within a single day. As is usually the case, this led

1.6. The elevated track of Dubai Metro.

to an oversupply and the bubble eventually burst and was followed by the Great Depression. But, and this is critical, the bubble left behind 'a lasting physical legacy of buildings and streets and beaches and man-made islands'. What was largely a swamp became a real city which today continues to draw visitors and residents from all over the world. Comparisons are also made to London's Canary Wharf, a creation of two booms, the 1980s and the last 10 years; thus 'an area that was derelict less than 30 years ago is now securely positioned as one of the world's major financial hubs'. In drawing an analogy to Dubai, one should remember that the city started from a much lower base – it was basically a fishing village until the 1960s (see Chapter 4) – and also that it has the support of the UAE's federal government, which will prevent a complete collapse.[11] More significantly, and as *The Economist* has pointed out, 'Dubai's developers fashioned a city out of the desert' – and that is a remarkable achievement.

Such an historical perspective will also correct a misconception about Dubai. Many critics seem to suggest that the city's growth and development only occurred within the last 6 years or so. This does, of course, make for good headlines – sudden growth, emerging from nowhere, and an even faster downfall. Yet, as I argue in this book, Dubai has been a thriving port and trading centre since the turn of the last century. Its modern urban transformation began in the 1960s, more than 40 years ago. It went through many stages of development, affected by various political and economic events impacting its growth to varying degrees. Furthermore, it should not be seen in isolation; it is part of a larger federation which in turn is connected to a financial powerhouse – the states of the Gulf Cooperative Council (GCC). Their fates are intertwined and it is not in anyone's interests to see the failure of one of its members. Dubai is not an overnight sensation that will somehow 'fade into the desert sunset'.[12]

What lessons can the city learn from this downturn? On the one hand many Emirati observers have in fact welcomed these events as some sort of cultural salvation. Political scientist Abdulkhaleq Abdullah, who until recently was extolling the virtues of the Dubai model, proclaims that 'the city needs to slow down and relax. It's good for the identity of our country'.[13] For many city residents there was a sense that these developments were not geared for them, that an entire city was being created for foreigners which had the result of creating an environment that can only be described as transient. As I describe here, this notion of transience is key in understanding and critiquing the Dubai project (Chapters 7 and 8). Its physical spaces do not foster a sense of attachment, they do not seem 'lived in', which according to urban sociologist Richard Sennett (2008, p. 293) is a key ingredient in the liveability of any city: 'time breeds attachment to place'. These lived-in spaces can only be found in Satwa and the older parts of Deira and Bur Dubai. While not having any distinctive architectural qualities, they are transformed through the mix of inhabitants into a set of vibrant spaces that

1.7. A weekly Friday market at the JBR Residential Complex.

1.8. The Deira district as seen from one of the city's *abras* (the boats which carry people across the Creek).

underpin a humanity and spontaneity that is lacking elsewhere. The superficial, homogeneous urbanity of Jumeirah Walk or Bastakiya Souq is no substitute for the real life mix of people in Meena Bazaar (an old market in Bur Dubai), or along the shores of its Creek, where the unexpected and the encounter with strangers reveal a unique set of spaces (figures 1.7 and 1.8). It is perhaps time to return to the simple ethos which Sheikh Mohamed (2006) articulated in his book *My Vision*, that Dubai is about the mixing of cultures; and it is also a time to reflect on the humanistic vision of Sheikh Rashid founder of modern Dubai whose Bedouin origins guided the city's growth, resulting in a measured and sustainable urban vision. In this way the city may go behind the spectacle and become a true model for urban living in the twenty-first century.

Epilogue: The City of the Future *IS* Dubai

Michael Winterbottom's movie *Code 46* (2003) deals with the future and the extent to which developments in genetic engineering and neuroscience have impacted our daily lives. But the most astonishing thing about the film – according to movie critic A.O. Scott – is that it was shot on location in the world of the present. Its vision of the future is of a network of high-rise, glass-and-steel cities, London, Shanghai, and Dubai, through which an empowered managerial class can move more or less freely. These centres of commerce and manufacturing are also open to workers who dwell in an updated version of the underground ghettoes of Fritz Lang's *Metropolis*. Some of them arrive illegally from a zone known as *afuera*

(Spanish for outside) that is a realm of poverty, lawlessness and freedom. Scott argues that the narrative of *Code 46* may be convoluted and preposterous, but it is nonetheless haunting because it seems, at the level of the image, to exaggerate so little. There is luxury and squalor, a mobile elite served and enriched by an army of transient workers, an architectural hotchpotch of pristine newness and ancient disorder which is 'the kind of thing you see everywhere'.[14]

In the movie, the city of Dubai offers the two protagonists a haven, a refuge. Parts of it are *afuera*, outside, but it is here that they are finally at peace, in the midst of a mix of cultures, languages and people. And, interestingly, these scenes were shot in the alleys of Deira and Bur Dubai, across the city's magnificent Khor (Creek), and in the shadow of its skyscrapers. The city of the future, for better or worse, lies here (figure 1.9).

1.9. City residents at a bus stop – a microcosm of Dubai's population.

Notes

1.   For a rather remarkable example of this see Greer, Germaine (2009) 'From its artificial islands to its boring new skycraper, Dubai's architecture is beyond crass', *The Guardian*. 9 February. http://www.guardian.co.uk/artanddesign/2009/feb/09/dubai-architecture-greer. Accessed 3 March 2009. She writes that her entire experience of the city is based on a 4-hour bus ride, which she was able to do because of an airport layover.

2.   There are numerous examples. For instance, noted journalist Roger Cohen writes the following: '... America's relative decline has become more manifest in stagnant or falling incomes, imploding markets, massive debt, and rising new centers of wealth and power from Shanghai to Dubai' (Cohen, Roger (2008) 'Palin's American exception', *International Herald Tribune*, 24 September). http://www.iht.com/articles/2008/09/24/opinion/edcohen.php. Accessed 3 March 2009).

3.   Kerr, Simon (2009) 'Emirate on the ebb', *Financial Times*, 29 January. http://www.ft.com/cms/s/0/a5e67266-ee1d-11dd-b791-0000779fd2ac.html. Accessed 5 March 2009. Also see Washington Times Global (2009) 'Financial centers of power have shifted over time', 5 March. http://www.washington timesglobal.com/content/story/global/89/financial-centers-power-have-shifted-over-time. Accessed 5 March 2009.

4.   Urbanist Nezar AlSayyad in his introductory remarks at the IASTE (International Association for the Study of Traditional Environments) conference held in Oxford, December 2008.

5.   Hope, Bradley and Khan, Sarmad (2009) 'Evicted Jumeira Gardens residents return home', *The National*, 7 January. http://www.thenational.ae/article/20090107/BUSINESS/599826714/1005. Accessed 4 March 2009.

6.   Worth, Robert F. (2009) 'Laid-off foreigners flee as Dubai spirals down', *New York Times*, 11 February. http://www.nytimes.com/2009/02/12/world/middleeast/12dubai.html?_r=1. Accessed 4 March, 2009.

7.   Sherwood, Seth (2005) 'The Oz of the Middle East', *The New York Times*, 8 May. http://travel.nytimes.com/2005/05/08/travel/08dubai.html. Accessed 4 March 2009.

8.   Fenton, Suzanne (2009) 'Construction sector on track; work on civil projects worth DH2.56tr continues despite overall slowdown', *Gulf News*, 5 February, p. 29

9.   Hope, Bradley (2009) 'Dubai to increase spending by 42%', *The National*, 11 January, p. 1; and Sambidge, Andy (2009) '$30bn business bay 'on track' despite global crisis', *Arabian Business*. http://www.arabianbusiness.com/544829-30bn-business-bay-project-on-track-despite-global-crisis. Accessed 4 March 2009.

10.   *The Economist* (2008). 'The beauty of bubbles', *The Economist*, 20 December, pp. 107–109.

11.   While there has been some debate about the degree of the UAE's federal government's involvement and the extent to which Abu Dhabi would be willing to aid its neighbour, the issuance of a $20bn bond, supported by the UAE central bank created an assurance of sorts. See, for example, Arnold, Wayne and Pantin, Travis (2009) 'Dubai launches US$20bn bond issue: central bank subscribes to $10bn', *The National*. 23 February, p. 1.

12.   Heathcote, Edwin (2009) 'No end in sight in quest for height', *Financial Times*, 25 February. http://www.ft.com/cms/s/0/dd1e647a-02de-11de-b58b-000077b07658.html. Accessed 5 March 2009.

13.   Slackman, Michael (2008) 'Emirates see fiscal crisis as chance to save culture', *New York Times*, 12 November. http://www.nytimes.com/2008/11/12/world/middleeast/12dubai.html. Accessed 4 March 2009.

14.   Scott, A.O. (2008) 'The way we live now', *New York Times Magazine: Metropolis Now*. 8 June. http://www.nytimes.com/2008/06/08/magazine/08wwln-lede-t.html?fta=y. Accessed 3 March 2009.

Chapter 2

Arab Cities and Globalization

In 2007 the world crossed a significant milestone – namely, for the first time in human history the urban population exceeded the rural. According to the UNFP (United Nations Fund for Population Activities, 2007) more than half the world's population – 3.3 billion people – would be living in urban areas in 2008. The figure is expected to swell to almost 5 billion, or 60 per cent of the world's population, by 2030. At that point, towns and cities in the developing world will make up 81 per cent of urban humanity. 'Many of the new urbanites will be poor' according to the report. Alarmingly, one in every three city residents will live in inadequate housing with no or few basic services (UN-Habitat, 2007).

Cities have thus acquired an unprecedented significance. Such rapid urbanization has been accompanied by what is referred to in the literature as 'mega-cities' whose population will exceed 10 million. They have become attractors for a rural population seeking to participate in their economic wealth, symbolized by the gleaming towers of their business districts (figure 2.1). Yet these migrants are forced to settle in slums – the only affordable housing alternative. These processes have resulted in a phenomenon well known in cities throughout history but is intensifying in the new millennium – what Marcuse and van Kempen (2000) refer to as 'the tower and the citadel' – the coexistence of pockets of extreme wealth with areas of extreme poverty and deprivation (figure 2.2). Such a phenomenon has historic precedence yet, due to various processes – economic, social, and cultural – collectively referred to as globalization, patterns of inequality have become more pronounced and visible. For some, such as Friedmann and Wolff (1982), this has become a defining character of world cities. Urbanization in the twenty-first century has thus become a phenomenon spawning a plethora of studies examining its impact on the growth of cities and on human lives. Another dimension of these processes involves the impact on the ecology of the planet. With cities increasingly consuming scarce resources such as water and energy, the search for alternatives and a mode of urbanization that is sustainable has become more relevant than ever.

An important question in the case of this book is, of course, the relationship between these issues and the urban development of Dubai. Given the rapid growth of the city since the 1960s and its position as a crossroads of sorts for travellers and migrants, it is critical to place the city's development within a wider

2.1. Shanghai's Pudong skyline.

2.2. Shanghai's rising economic power has led to a growing contrast between old and new buildings.

context. Specifically Dubai's status as a migrant city – it is estimated that non-residents comprise more than 90 per cent – makes it particularly susceptible to trends occurring in developing countries. Portrayed as a model city for neoliberal economic policies, with all its successes and failures, the spatial implications for such directions are evident. It aspires to be a global city, and in doing so is claiming that it has developed a unique model – evidenced spatially in its gleaming towers, financial centre, spectacular architecture and so on. That such developments occur within a Middle Eastern context adds another provocative dimension. Thus, examining the city is particularly relevant both for the global city debate and issues pertaining to Middle Eastern urbanism. But before I address the implications of this for Dubai in more detail, not just in this chapter but in the remainder of the book, I outline first some of the constructs which will be used such as globalization, sustainability and urban governance, focusing on their spatial ramifications. My point of reference is taken from the West, where these constructs initially emerged and developed. I then explore the extent to which these categorizations are related to the Arab city in general and in subsequent chapters use these as a theoretical framework for critiquing the *Dubai Project*.

The Meaning of Globalization

While the prevalent view of the world's interconnectedness focuses on its uniqueness there are some who argue otherwise – aiming to establish a historical continuity. Hirst and Thompson (1996), for instance, claim that globalization is a myth propagated for ideological reasons. They argue that there has always been an international trading system of some sort and that, in fact, there was more internationalization in the economy in the late nineteenth century than there is at present. In a widely cited article, Janet Abu-Lughod (1995) draws to attention the historical dimension of current globalization processes. Of particular significance is her argument that the connectivity of cities, being part of a larger network, constitutes an essential feature of being a city in the first place – it is thus not a new phenomenon. She develops a strong argument for the cyclical development of what she terms world systems, which at the present is in its fifth iteration. There are some, however, who while in essence agreeing with the historical component of globalization nevertheless argue for the uniqueness of contemporary processes. Brenner and Keil (2006), for example, note that urbanization processes are being *consolidated*, *intensified* and *accelerated* under contemporary conditions of globalization, which is a view widely held by many urban observers. Friedmann and Wolff (1982) recognize the historical continuity of urbanization processes but argue that the present situation is substantially different since the world economy is now truly global, involving the entire world rather than specific geographic regions.

For many in the Arab world today's globalization is yesterday's imperialism and colonization, which is, of course, an oversimplification.[1] The term itself is complex, laden with meaning. Scholars, academics, economists, planners, geographers, all tend to emphasize certain aspects relevant to their background and viewpoint. For example, Peter Marcuse (2006), a planner, defines globalization as a further strengthening and internationalization of capital using substantial advances in communication and transportation technology. Newman and Thornley (2005, p. 2), political scientists, citing Held *et al.* (1999) define globalization as the 'widening, deepening and speeding up of worldwide connectedness in all aspects of contemporary social life'. The aspects of social life seen to have been affected by globalization have included not only economic restructuring but also social polarization, international crime, dominant cultures, patterns of international migration and patterns of governance. Popular accounts refer to globalization as the complex of forces that tend towards a single world society. Among these forces are mass communications, commerce, increased ease of travel, the internet, popular culture, and the increasingly widespread use of English as an international language.

Of particular importance is the extent to which major players in world city affairs, such as the IMF (International Monetary Fund) and the World Bank, and in turn national governments, view the term. Newman and Thornley (2005) argue that agencies such as the IMF and the US government have a particular view of globalization, based on what is known as the Washington consensus.[2] This sees the inevitable adaptation of all national economies to the new global economic imperative (p. 5) – a view sometimes equated with neoliberalism. Among its ten points, three are significant in the context of this book. States are advised:

7. To remove all barriers to foreign direct investment and enable foreign and domestic firms to compete on equal terms;

8. To privatize state enterprises;

9. To abolish regulations impeding the entry of new firms or restricting competition and insure that all regulations of a given industry are justified.

While these definitions tend to emphasize the economic dimension of globalizing processes there are also socio-cultural aspects and, more significantly, spatial ramifications. I should also note that the actual application of these principles has varied quite substantially. The notion of privatization, for instance in the context of Arab Gulf monarchies, can be subjected to varying interpretations. The case of Dubai is particularly interesting as I illustrate in Chapter 5.

The Dimensions of Globalization: Economic, Social and Cultural

Globalizing processes – opening up borders and the free flow of ideas and exchange of information – has resulted in an increased rate of migration. The United Nations in 2002 evaluated the total number of international migrants at some 175 million, including refugees but excluding an estimated 15 to 30 million illegal or irregular migrants, whose numbers are rapidly increasing (United Nations Population Division, 2002). A breakdown by major regions shows that some 77 million international migrants reside in industrialized countries, 33 million in transition economies, 23 million in Eastern Asia, 21 million in the Middle East and North Africa and 14 million in Sub-Saharan Africa.

Remittances are another factor related to globalizing processes. According to the World Bank, mass migration has spawned an underground economy of staggering proportions. Globally, remittances – the cash that immigrants send home – totalled nearly $276 billion in 2006. Across Latin America, remittances hit $62 billion in 2006 and are projected to top $100 billion by 2010, according to the Inter-American Development Bank. Mexicans wire home the most cash – nearly $22 billion – most of it earned in the United States. India is the world leader in remittances, taking in $23.7 billion in 2005 and an estimated $26.9 billion in 2006.[3]

According to UN-Habitat (2007) current international migration flows display three main features which make them significantly different from past experience: (a) the direction of the flows; (b) their nature; and (c) their focus on conurbations. Furthermore, since the early to mid 1990s, these migratory flows are between developing countries, such as those from Southeast Asia to the Middle East; women represent more than half of all transnational migrants (in the 1990s, 84 per cent of all Sri Lankan migrants to the Middle East were female as were two-thirds of Filipino migrant workers), in what has been called 'the female underside of globalization' (Ehrenreich and Hochschild, 2002). International migrants are heading increasingly for urban areas, particularly large cities, where they have more chance of finding income-earning opportunities. However, one particular negative outcome is that the integrating role of the city seems increasingly to be giving way to an exclusionary trend, as highlighted by increasing social and economic segregation as well as spatial fragmentation. Exclusion, poverty and violence are on the rise as the sense of belonging, social cohesion and the very notion of citizenship are threatened.

Scholars have introduced a term to describe this intensifying phenomenon, 'transnational migration', where individuals belong to two or more communities at the same time. The difference between international and transnational migrants is often blurred and is becoming increasingly so as more and more individuals reside in a host country while maintaining strong ties with their countries of origin. As a result remittances are beginning to play a major role in world economics. Financial transfers to developing countries in 2004 amounted to a combined equivalent of $75 to $100 billion per year, or significantly more than official development aid (ODA) from developed countries and second only to oil revenues (World Commission, 2004). I discuss this as it applies to Dubai in Chapter 7.

The Spatial Dimension: Definition of the Global City

The discussion so far has centred on the economic and socio-cultural ramifications of globalizing processes. However it is important to highlight the spatial impact of cross border flows. These have resulted in what many scholars are calling the *Global City.* Viewed as a city which concentrates financial services and acts as a command and control centre for the rest of the world. Three cities in particular are singled out – London, New York and Tokyo. While this concept can be attributed to many scholars, the work of social geographer Saskia Sassen is typically cited in this context. However the whole notion of a Global City is highly problematic.

Brenner and Keil (2006), in their introduction to the *Global Cities Reader* and based on recent trends in research, argue for a contextualization of world city research and global city theory. This is based on the emergence of new trends which focus on marginalized cities, and a realization that local agents shape and interact with global processes. Marcuse and van Kempen (2000), recognizing that cities engage in globalizing processes in different ways, introduced the more appropriate term *globalizing cities.*

Space is transformed in these cities to cater for a consumerist society, transnational migrants and so on. The most visible manifestation of the sizeable new consumer elite is the striking transformation of the city centre to be found in virtually all our cities. Offices, hotels, luxury housing, and up-scale shops and restaurants have displaced low-income residents (Gugler, 2004). This also ties in with the work of geographer David Harvey (1989) in his examination of enterpreneuralism and urban governance which favours entrepreneurs at the expense of inhabitants. Buildings are important in this context because they give the *appearance* of a global city. Peter Marcuse (2006) discusses spatial patterns in cities and the extent to which they have changed due to globalization (if at all). For example, one outcome is a variety of juxtaposed and sometimes overlapping residential cities and a city of unskilled work and an informal economy.

Cities are assuming a powerful role, and as a result of such processes they are increasingly being viewed as a product that needs to be marketed. These marketing efforts involve attracting headquarters or regional branches of international companies and staging of 'mega-events'. According to *The Economist* (2007), when wooing investors or companies ready to move their headquarters, rival cities will now flaunt their galleries, theatres and orchestras as much as their airline connections, modern hospitals and fibre-optic networks. Other projects include luxury housing, dining establishments and entertainment amenities to attract the professional personnel required to operate these global activities. Urban projects, such as trade and conference centres and hotels, are used to act as catalysts to further encourage investment and tourism. Architecture, in many instances, is used as a tool to create 'eye-catching' impressions – the Guggenheim Museum in Bilbao is an example of this (UN-Habitat, 2001). Such projects are used to revitalize an otherwise 'stagnant' city – also called the 'Bilbao effect'.[4] Thus these megaprojects transform the image of a city – but not the reality – into an ultra-modern, arty, fun-filled metropolis (*The Economist*, 2007). I discuss this in greater detail in Chapter 6.

But there is a downside to this increased opening up of borders. Insecurity due to the increasing numbers of migrants, for example, as well as economic disparity have resulted in the abandonment and stigmatization of certain neighbourhoods, the development of an *architecture of fear*, and the gradual establishment of so-called 'fortress cities' where response to crime has led to spatial transformation that has changed parts of cities into protected enclaves and 'no-go areas' separated by high walls, gates, electronic surveillance cameras and private security guards (UN-Habitat, 2007, p. 145). Such protected enclaves are the result of '[a] decision to create private urban spaces which are set apart from the rest of the city with the aim of providing an escape from undesirable social disorders' (*Ibid.*, p. 146).

They consist of large or small housing estates typically aimed at the middle and upper classes and are usually surrounded by a wall or fence. As noted, the main reason for their proliferation is a growing sense of insecurity, the deterioration of public areas, and the guarantee of a high social status (figure 2.3). The real estate market has a vested interest in promoting paranoia about insecurity and environmental degradation. Thus there is a proliferation of enclosed neighbourhoods – and marking out, physically and symbolically, the boundaries of the residential estate. Aside from their negative social implications they are a waste of resources such as water and electricity, because of their horizontal spread and typically low densities. Gated communities are also major consumers of land. For example, in the metropolitan area of Buenos Aires, enclosed urban estates occupy approximately 30,000 hectares yet house only 1 per cent of the city's population, while in the case of Guadalajara in Mexico, enclosed communities occupy 10 per cent of the city's land space yet house only 2 per cent of the population (UN-Habitat, 2007).

Thus perceptions are driving policies which are increasingly resulting in polarized urban spaces since they cater for a specific, small segment of society and exclude a large majority, which is one of the main criticisms directed at Dubai's urban development as I discuss in this book. This leads us to the notion of inequality, social polarization and so on – a favourite subject for research in global city theory. It is tied to what has been called *the global city hypothesis*.

2.3. The imposing gateway to Emirates Hills, one of the most exclusive gated communities in Dubai.

The Global City Hypothesis and Social Polarization

The idea of a global city hypothesis – i.e. a set of propositions defining the emergence of this new type of city – was articulated in the key 1982 article by John Friedmann and Gerald Wolff, which in turn generated a wide array of studies to test their propositions. One of their main arguments pertains to the notion of inequality created in global/world cities. They note that contradiction and inequalities in world cities are due to what they call the 'new international division of labor'. Thus, cities are simultaneously viewed as spaces of hope and spaces of gloom – the 'citadel' and the 'ghetto' exist side by side. The notion of inequality is, of course, central to all these arguments. Friedmann and Wolff devote considerable attention to this, noting the functional necessity for having both rich and poor in close juxtaposition, since they define each other. Accordingly, there is an 'underclass' which serves the economy, and also 'distinguishes' the ruling class and its dependent middle sector – 'they are the city'. Moreover, 'the underclass lives at its sufferance'. The ghetto/citadel metaphor is frequently evoked, and has since become one of the main themes of global city research. Consider the following quote:

> With its towers of steel and glass and its fanciful shopping malls, the citadel is the city's most vulnerable symbol… The overcrowded ghettos exist in the far shadows of the citadel, where it is further divided into racial and ethnic enclaves. (Friedmann and Wolff, 1982, p. 64)

These arguments were further developed in Friedmann (1986) in his widely cited article 'The World City Hypothesis'. In it, a series of hypotheses are proposed dealing with the relationship between urbanization and global economic forces. Two are of particular importance: Hypothesis 5, in which it is argued that world cities are points of destination for large numbers of both domestic and/or international migrants; and Hypothesis 6 which explicitly states that one of the defining characteristics of world/global cities is spatial and class polarization.

Friedmann and Wolff classify globality of cities as those in the core (truly global); semi-periphery (rapidly developing, but relying on the core); and those on the periphery (confined to 'peripheral obscurity'). In citing examples for these cities it is interesting to observe that Arabian Gulf cities – among Arab scholars considered to be the most global in the region – are not mentioned at all. But as this was written in the 1980s significant advances had taken place in the GCC area in particular and it could be argued that some centres, such as Dubai for example, had in fact moved to the semi-periphery region – aspiring to be global but not quite there yet. These aspirations have been depicted by some observers as representing a *model* for the Middle East. I will explore this in the concluding chapter of the book where I look at the merits – or lack thereof – of the Dubai *model*.

However, as discussed earlier, there is a growing body of literature which disputes this deterministic argument. Susan Fainstein (2001), for example, argues that it is deeply problematic to generalize about global cities, and that individual cities are situated within a specific national context. Furthermore, she claims that immigration patterns influence patterns of inequality within each city. The implication of all this is that more contextually-grounded case studies and explanations are required (a 'globalization from below' approach). Conventional global city theory posits that there is a widening gap between a shrinking middle and a growing bottom. This is due to a demand by upper-income people for services from the poor – immigrants, labourers, etc. Fainstein's work does not support this; in fact she argues that exclusion from the work force is a major cause of poverty together with factors related to public policy. Thus, while the notion of the spatial impact of globalization is not essentially in dispute, there are calls for both theoretical and methodological reconsiderations. Transnational urbanism is one particular modification for global city research which I discuss briefly below and elaborate on further in Chapter 8, showing that Dubai is perhaps the ultimate transnational city.

Critique of the Model: Transnationalism/Globalization from Below

Within the global city theory there is a bias towards certain regions. In this regard maps become ways of articulating and representing power. Brenda Yeoh (1999, p. 608) describes this as an 'image of the world that is empty beyond global cities, a borderless space, which can be recorded, neglected or put to use according to the demands of globally articulated capital flows'. Response to this new way of looking at cities considers other ways of becoming global, for example, Robinson (2002) and also Marcuse and Van Kempen (2000) who introduced the notion of globalizing cities which addresses 'multifaceted processes of urban globalization', as noted earlier.

Conventional global city theory focuses on a paradigmatic model to which all cities must aspire. Some scholars have searched for ways to expand categories of global cities working within the framework of the theory; Robinson (2002) aims her critique at the epistemological core of the theory itself, which she argues represents an 'imperial approach to cities'. Based on the work of Amin and Graham (1997), she argues for the use of 'ordinary cities' as a conceptual category which would account for the diversity and distinctiveness found in most cities.

The conventional approach, according to her, can have devastating consequences. Many cities will never become 'command & control' centres so they need to pick up other *global functions* identified by Sassen and others. One of them is the promotion of attractive global tourist environments; this, however, can place a city at the opposite end of power relations in a global world and could undermine the provision of basic services to the local economy. This in turn would place 'the city concerned in a relatively powerless position'. In her critique of global city theory Robinson draws an interesting analogy to first/third world characterization and how postcolonial literature began to critique that. Thus urban studies would have to adopt a similar approach – in essence deconstructing conventional global city research. In her words, 'there is a need for alternative formulations of city-ness'.

The socio-spatial restructuring of global cities has led to new research which examines socio-economic inequality and everyday life. The work of Sassen and Peter Smith for instance looked at immigration as a form of transnationalization. Arjun Appadurai (1996) uncovered the racist, exclusionary progressive policies within global cities. Using the case of Mumbai, he develops the concept of *de-cosmopolitanization*, which means an ethnicization of formerly cosmopolitan cities. Similar themes can be found in the writings of Harvey.

The work of Michael Peter Smith is of particular importance. He represents an agent-centred critique of global cities. Underscoring the role of social mobilization 'from below' in the production of globalized urban spaces, he notes that 'the global cities discourse constitutes an effort to define the global city as an objective reality operating outside the social construction of meaning' (Peter Smith, 2001, p. 378). His main argument is that 'there is no solid object known as the "global city" appropriate for grounding urban research, only an endless interplay of differently articulated networks, practices, and power relations' (*Ibid.*). I use this new categorization to both critique and uncover spatial practices in Dubai.

Sustainability and Globalization

Sustainability is a contested concept. It means different things to different people, depending on whether they stress environmental sustainability, economic growth or human development.[5] William Rees argues that sustainability includes political recognition of environmental decay, economic injustice, and limits to growth. Reminding humans that they are not isolated, but deeply embedded in natural systems with inescapable limits, Rees raises moral and normative considerations such as 'the need in a finite world for an equitable sharing and conservation of natural bounty' (Rees, 1990, p. 1). Other writers emphasize the rights of future generations to access the earth's resources, and the right of every person to equal access to an intact environment (Sachs *et al.*, 1998). From a different perspective, the United Nations Human Development Report (1999) argues that human development is the end, and economic growth simply a means to that end. There is, however, intense disagreement about the extent to which sustainability and human development should restrict the pursuit of economic growth. The UN Human Development Report supports the search for rules and institutes for stronger governance, but argues that the challenge is not to stop the expansion of global markets.

Socio-cultural sustainability is inextricably linked to the above systems, centred on the normative ideal of democratic communities. Socio-cultural sustainability refers to social systems which provide room for independent and autonomous cultural development, as well as democratic relationships at various levels of society. Variables include levels of independent cultural expression, concentration of control over the mass media, the power of consumerism as a cultural force, trends in crime, and other indicators of social upheaval and instability. Cultural disintegration is a threat as well. Many nations and their arts communities are disturbed by threats the American entertainment industry poses for the sustainability of their unique national and local cultures.[6]

Thus while the mainstream media and popular opinion focus on the ecological dimension of sustainability, which no doubt is a critical issue, it loses meaning and relevance if other aspects are not taken into account, particularly socio-cultural sustainability with its significant dimension of a just society. As Graham Haughton (1999) argued, moving towards sustainable development requires achieving economic and social systems which encourage environmental stewardship of resources for the long-term, acknowledging the interdependency of social justice, economic well-being and environmental stewardship. He further notes that the social dimension is critical since an unjust society is unlikely to be sustainable in environmental or economic terms in the long run, since the social tensions which are created undermine the need for recognizing the reciprocal rights and obligations, leading in all manner of ways to environmental degradation and ultimately to political breakdown.

Applying this to cities, a sustainable city – from a social and cultural perspective – would be a city where citizens, irrespective of socio-economic background, education etc, have access to all its facilities; where its public spaces are a true space for mixing with diverse people, what urban sociologist Richard Sennett refers to as encounters of strangers; and where its various groups are not relegated to ghettos and gated communities.[7] While a city such as Dubai defines itself for the most part as a multicultural melting pot of sorts, it is more of a polyglot, a confused mix of ethnic groups, where, in spite of the existence of numerous nationalities, each has its own dedicated space and encounters take place only in controlled settings such as shopping malls. True public spaces – the essence of a socially sustainable city – are seriously lacking, but the city's urban policy seems to be directed towards effectively discouraging the formation of such settings, as I argue in the following chapters.

The discussion so far has defined the terms globalization and sustainability, illustrating that these are multi-dimensional constructs encompassing a variety of viewpoints – in many instances influenced by specific political orientations. However, there is agreement that globalization entails an unprecedented flow of capital, goods, people and ideas. While these processes have existed in the past they have intensified and, more importantly, they encompass the entire globe rather than specific regions. Because of this opening up of borders, cities have become particularly attractive for migrants, which has added pressure on their limited natural resources. As a result the sustainability of these cities' economic, environmental and social dimensions, is threatened, as I have tried to illustrate in the preceding sections. The increasing number of people in cities and their concentration in ghettos – whether of the rich or the poor – threatens the 'integrating role' of cities which in turn undermines socio-cultural sustainability. These issues are present to varying degrees in the city of Dubai and an understanding, as well as a critique, of its urban development needs to take them into account. All this takes place within a political context, which I discuss briefly in the following section.

Urban Governance

The term 'urban governance', formerly equated with urban management, has come to be understood as both government responsibility and civic engagement. Generally, it refers to the processes by which local urban governments, in partnership with other public agencies and different segments of civil society, respond effectively to local needs in a participatory, transparent and accountable manner (UNFPA, 2007). In short, it involves participatory decision-making in cities and devolution of power from central to local governments.

This definition may run counter to existing political realities in the Arab world, which in many instances are still effectively governed by one-man institutions. However, UN-Habitat (2007) notes that for some countries having a 'benign' central government system may prove to be beneficial as it is a guarantor of sorts that policies will be implemented effectively. Thus it suggests that highly centralized systems of governance cannot benefit the urban poor if they are being run by regressive, anti-poor political leaders. For example, Morocco's centralist tradition has benefited from the monarch's pro-poor stance towards upgrading. Furthermore, the government of Morocco is now trying to introduce greater participation in the planning and implementation of slum upgrading projects through a new concept called 'Social Project Control' and laws on promoting participation. In Egypt, too, there are signs of change. The entire regulatory and policy framework, including the constitution, is being examined and revised in a massive effort to broaden democratic processes within the country (UN-Habitat, 2007). The Gulf monarchies are implementing policies which rely on a highly centralized form of government which has proved to be very effective (for its citizens at least).

Key changes occurring in cities due to globalizing processes are the relative decline of the nation-state (which is debatable) and the increasing turn towards the private sector as a main actor in development. This can be seen through the proliferation of NGOs in various countries, and the emergence of powerful real-estate companies which are increasingly shaping the skylines of globalizing cities. In that vein, governments are engaged in a process of selling public assets – such as land formerly occupied by the military, for example – to foreign (and local) developers. Of course, one drawback is that the role of the state as providing and ensuring welfare for its citizens is increasingly in decline, thus further exacerbating inequality.

As a result of increasing rates of migration between cities, a new form of citizen is emerging – a transnational subject. This is an individual with ties to both his/her home country and country of residence. Within cities such a phenomena manifests itself through the presence of multi-ethnic neighbourhoods, for example; a political engagement by residents in both affairs related to their country of origin and their place of residence, facilitated by the proliferation and prevalence of various modes of communication. For some observers such as Warren Magnusson (1996), this has become the defining character of urbanity itself, which he characterizes as a kind of nomadism; a presence within the space of flows connecting different parts of the world. For the cosmopolitan citizen 'it is a sign of parochialism – or poverty – if one fails to inhabit the whole world' (p. 257). This can be observed in the Arab countries of the Gulf where in some instances the local population does not exceed 20 per cent. In Dubai the percentage of locals is even lower – 5 per cent according to some estimates. Thus one could argue that these global networks may result in new types of citizenship claims.

Status of the Arab City: The Great Economic Divide

Scene 1: *Summer 2007; extreme water shortage in Egypt*

Dalal, a 12-year-old villager in Al-Hammad [Egypt], said she only saw tap water and tubs in the movies she watches on TV. Her dream is to have a faucet, a shower and a sink in their house one day. She heard about the demonstrations in Al-Borg and asked her father if he, too, could demonstrate so that her dream may come true.[8]

Scene 2: *Winter 2005; after the Amman Hotel bombings*

Those in upscale neighborhoods, like Abdoun, for example, have waved flags and festooned their cars with pro-Jordanian banners, while residents of more depressed neighborhoods, like the Palestinian refugee camp at Al Wehdat, have joked that *there is finally some benefit to being poor: the attacks occurred in hotels they could never afford to set foot in.*[9]

These scenes which took place in Egypt and Jordan illustrate two main problems within the 'traditional' Middle East. On the one hand, we have a strong sense of inequality, demonstrated by a lack of basic services such as water provision in Egypt's villages. On the other hand, because of this inequality, there is a sense of social injustice to the extent that it may contribute, directly or indirectly, to social unrest (figure 2.4). But these scenes also show the vast gap that exists in the region – cities such as Dubai and Doha, for example, are seemingly immune from these disturbing images.

Such patterns of inequality are observable not just within cities but also across cities in the Arab region. Various economic statistics indicate that the pace of economic growth in the GCC is stronger than the rest of the Arab world. Several indicators of economic growth and development show a wide gap between the GCC and other Arab countries. Furthermore this gap appears to have widened in recent years. Some of the numbers are quite striking. The total population of GCC countries was approximately 37 million in 2006, which was roughly 12 per cent of the Arab population of the Middle East and North Africa. However, the economy of GCC countries in 2006 accounted for more than 55 per cent of the Arab world's $1.25 trillion economy. In 1995 the GCC countries had an average per capita income of $8500, which was 7.3 times larger than the per capital income of the remaining Arab countries. In 2006 the GCC per capita income rose to $19,300, which was 10.4 times larger than the average for other Arab countries. The per capita income in some GCC countries such as Qatar ($63,000) and the UAE ($38,000) were higher than many advanced Industrial countries in 2006.

The 2005 Human Development Index (HDI), which is reported annually by the UN, shows that Kuwait, Bahrain, Qatar, the UAE and Oman achieved the five highest scores among Middle Eastern countries, while Saudi Arabia stood at seventh place, after Libya. Another gap between the GCC and other Arab countries

2.4. The grinding poverty of Cairo's informal settlements or *ashwaiyat*. Railway lines and highways intensify their isolation.

is governance which measures six parameters: voice and accountability; political stability; government effectiveness; regulatory quality; rule of law; and costs of corruption. According to the World Bank's governance indicators for 2005, on average GCC countries achieved higher scores in all parameters. The high quality of governance in GCC countries has led to a sharp increase in foreign investment inflows. The share of the GCC in total inflow of foreign investment into the Arab world has also increased.[10]

This divide in the region is, of course, based on oil wealth. According to the IMF, the bulk of the oil windfall will be invested in the region where more than $1,000 billion of projects were planned (as of 2008). A study by McKinsey estimated that over the period 2005 to 2020 the Gulf was likely to have a $3,000 billion oil surplus, half of which would stay in the region, with another $750 billion or so of capital going into investments in the wider Middle East and North Africa.[11] While these numbers may change downward given fluctuation in oil prices, they indicate that there is such a trend leading to a division in the region.[12] For example, based on a World Economic Forum report ranking Arab economies, the region is divided into three groups according to their stage of development. The GCC is in the first, Tunisia and Oman rank first in the second, and Egypt ranks best in the third – and last – group.[13] The global financial crisis is not very likely to change this grouping and may in fact intensify them, given the cash reserves available for GCC countries as a whole.

This 'great divide', as it were, has led to many problems. Among them an increased rate of migration from poor Arab countries to the richer ones in the GCC. This can be observed, for example, at the border between Yemen and Saudi Arabia which is crossed yearly by vast numbers of illegal immigrants. According to one observer: 'GCC countries like all other rich countries in the world, need to understand that maintaining a bizarre status of economic inequality between neighboring countries would inevitably mean more illegal immigrants and hence more problems for all'.[14] In addition there are spatial repercussions for such economic disparity across countries. Cities, in particular, are sites where such divisions are made visible and are greatly intensified. Dubai is a poignant case for observing these inequalities at a political, cultural and spatial level, as I illustrate in this book.

Notes

1. For more on this see my introductions in Elsheshtawy (2004) and (2008a).

2. The concept and name of the Washington Consensus were first presented in 1989 by John Williamson, an economist from the Institute for International Economics, an international economic think tank based in Washington, DC. Williamson used the term to summarize the commonly shared themes among policy advice by Washington-based institutions at the time, such as the International Monetary Fund, World Bank, and U.S. Treasury Department.

3. Kole, William J. (2007) 'Migrant cash is world economic giant', *Guardian*, 18 August. http://www.guardian.co.uk/worldlatest/story/0,,-6860055,00.html. Accessed 3 October 2007.

4. Other examples exist such as the Liebeskind Imperial War Museum North in Manchester. Such trends began perhaps in the 1960s with the Sidney Opera House, which became a symbol for the city.

5. The Globalism Project (2000) *Neo-Liberal Globalism and its Challengers: Sustainability in the Semi-Periphery*. http://www.ualberta.ca/GLOBALISM/about.html. Accessed 19 November 2007.

6. *Ibid.*

7. Sennett, Richard (2001) 'A flexible city of strangers', *Le Monde Diplomatique*, February. http://mondediplo.com/2001/02/16cities. Accessed 25 February 2009.

8. Ezzat, Dina (2007) 'Not a drop to drink', *Al-Ahram Weekly*, 12–18 July. http://weekly.ahram.org.eg/2007/853/eg9.htm. Accessed 13 August 2007.

9. Slackman, Michael and Al-Naggar, Mona (2005) 'A saddened, but ambivalent, Jordan muses on bombings' aftermath', *International Herald Tribune*, 18 November, p. 5.

10. Habibi, Nader (2007) 'Economic divide among Arabs', *Gulf News*, 13 November, p. 52.

11. Khalaf, Roula (2007) 'It's boom time', *Gulf News*, 22 November, p. 22.

12. According to ESCWA (2000) the wide disparities between GCC countries and others in the region are demonstrated by the fact that, while 100 per cent of the urban population have access to fresh water in Qatar, Bahrain, Kuwait, and Lebanon, the percentage drops to 82 in Egypt. One hundred per cent of the urban population in countries like Saudi Arabia and Kuwait have access to sanitation. In Oman and United Arab Emirates, which are also part of GCC, it is 98 and 93 per cent respectively. By contrast only 20 per cent of the urban population in Egypt have access to sanitation, 40 per cent in Yemen and 77 per cent in Syria. These are all non-GCC countries. The figures also show the differences in access to opportunities for a safe and healthy life, and the situation of the urban poor.

13. Arab World Competitiveness Report, 2007. http://www.weforum.org/en/initiatives/gcp/Arab%20World%20Competitiveness%20Report/index.htm. Accessed 11 March 2009.

14. Al Saqaf, Walid (2007) 'How to stop illegal aliens', *Gulf News*, 28 September.

Chapter 3

The Other Dubai: A Photo Essay

'To take photographs means to recognize – simultaneously and within a fraction of a second – both the fact itself and the rigorous organization of visually perceived forms that give it meaning. It is putting one's head, one's eye and one's heart on the same axis.'
Henri Cartier-Bresson (quoted in Galassi *et al.*, 2006)

Our image of Dubai is shaped by its megaprojects and spectacular developments. This obscures the fact that behind its flashy exterior are places which are full of life and character. Thus, I have included a selection of images which uncover these hidden spaces thereby moving the discourse away from one merely fixated on flamboyant architecture and mega-developments. With that in mind the essay is structured in three parts – *Distance*, *Framing* and *The Inner Life*. First I show the city from a distance, establishing its location within a desert (pp. 32–33). Then, the attention shifts to the city's iconic projects – particularly the Burj Dubai, Burj Al Arab and the Sheikh Zayed Road skyline. But here I am framing these structures in a manner that is unconventional, intentionally showing the surrounding context. Through these juxtapositions a certain dynamic is created that allows for these icons to be seen not just in isolation but as parts of a wider urban setting (pp. 34–37). The third part, 'The Inner Life' delves into the city's low-income districts, focusing on its residents and the extent to which they are interacting with its spaces. The built environment does allow activities to take place but in many instances

A flock of camels in the desert surrounding the city. The city skyline in the background is dominated by the Burj Dubai (February 2007).

it also hinders them. At other times it is irrelevant. People construct their own narratives and stories – irrespective of any physical structure or layout. Sometimes a conscious act of resistance – a subversion – takes place through which they are actively engaged in re-shaping their physical surroundings. My observations and the resulting images, in my view, support this (pp. 38–59).

I have intentionally refrained from capturing extremes: the 'abject squalor' of Dubai's labour camps or the ultra-luxurious settings of its gated communities or hotels. For most residents these settings are quite remote from their daily lives, exotic even. While not disputing the relevance of looking at these places and the extent to which they contribute to the city's urbanity (or lack thereof), this is not the subject of this essay or the book as a whole. My focus is on the settings of the everyday.

The images here are the result of a mapping project which I conducted in the city, starting in 2004 (see http://www.sheshtawy.org/hidden.htm), and follow in the tradition of such pioneering documentary and street photographers as Henri Cartier-Bresson. Through their images they captured some of the fleeting moments of everyday life, showing people interacting in everyday settings. But it is also useful to observe traces, left-over objects which illustrate the lived-in quality of some of these settings. The images are shown here in black and white which is not merely a choice given printing restrictions, but a conscious one giving a timeless quality to this portrayal. In addition, some images have been tilted – a technique sometimes used to evoke a dynamic quality and suggesting a different way of seeing for the spaces and buildings constituting the city of Dubai. In other instances there were also practical considerations: narrowness of alleyways, speed of shots to capture fast moving objects (which did not allow for careful compositions), etc. To capture the constant flow of people some images were taken with long exposure times. As a result moving figures appear blurred, while people standing appear in sharpness, thus highlighting the difference between movement and stillness.

A slightly older image of the Sheikh Zayed Road skyline with the World Trade Center (far right) and the twin Emirates Towers (2004).

The Toyota building, one of the oldest high-rises on Sheikh Zayed Road, built in the early 1970s. An oddity – both in style and level of maintenance – in the midst of gleaming high-rises.

Back entrance to the Toyota building. The billboard on the left indicates the number of storeys completed for the Burj Dubai in December 2007.

Burj Dubai as seen from a construction storage site for pipes near the Toyota building (December 2007).

An abandoned school building behind Sheikh Zayed Road.

Burj Al Arab – Dubai's original iconic landmark and symbol – as seen from an entrance to a construction site.

Trucks making a stop near the Burj Al Arab in the upscale Um Suqeim district.

Dubai's skyline as it appears from the Satwa district, home to low-income labourers mostly from South Asia.

A house in Satwa. The name is derived from the Arabic for 'wet sand' due to its close proximity to the Gulf, as well as its remoteness from the city's original urban area.

The narrow alleyways of Satwa offer a stark contrast to the luxurious towers on Sheikh Zayed Road.

Near the Ghubeiba bus stop in Bur Dubai. Street corners and empty lots become major gathering sites for the city's low-income migrant population.

The district of Ghubeiba is characterized by the presence of restaurants that cater for various ethnic groups.

The back alleys of the Ghubeiba district suggest a human scale and a lived in quality that is absent in the city's spectacular spaces.

A city resident uses his mobile phone
in the midst of the flow of people in the
Ghubeiba district during the evening.

Meena Bazaar, a commercial district in Bur Dubai. Lamp posts are used for informal modes of advertising. The name, according to popular perception, is based on a similar setting in New Delhi.

The backstreets of Meena Bazaar reveal vibrant settings dominated by commercial establishments.
Outdoor seating areas are provided by coffee shops.

A surreal stage set. Mannequins dressed
in traditional South Asian clothing are
displayed in a side alley. In the background
is a person talking on his phone.

An elaborate display window mostly geared to a South Asian clientele near Meena Bazaar and in close proximity to Dubai Museum and the gentrified Bastakiy'ya district.

The Naif market area in Deira – a traditional commercial setting. Its open spaces are gathering places for merchants.

A side alley next to the Hindu Temple in Bur Dubai. The temple caters to Dubai's large Indian community.

A narrow alley behind the Hindu temple leading to the *abra* (water taxi) station on the Creek.

Hindi magazines displayed on the temple's back walls catering for the dominant population of
South Asians.

Approaching the Hindu Temple which is on a site given by Sheikh Rashid to the Hindu community.
It is adjacent to the Diwan – the original location of the ruler's office.

Low-income workers use an electricity box for posting advertisements which range from lost labour cards to a search for residences.

The city's high rises are a distant dream for many labourers.

The Dubai skyline seen from Al Quoz industrial district. Trucks and labour camps characterize its desolate landscape.

Two workers take a rest along a major road in Al Quoz while the city skyline appears in the distance.

Rashid Colony, a public housing development built for the city's low- to medium-income population. It is located in the Al Qusais district behind the city's international airport.

The project has been marked for demolition, yet residents have offered resistance to eviction.

Alongside the project are commercial establishments. In a place without any viable public settings, these become the only option for an evening out.

A residential community near Rashid Colony – some areas appear lifeless, lacking any visible signs of residents.

A colony – governmental housing project – in Karama, built in the 1970s. These projects are an affordable housing option for the city's medium-income population.

Karama, a multi-ethnic neighbourhood characterized by a variety of housing styles. Its central location makes it particularly attractive for many residents.

Graffiti written in Arabic along the backstreets of Karama – 'Only Karama.', and 'Only Ajman'.

Workers at the World Trade Center Roundabout bus stop.

Chapter 4

The Illusive History of Dubai

In 1822 an English traveller described Dubai (or Debai as it was known then) as follows:

> Debai the next town in succession to Sharga... The town is a miserable assemblage of mud hovels surrounded by a low mud wall in which are several breaches & defended by three round towers, and a square castellated building, with a tower at one angle much dilapidated, and having only three or four guns mounted, which are old & rusty... There are two or three small date groves, in which are contained the only fresh water wells in the place, at the back of the town; otherwise the country is uncommonly barren. From the tower the creek was observed taking a winding course to the [south-]eastward ... where it was lost in a marsh... Debai may be considered as the termination of the Pirate Coast as the natives to the southward and westward, have been generally less addicted to plundering & always were friendly inclined to, or perhaps stood more in awe of, the English. (Burdett, 2000, pp. 3–4)

A map from that time, titled *Trigonometrical Plan of the Backwater of Debai*, confirms the above (figure 4.1). The city was indeed a *miserable collection of mud huts*, in what is now known as Bur Dubai, specifically the Shindagha area. This is the earliest record of Dubai – although some historical accounts have suggested that a settlement existed there at the end of the eighteenth century. The population in the first quarter of the nineteenth century was estimated at 1,200 inhabitants – a small insignificant fishing village whose inhabitants were viewed by the outside world as primitives *in awe of the English*. A series of events in the area, however, were to transform this *backwater*, setting the stage for a modern, contemporary metropolis.

One of the myths which I hope to dispel in this chapter is the notion of an oil city which emerged out of nothing, from the desert. While this is the typical Western view, one cannot discount the hand of officialdom in propagating this myth – a narrative of miraculous development, guided by the wisdom of the city's rulers. Nothing could be further from the truth. As this historical depiction will show, Dubai, unlike many of its neighbours such as Abu Dhabi, has a distinguished history (recent perhaps, but a history nevertheless). Similar to other modern cities, in North America, for example, it has humble beginnings but a shrewd ability to optimize its limited resources and its geographical position, all played a role in the city's 'miraculous' urban development.

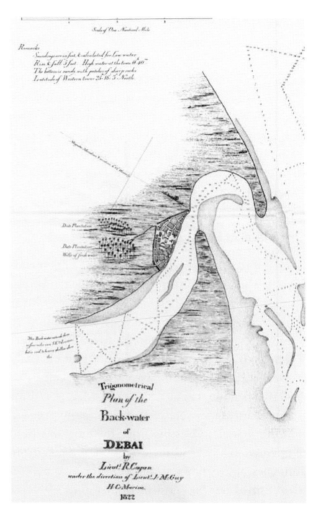

4.1. 'Trigonometrical Plan of the Back-water of Debai by Lieut R. Cogan, under the direction of Lieut J.M. Guy, HC Marine, 1822'. This is the oldest available record of the city's built environment. (*Source*: India Office Records, by courtesy of the British Library)

To that end, in the first part of this chapter I will discuss the city's origins and its development. The narrative interweaves the political, social and economic to show the extent to which they impacted on the city's urban form and architecture. I will complement this by providing travellers' portrayals and media reports, the latter relying on an extensive search in the *New York Times* and *The Times* archives. Interestingly, this search shows that in the first half of the twentieth century, and indeed until the late 1970s, its neighbour Abu Dhabi had far more coverage. Regarding travellers, one particularly interesting description of the city in the 1950s is provided by Lela Headley, a New York based public relations specialist, in her book *Give Me the World*. Of course at that time neither Dubai nor any other city in the region, with the exception of Muscat and to some degree Manama, provided the kind of 'Eastern' experience that was found in places such as Cairo and Damascus. I will follow this by discussing two case studies involving areas of the city whose development and transformation , in my view, encapsulate the kind of changes that have resulted in contemporary Dubai. They are the Bastakiy'ya district in Bur Dubai, the area perhaps most widely portrayed as representative of historic Dubai, with its wind towers (or windcatchers) and narrow alleyways; and the lesser known to tourists and visitors, Baniyas (or Nasser) Square in Deira. I will conclude by discussing how Dubai is using these historical settings as devices to establish (or reconstitute) an 'illusive' identity – and here I am using Eric Hobsbawm's notion of invented traditions – which needs to be constantly recast, redefined, and redeveloped. This will be set within current efforts to establish historic preservation guidelines, the recently formed Dubai Culture and Arts Authority, and the Creekfront Project, which aims to revitalize the historic importance of the Creek.

Origins and Developments

The Gulf region has been an area of contention and struggle since the fifteenth century when the Portuguese, followed by the British, attempted to gain control over parts of what was then known as 'Historic Oman'. Motivation was primarily commercial, to control the vital spice trade, an important commodity at that time due to its use in the preservation of food. The United Arab Emirates or UAE – as it is now known – was initially part of Historic Oman. As an important trading centre, it dates back to antiquity and Mesopotamian documents from as far back as 2000 BC mention trading activities in 'Magan' as it was then called.

The Portuguese were the first Europeans (i.e. Western) powers to 'colonize' the Gulf in a period lasting from 1500 to 1750. Some have argued that the fall of Grenada in 1492 and the expulsion of Moslems from Spain, followed by the Portuguese invasion of the Gulf, could be seen as a continuation of the war against Islam carried out on Moslem lands (Smith, 1991). No doubt such ideological conflicts cannot be discounted, but the area was also attractive as a centre of trade, being centrally located between European markets and those in Africa and Asia. While Portugal was emerging as a major power in the region other developments taking place were influential, such as the fall of Constantinople in 1453 and the emergence of the Ottomans as another hegemonic entity. Meanwhile the Portuguese continued their expansion with a series of battles culminating in the capture of Hormuz, Persia in 1507 and the battle of Ras Al-Khaimah.[1]

While there was an indigenous population in the area, a series of tribal migrations occurred in the eighteenth century which formed the nucleus for the current local population's make-up. These tribes settled in Historic Oman, attracted by the promise of prosperity from trade. Of significance are the *Qawasim* who came from Persia and the *Bani Yas* tribal grouping who came from the Najd area, in what is now Saudi Arabia. At that time the British showed interest in the area, and the *Qawasim* were perceived as a serious threat to their territorial ambitions. The influence of that tribe extended from Sharjah to Ajman, Um Al-Quwain and Ras Al-Khaimah (current Sheikhdoms or Emirates). They also had a significant maritime fleet numbering close to 500 ships. The *Qawasim* formed an alliance with the newly created *Wahabi* – or *Muwah'hidin* – movement in Central Arabia between 1795 and 1799.[2] The Ottomans and British saw the *Muwah'hidi* expansion as a threat to their dominance. As a response to this alliance, and to the *Qassimi* attempt to charge the British for navigational rights in the Gulf, it was decided to launch an attack against Ras Al-Khaimah in 1805. The *Qawasim* were ultimately defeated in 1819 thus establishing British colonial rule in Historic Oman which lasted until 1971 – although some have divided this period into two parts: 1820–1945 (end of World War II) and 1945–1971 (Kazim, 2000).

As opposed to outright physical occupation with all the responsibilities it entails, the British preferred to construct a series of treaties with a few select sheikhs (tribal leaders). These came to be crucial factors in the formation of the UAE and the emergence of the various emirates such as Abu Dhabi and Dubai. One of the most significant is the 1820 treaty signed by the Sheikh of Abu Dhabi, to be followed by other sheikhs including the Sheikh of Dubai, which officially designated the British as the rulers of Historic Oman. This treaty extended to the sheikhs' descendants as well. In 1922 another important treaty was signed specifying that, in the case of oil discovery, concessions would not be extended to any non-British entity. This was mainly prompted by oil discoveries in Abadan, Iran in 1908 and in Trucial Oman during World War I. During British dominance in the area some measures of resistance did exist which eventually culminated in Independence, but these were short-lived and did not take the form of armed, organized opposition as was to be found elsewhere in the Arab world.[3]

These agreements had a number of significant consequences. First, Historic Oman was divided into two parts: Oman and Trucial Oman. Trucial Oman was divided into separate sheikhdoms, 'conferring' an identity on each – thus leading the way towards cultural, political and economic segmentation. Also, a social hierarchy was 'constructed' as a result of designating treaty signatories and their descendants as *de facto* rulers, with all the power and prestige that entailed. Through this shrewd policy, power was conferred on the mercantile/trade families who signed these treaties thereby establishing hierarchical relationships – thus giving rise to the current power base of *Shuyookh* (elder, rulers). Also, most importantly, because of such arrangements the area was politically separated from the rest of the Arab/Moslem world.[4]

The Foundation of Modern Dubai[5]

As noted, the *Bani Yas* was a tribal grouping competing with the *Qawasim*, whose territory extended from Dubai to Qatar along the coast, and inland towards Bureimi. The 1820 treaty divided *Bani Yas* further by having Sheikh Tahnoon bin Shakhbout of Abu Dhabi and Sheikh Hazaa bin Za'al of Dubai (at that time 11 years old) each sign independently, thus 'creating' the emirates of Abu Dhabi and Dubai. A significant development strengthening the independence of Dubai occurred in 1833 when, due to political turmoil in Abu Dhabi, the *Al-Bufalasah* section of *Bani Yas* migrated to Dubai, eventually settling there. They numbered almost 800 people, a figure which effectively doubled the reported population of the fishing village at the time. The Al-Maktoum family, the current rulers of Dubai, were part of this 'wave of immigrants' who had decided to separate from Abu Dhabi. The mid eighteenth century saw expanded economic prosperity resulting in greater urbanization. While the bulk of the income was generated from fishing and pearling, Dubai's *souqs* were bustling with mercantile activity, in part as a result of the tolerance and openness of its rulers. Towards the end of the eighteenth century the population was estimated at around 3,000. Dubai's importance in the late 1800s and early 1900s was primarily due to the British bringing their goods by steamer and because it became Trucial Oman's main pearl exporter, because of developments in neighbouring Persia (currently Iran).

In the 1870s, political instability in Persia gave the ports on the coast of Oman, among them Dubai, an opportunity to become the major trading centres of the area. In addition, due to tax increases commissioned by the Shah in 1902, Arab Sunni merchants migrated *en masse* to Dubai where they established a trading base. By 1925 the Persian taxes had become even more onerous and were seen to be permanent; consequently the merchants who had been in temporary residence accepted the Dubai's ruler's offer to settle in Dubai and brought their families over. These merchants of mixed origin were given an area of land immediately to the east of Al Fahidi Fort on which to build themselves houses. The district became known as Bastakiy'ya since many of the settlers came from Bastak, part of the sub-province of Lâr in the Fârs province.

In the nineteenth and early twentieth century Dubai attracted a variety of immigrants, not just the Persians from Bastak. Other Persian and *Shi'i* groups arrived; Bahraini pearl divers had their own special district – Firj al-Bahrainah; migrants came from Iraq to work as accountants and clerks for Dubai's merchants. Another round of migrants in the 1930s were *Baluchis* who came mostly from an area in what is now Pakistan, bordering Iran and Afghanistan; they worked as porters and in other low-level employment (Kazim, 2000). Thus by early last century Dubai's population was made up of several classes and ethnic groups.

British influence was strong because of their interest in maintaining ports of call in the Gulf which was for two reasons: first they wanted an alternative overland and maritime route between India and Britain; second they wanted to reinforce their presence to prevent Russian influence in Persia. In 1904 steamers were calling at Dubai on a weekly basis, encouraged by the abolition of a 5 per cent customs duty following the declaration of Dubai as a 'free port'. The city also became a distribution centre for goods to other cities along the Gulf as well as to the interior and to the Sultanate of Oman.

As the population grew, Dubai developed into three distinct areas, separated by the Creek: Deira on the east bank was the largest and the main commercial centre, while on the west bank Bur Dubai – considered the government centre – and Shindagha were separated by a wide stretch of sand called Ghubaiba, which would flood at high tide. Shindagha, situated on a narrow strip of land separating the sea from the Creek, was the smallest area and the main residential district. The ruling sheikhs traditionally lived here and the late Sheikh Saeed's house is still standing. Shindagha was probably the site of the original *Bani Yas* village. Ferries connected the two main parts – Deira and Bur Dubai.

During the period 1947–1971, following World War II, Dubai continued to maintain itself as a mercantile city. However, it still remained more or less a British protectorate, a status enhanced by a series of political measures and development projects. For example, numerous contracts were extended exclusively to British firms: in 1947 the British Bank of the Middle East was established, while the construction of Al-Maktoum Hospital was a joint project with the British begun in 1951. At that time Dubai replaced Sharjah as the seat of the British political agent.[6]

Under Sheikh Rashid bin Saeed Al Maktoum, a series of development projects – all carried out with British assistance – greatly helped strengthen the city's position as a centre of trade. These included the electrification of Dubai in 1961, a year which also saw the dredging of the Creek for which funds were borrowed from Kuwait to pay the British firm of Halcrow & Partners. In this project the port was deepened through dredging and the building of breakwaters. Financing for many of these projects was based on anticipated oil revenues. And, as expected, oil in commercial quantities was discovered in 1966. British companies, to which all these contracts were granted, needed cheap labour which was readily available from India and Pakistan. Many came from other parts such as Iran, Europe and Arab countries. In 1968 immigrant labour constituted 50 per cent of Dubai's population. These workers had considerable cultural impact but they had no political power within Dubai's civil society – for example, they were not permitted to form unions. The influx of these 'foreigners' strengthened the identity of locals in relation to the immigrants, creating a sense of nationalism. Also, 'Dubayyans' perceived themselves as superior to the northern sheikhdoms (Ras al Khaimah, Ajman, Um al Quwain) due to their economic privilege.

Even with the presence of diverse cultures the city enjoyed relative stability – a fact paradoxically enhanced by this fragmentation. Each segment of society became too self-contained to unite with others and, in turn, challenge the *status quo*. Furthermore, tribal divisions were less significant in Dubai than in Abu Dhabi, for example, which is where most of the tribal groupings resided.

Forms of Resistance and Anti-Colonialism

Attempts at reform and in turn removal of colonial power did occur. In 1930 an armed conflict took place between Sheikh Saeed Al Maktoum and the *majlis* (a grouping of merchants acting as advisor to the sheikh) led by Sheikh Maani which eventually led to a British intervention, the installation of a new *majlis* and Sheikh Maani going into exile. Also termed the 'Reform Movement', they were pearl merchants reacting to the declining income from pearl revenue. Other mercantile groupings refused to join, however. This event prompted some to declare that '... behind Sheikh Saeed was British colonial power' (Kazim, 2000, p. 203). Interestingly, however, this movement began for a series of reasons: the opening of the Suez Canal in Egypt, the development of steam shipping and of a postal system, all of which led to the spread of ideas through the newspapers and other media, which advocated nationalistic movements and the creation of an 'Arab' identity to confront colonial powers. Another relevant event pertains to the construction of the airport. The British, encountering resistance in Ras Al-Khaimah, at the end of 1931 set their sights on Dubai. Many of the sheikh's relatives, as well as merchants, wanted to prevent Dubai from becoming a centre for British hegemony in the Gulf. A small airport accommodating flight services between Alexandria and India was, however, finally built in 1937.

The period following World War II saw a weakening of British hegemony and the emergence of the United States. This was, of course, linked to a rising global anti-colonial movement in the period between 1945 and 1965, which manifested itself in the forced withdrawal of colonial powers from many Arab countries. This was not what happened in the Gulf however which, for a number of reasons, witnessed an early, voluntary British withdrawal. By making the transition more peaceful they would ensure that oil concessions would remain intact and that British firms would be hired for maintenance and expansion of infrastructure. A stable political structure in place ensured the continuity of ruling entities and the prevention of armed insurrection.

In spite of this, the region did witness anti-colonial activities which, while not going as far as armed conflict, were nevertheless critical in establishing – or constructing – a 'UAE' identity. The first stage of this struggle was, of course, the short-lived Reform Movement in the 1930s which was not explicitly anti-colonial, its focus being mainly on governmental reform. The second stage made British withdrawal one of its key demands – deriving inspiration from Egypt's Nasser. A third – armed stage – as happened in Oman and Aden – did not occur mainly because oil revenues led to massive development projects, bringing prosperity and the beginning of consumerism. Furthermore, the failure of the development of an indigenous working class contributed to this. Workers, brought by the British retained identification with their home countries.

On 2 December 1971 what had been known as 'Trucial Oman' became the United Arab Emirates. There were many unifying factors which paved the way for a smooth transition: the same series of treaties being imposed on each emirate; pearl fishery; tribal interconnections; and, of course, being subject to the control of the British government of India. Ironically, the occupation of the islands of Greater and Lesser Tunbs by Iran – one day prior to the announcement of Independence (!) – helped in strengthening the newly emerging UAE identity.

Travellers' Accounts

The previous section outlined the main political factors which contributed to the development of Dubai, relying on primary sources such as *Records of Dubai*, but also on such studies as Aqil Kazim's comprehensive work on the socio-political development of the United Arab Emirates. However, the picture is incomplete. One does not have a sense of the city's inner life or its urban character. For most cities in the world there is usually an extensive collection of travellers' writings and works of fiction or poetry to draw upon. For the Gulf such resources are scarce, particularly if one is looking for early twentieth-century depictions, but in the case of Dubai a number of excellent sources do exist. The first is by Peter Lienhardt, an Oxford University Middle Eastern scholar, whose *Sheikhdoms of Eastern Arabia* is an anthropological study undertaken in the Gulf region between 1953 and 1956. The second was written in the 1950s by Lela Headley a 25 year old woman from Manhattan, New York who left a PR position and set out for Hong Kong with her 6 year old son. In the course of her long boat journey she encountered a variety of characters, visiting places such as Ceylon, Bangkok, Bombay and, of course, Dubai. These encounters and experiences are depicted in her book *Give Me the World*. Then there is, of course, the work of traveller Wilfred Thesiger who, in his journeys through the deserts of Arabia in the 1940s, offered a unique glimpse of the region which included a brief incursion into Dubai; a 1956 *National Geographic* article written by Ronald Codrai completes the selection.

Dubai in the 1940s

Given that Dubai was in a region considered inhospitable it did not receive much attention from travel writers. In 1949 Wilfred Thesiger, who travelled the empty deserts of Arabia, made a brief stop in Dubai. His dislike for urban settlements and preference for the open desert are evident in his portrayals. For instance, he describes his first encounter with Dubai as follows:

> We approached a small Arab town on an open beach; it was as drab and tumble-down as Abu Dhabi, but infinitely more squalid, for it was littered with discarded rubbish which had been mass-produced elsewhere. (Thesiger, 1959, p. 275)

During his brief stay in the city he lived in a large house overlooking the Creek owned by Edward Henderson the British representative in the area. From such a vantage point he made frequent references to both the poverty and primitive nature of the residents as well as the windcatcher houses of Bastakiy'ya. Hidden behind these is the *souq*:

> Naked children romped in the shallows, and rowing-boats patrolled the creek to pick up passengers from the mouths of alleys between high coral houses, surmounted with square wind-turrets and pleasingly decorated with plaster moulding. Behind the diversity of houses

which lined the waterfront were the *suqs*, covered passageways, where merchants sat in the gloom, cross-legged in narrow alcoves among their piled merchandise. (*Ibid.*, p. 276)

The *souq*'s inhabitants and users are noted for their varied background, hailing from a variety of regions in Asia as well as Africa. Of particular interest is Thesiger's description of his own experience walking through the market which according to him offered a slightly nostalgic version of a past time:

Here life moved in time from the past. These people still valued leisure and courtesy and conversation. They did not live their lives at second hand, dependent on cinema and wireless. I would willingly have consorted with them, but I now wore European clothes. As I wandered through the town I knew that they regarded me as an intruder; I myself felt that I was little better than a tourist. (*Ibid.*, p. 276, my emphasis)

Another significant source concerning Dubai's daily life in the 1940s is by Ronald Codrai – a Thesiger contemporary – who served in the Royal Air Force in the Second World War and lived in the region from 1948, working for an international oil consortium and travelling widely. His descriptions, like those of Thesiger, convey a setting of primitiveness, but also a teeming and vibrant community deeply rooted in rituals and well-established traditions. Writing in a 1956 article in the *National Geographic*:

Beneath my veranda lay grunting camels, left hobbled while their owners – tribesmen from the great sand seas of Arabia – shopped in the crowded bazaar. At the beginning of summer I would listen to the chanting of boat crews as they rowed out of the lagoon for the start of another pearl fishing season. And each Fall, when flights of turkey-sized bustard's came to the desert, the Sheikh's falconers would appear again, swaggering about the town with hawks perched on heavy canvas cuffs. (Codrai, 1956, p. 68)

He also devotes considerable attention to the city's marketplace, listing the various nationalities that constituted its population:

Dibai's teeming market has changed little through the centuries. Arabs, Iranians, Baluchis, Negroes, Pakistanis and Indians sit in the doorways of little open-fronted shops before colorful bales of cloth worth thousands of rupees. Other merchants squat in the open with only a few odds and ends spread on the ground before them. (*Ibid.*, p. 68)

Both Thesiger and Codrai evoke a setting that is exotic and different – perhaps having in mind their expected readership. It is possible to read this through an orientalist lens where the city's otherness – in its architecture as well as inhabitants – serves as a reminder of the West's superiority and as a justification for its hegemonic ambitions in the area. But it is also possible to construe this as an admiring, even romantic, illustration of a bygone area. But these are, of course, selective perceptions. In fact the city was engaged in modernizing as I will show in the following section.

Dubai in the 1950s

Perhaps not as romantic is Peter Lienhardt, who in his book represents an analysis of the Arab sheikhdoms of the Gulf. He discusses the common social patterns manifest in their tribal structure, the relations between men and women, the economics of pearl fishing, the growth of towns, and the complex relationship between the ruling sheikhs and their subjects. The book also addresses some of the traditional social, economic and political systems of the Arab sheikhdoms of the Gulf. Of particular interest are his depictions of the everyday life of residents as well as the overall urban character of cities – including Dubai. Here the primitive nature of the settlement is highlighted. He describes Dubai in the 1950s as a city that was still underdeveloped, noted for having extensive quarters of 'palm-houses' but there were also three and four-storey 'solid buildings' (Lienhardt, 2001). He argues that it was the only thriving town along what was then known as the Trucial Coast:

> Of all the towns and villages in the Trucial Coast, Dubai alone was in any way flourishing at that time. Dubai had extensive quarters of palm houses, but also had wide areas of more solid buildings, many of them two and a few three storeys high and most of them in good repair, surmounted by handsome wind towers in the Persian style. Heaps of coral for further building stood along the shore drying out. (p. 122)

Contrasting with these rather factual, objective depictions is Lela Headley's travelogue. She paints a romantic picture of a town rising from the midst of the desert:

> … toward the desert sheikdom of Dubai. The sun had just risen when we moored in the lee of the harbor curve of Dubai. The fretwork of the town, its minarets and mud walls and watchtower, rose like a mirage from the scimitarlike sweep of the littoral, with the pale sand of the desert stretching away on either side in sun-bleached levels to the horizon. (Headley, 1958, p. 253)

Minor dredging operations took place along the shore of the Creek, and these were responsible for reclamation of new areas of land, significantly expanding areas for building.[7] The overall hygienic conditions were below acceptable levels (an interesting observation considering that these depictions were in the 1950s) to the extent that many people would refuse to eat fish caught in the Creek since the waterway was treated as a 'sewer'.[8] Also, public services were lacking. Some people used electric generators but most had pressure lamps or oil lamps. Garbage was either thrown into the street or taken to the Creek. Water was delivered using Baluchi water carriers.[9]

This lack of basic services was also described by Headley in her one-day excursion to Dubai. Noting an invitation to dinner from a Dubai merchant, she describes romantic scenes of a candle-lit dinner, the presence of a refrigerator (powered by a special generator) containing among other things, a revolver![10] She also provides some insights into the town's morphology which, typical of desert cities, is one of intricate, maze-like alleyways, bordered by windowless walls, occasionally leading to a small open space. Her first encounter with the city paints a scene of primitive modernity and of a medieval oriental cityscape:

> The landing stage was enclosed in a cavern of concrete with a rounded archway that led out to a gray sand street flecked with rind and refuse, a sinuous passageway flanked by windowless walls of mud and screened from the light of the sky by a canopy of wooden gutters overhead. Out of necessity we walked in a single file along this alley. Rapidly twisting and turning, we met no one until the alley unexpectedly debouched into the souk, which was unlike any other market place I had ever seen. It was mud-walled and shadowy beneath a wattle thatch – a cool, smoky mole burrow with a blinding bright square at the far end where it tunneled through to an open courtyard. There was a charred, burned-meat, roses-after-rain smell, a general hubbub of noise, and again the feeling, which I never got used to in the East, of unreality, of a tableau vivant to amuse the senses and the mind. (*Ibid.*, pp. 255–256)

In another passage she notes how the city closes down outside the *souq* area:

> Outside of the little souk area Dubai closed down, contracted again into a sandy labyrinth of paths pinched between thick mudwalls. Occasionally, from an open postern let into the panel of a nail-studded door, there seeped small sounds of life from a hidden inner court… I followed Sherif down a maze of dark alley-ways and up a wooden ladder to the roof-top level of the town, across narrow plank bridges spanning wattle roofing, over inexplicable ridges and hummocks, down steps, up steps, jumping from one rooftop to another, never quite sure that I was not going to crash into the street below… On the roofs about us and in the courtyards and streets below the firefly flashing of lanterns began. The desert air, tonic and distilled, was freshened with a sea breeze, and from the tops of the lime-plaster minarets the muezzins arrowed their voices through the darkness… (*Ibid.*, p. 258)

The city at that time had a vibrant marketplace, although the shops were typically oriental – i.e. stores had no glass fronts, but were raised above street level with the merchant sitting on a ledge.[11] Headley paints a 'chaotic' scene of mixed uses in which such modern signs as a store's advertising – in English – and its tailoring activities, are viewed with curiosity.[12]

Absent from Headley's description are any signs of modernity – aside from the refrigerator – which is illustrative perhaps of an orientalist mentality. One could speculate that her main interest was in depicting an 'Eastern' setting, and how she as a Western, female subject was 'violated' by the gaze of the 'primitive' oriental. However, Dubai at that time had some modern institutions such as a bank[13] and an open air cinema.[14] The latter is an example of the city's liberal policies, since such modern Western settings were deemed as 'immoral' elsewhere in the area.

In general these depictions are confirmed by historic photographs which convey a similar atmosphere. Photographs of the *souq* are a visual embodiment of these travel accounts. It is also interesting to note that official portrayals of the city's heritage do not attempt to hide its underdeveloped state. Rather, Dubai's current high-tech progress is contrasted with these images, to underscore the 'miraculous' development witnessed within the last two decades (from the 1980s onwards). The city has in fact changed significantly and only traces remain of the 'Arabian', 'Eastern' setting depicted above. These remnants of the past, as it were, can be seen in Dubai Fort, a reconstruction currently housing the Dubai Museum, and the Bastakiy'ya district. A setting symptomatic of the city's modern transformation is Baniyas Square.[15]

Dubai in the Media

Examining historical media archives offers another way to get a glimpse of the city's inner life as well as providing a better understanding of the political context. Particularly in the 1950s and 1960s, the Gulf region and the Arabian peninsula began to attract the attention not only of many travel writers and historians, but also journalists who were drawn to the region's history as well as its emergence on the world stage due to the discovery of oil. *The New York Times* archives, which date back to the nineteenth century, are an excellent resource in this regard. I have also researched the UK's *The Times* archives which date back to the eighteenth century and provide extensive and interesting observations – understandable given British involvement in the area.

Dubai through American Eyes: The New York Times

A search for Dubai in *The New York Times* archives reveals that one of the earliest references to the city is in a 1956 article investigating slavery in the Arabian peninsula. While the focus is on Saudi Arabia and the 'extensive slave hunting in the sheikdoms of the Persian Gulf coasts', the article notes that there are more than 500,000 slaves in the area and, interestingly, Dubai – according to the report – represents 'a key node in a "slave route" linking Qatar, Muscat and Buraimi to the markets in Riyadh'.[16] Another reference to the city appears in a 1961 article by Marion Stelling who describes her voyage to the Orient, which included a stop in Dubai. Her depictions centre on the market which she views as one of the 'high spots of the cruise'. The city – or ancient town according to her description – follows a traditional oriental town in its layout and features: 'The bazaar under a thatched roof, the fish market by the shore, the tall buildings shading three-foot-wide streets'. Furthermore her observation concerning the city's daily life evoke poverty and exoticism:

In the bazaar, beggars cry out for baksheesh, alms. But they will not accept the Indian rupee coins that are used aboard ship, hence available to passengers at a value of roughly 20 cents. It appears that only the Gulf rupee is current in Dubai, and the Indian variety is rejected in the community... The women of Dubai wear ornate dresses and filmy black head coverings. Their oddest adornment is a curious mask worn over nose and mouth. Such masks are constructed of leather over a frame of bone.

She is particularly fond of the harbour which she sees as the city's 'pleasantest feature'. She views with suspicion the comparison that is made to Venice as the harbour has been given the title 'Venice of the Middle East' – a designation she describes as 'dubious'.[17]

Another reference appears in a 1968 article which deals with the political situation in the Arabian Peninsula, showing rivalry between Abu Dhabi and Dubai and the extent to which Saudi Arabia is playing a role in supporting Dubai. The article notes that there was a war between the two emirates in 1948 but that their rivalry 'takes the form of outbuilding, outdeveloping, outeducating and outgrowing each other'.[18] Within that same time frame Abu Dhabi received much more coverage, due mainly to the early discovery of oil, and because it was the capital of a newly emerging nation embarking on a massive development programme which more or less entailed the creation of a new city (see, for example, Elsheshtawy, 2008). This evoked the curiosity of many journalists and travel writers such as Jonathan Raban who describes a visit to Dubai in the 1970s which I will discuss in the next chapter.

Dubai through British Eyes: The Times

One of the earliest references to Dubai appears in a 1911 article titled 'Gun running in the Persian Gulf; the Arabs and British action'. It attempts to explain resistance encountered by British forces in what was then known as Debai. According to an official: '... pro-British sentiment on the Pirate coast has grown weaker. Misled by the Egyptian Pan-Islamic press, the Arabs believe that a departure from our policy of non-intervention is contemplated and they fear a partition of Persia, followed by annexation in Arabia'. The article then goes on to describe 'fighting at Debai' which resulted in British casualties.[19]

In 1956, an article titled 'Britain's burden in Arabia' discusses the desired level of British engagement in the region, given that oil had only been discovered in a few select countries. The article is prefaced by a description of Dubai emphasizing its primitiveness, drawing references to Joseph Conrad's *Lord Jim*, a nineteenth-century novel about a sailor redeeming himself in the midst of Moslems in South East Asia:[20]

One look at Dubai, and you think of Conrad. Somewhere surely along this exotic creek, where the dhows lie bow to stern under ragged and piebald flags and the boatmen leave their passengers under white awnings from shore to shore, like Venetian gondoliers, somewhere a broken giant of a white man must be expiating a fearful sin – the Lord Jim of the Trucial Coast. The thought has its significance, for it places Dubai where it belongs, squarely in the nineteenth century. It is the Persian Gulf before oil. There could be no Lord Jims in Kuwait.

Somehow the reference to Conrad and his fallen hero seems to justify British engagement in the region – a duty of sorts to take the primitives from the nineteenth century into the twentieth. The writer goes on to emphasize the exotic nature of the place and that its citizenry are awaiting promised riches: 'Their life is devoted to dreams of oil'. Another reference to Dubai appears in a 1965 report detailing a trip taken by dhow from Kuwait to Dubai which evokes in lyrical language the hardships as well as the camaraderie among the boat's crew.[21] In 1966 oil was finally discovered which was duly noted by *The Times* in an article titled 'Now Dubai becomes an oil state'.[22]

A significant number of articles are devoted to Dubai's reputation as a 'gold smuggler'. A 1969 report describes in great detail the mechanisms involved in this trade: 'Now dhows driven by diesel engines make the voyage in rough weather from Dubai to rendezvous with Indian boats outside Indian territorial waters of Bombay'.[23] The reason behind the proliferation of the trade, according to the writer, is that '… gold is interwoven into the religious, social and economic life of India'. However, because of the trade there has been an outflow of foreign exchange, which represents a substantial drain on its economy – hence efforts by India to make it illegal. Yet the article notes that the trade, in which both London gold merchants and Dubai traders are involved, is not illegal. Of course the trade had a positive impact on Dubai's development: 'it has helped to finance the building of an international airport and several good hotels and the expansion of the harbour'. But the writer observes that this may change: 'Black gold has now been found in Dubai and may eventually supersede yellow gold in importance'.

Dubai's historical focus on trade is the subject of another 1969 article which points out that the city distinguishes itself from its neighbours precisely because of this trait – it is not simply an artificial oil creation.[24] Along those same lines another article details the city's advances and heritage – making it an attractive proposition for outside investors and visitors. The writer describes the dhow as 'a symbol of Dubai'.[25] He observes the advanced state of the city in relation to its neighbours; the consistency of electric supply and the cleanliness of the water which until recently 'was brought, greasy and full of dead flies, in kerosene drums on the backs of donkeys'. Considerable attention is devoted to one particularly noticeable aspect, namely the multicultural nature of the population and the tolerance displayed towards any sign of otherness.[26] Another sign of progress is the presence of cinemas:

> The Kuwaitis have long been speaking about building a booster transmitter in Dubai, but for the next year at least the main recreation will continue to be the cinema. There are four cinemas in

Dubai and the films, mostly Indian, still tend to be advertised by the foot in contrast to quality. An enormous cinema is being built near the centre of the town by a retired Pakistani gold dealer and it is rumoured that the owner may speculate in MGM and Twentieth Century-Fox.

Dubai's reputation as a smuggling hub is the subject of yet another article arguing that its main economic activity still relies on gold trade, despite the fact that its economic figures at the time put the city near bankruptcy. The article also notes that the city is becoming a main centre for smuggling in the East on a par with Macao and Bangkok.[27] Dubai's distinction from its neighbours, particularly its liberal attitude and its 'charm', is depicted in a 1969 article, where the city is portrayed as becoming the region's Beirut, i.e. a centre for entertainment and leisure:

> Dubai has the potential of becoming the Beirut of the Gulf. It had three luxury hotels when one still had to drive across sand to get to them and, when I first went there three years ago, a most daring innovation for a strict Muslim community had been made – a Jazz band was playing for dancers at one hotel. The creek, with its picturesque dhows is a delight in a desert land, and the Persian wind towers which serve to air condition the older buildings, give the town a charm wholly lacking in Abu Dhabi or indeed in Qatar and Bahrain.[28]

In 1974, another article argued that Dubai was set to become the business centre of the Gulf. The piece is accompanied by images of the newly constructed Garhoud Bridge with two sailors and their dhows in the foreground – their antiquated image contrasting with the elaborate concrete structure of the bridge. Another image shows the Bastakiy'ya district with a lone Arab walking in the foreground. The caption reads: 'Old houses in the town of Dubai where merchant families still live. Sheikh Rashid has ordered that some must be preserved as a part of the country's history'.[29]

The notion that the Gulf states, particularly Dubai, emerged from a primitive past to a modern present begins to take hold in the mid 1970s as a result of the extensive construction activity. A 1975 article characterizes these developments as 'ruthless',[30] while an architectural critic notes 'the absence of planning controls'.[31] Yet in spite of these criticisms it is observed that the people are 'arriving in the thousands' and that shops and restaurants are full of 'elegance'.[32] And in an insightful and eloquent quote the writer captures the tolerant nature of the city:

> Tolerant of all comers the resident of Dubai blinks an eye on Burns' night as the sound of bagpipes rises about Jumeirah from the Caledonian Society chieftain's house. All manner of clubs and societies, three English-language libraries, church services of small Asian denominations, hotels, restaurants, shops, theatre, international trade exhibitions and fairs, teeming dhows and suks, the muezzins and baggy-trousered Baluch keep this melting pot on the boil.

The Bastakiy'ya District

More than any other setting in Dubai the Bastakiy'ya district located in Bur Dubai encapsulates what for many is the true essence of Dubai (figure 4.2). Its houses crowned with towering windcatchers are the quintessential image luring tourists to the city. Such images are also used to convey a sense of history, that the city has roots to its past. Yet it is surprising, given the importance currently being placed on the district, that it was seen as an eyesore in the 1970s and that many of its original buildings have been demolished. In fact Bastakiy'ya would have been obliterated had it not been for the intervention of the UK's crown prince who, visiting Dubai in 1989, encouraged the authorities to recognize the value of preservation, which led to its current situation – an open air museum housing upscale galleries and restaurants for the elite connoisseurs of traditional architecture and urbanism (figure 4.3).

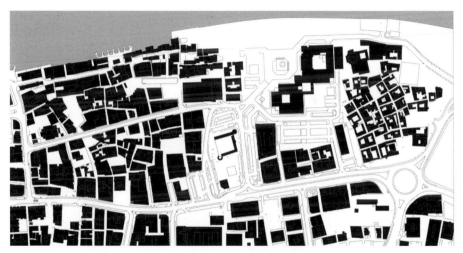

4.2. Figure-ground diagram of the area surrounding Bastakiy'ya. (*Source*: Dubai Municipality)

4.3. The meticulously preserved houses of Bastakiy'ya, currently housing art galleries and restaurants.

This image contrasts sharply with the district's origins and the place it occupied in the history of Dubai's urban development. Reading this history and listening to the stories of its original residents reveals a place that is alive, filled with memories, and playing a substantive role in the city's growth – unlike the current fossilized version. In examining the district's history and transformation I will be looking at its early beginnings and its subsequent decline – essentially becoming a home to squatters. Its subsequent revival and transformation into a symbol of national heritage illustrates a shift as well as a recognition of the importance of such places not just at a local level, but regionally and even globally. Complementing this narrative I will examine the surrounding area which seems to be a more authentic representation of history and heritage.

Early History and Origins

The origins of Bastakiy'ya go back as far as 1896 with the arrival of Iranian merchants from the towns of Lingeh and Bastak. These merchants initially settled

4.4. The Fahidi Fort and a reconstructed part of the wall which surrounded the city in the nineteenth century.

in an area known as Hamriya, next to the current Bastakiy'ya district. They lived in rooms above their shops in the nearby *souq*. The area was close to the fort as well as Sheikh Saeed House, the ruler's residence in Shindagha, giving it added importance (Coles and Jackson, 2007). Prompted by changes in Persian taxation laws, as well as imposition of rules that contradicted well established cultural traditions these merchants found Dubai receptive to their presence.[33] In addition Dubai's shrewd rulers recognized the commercial benefits of having such a community of merchants in their midst. Thus, these merchants of mixed origin were given an area of land immediately to the east of Al Fahidi Fort on which to build themselves houses (figure 4.4). As noted above the district became known as Bastakiy'ya because many of the settlers came from Bastak.

The influx of wealthy merchants created a rich architectural neighbourhood. Their houses were built by masons who designed and constructed the buildings to minimize the discomforts of the heat and humidity on the Gulf coast. Also, the influx of people from the Persian coast introduced windtowers (also known as *barajil*). The expansion of the Bastakiy'ya area can be seen as a symbol of the changing emphasis in the economy of Dubai as well as of the new cultural and social influence and as a new dimension to the social structure of the city-state.

One pearl merchant recounting the early days of settlement in Dubai illustrates the extent to which the ruler played a strong role in encouraging migrants to come to the city and reserving a special area for these newcomers:

> I was born on January 5th, 1916 at the Bastaki family house in Bastakiy'ya . My family came from Bastak, a town in southern Iran, close to Dubai. Then we came to stay in the Bastakiy'ya area here. It was our home. Sheikh Maktoum, Sheikh Saeed's father wanted us to come to Dubai. We were coming and going for 20 or 30 years, but around 1900 we settled because Sheikh Maktoum told us to come and stay home. He said people would shift from the area we called Bastakiy'ya to Deira and leave this area for all of us. 'You bring your family,' he told my father.[34]

Another depiction shows the transnational connections which were established by these merchants who had ties to Iran, India and Africa, thus turning Dubai into a major node in trade routes at the beginning of the twentieth century - a role that defines the city to this day:

> Mohamed Sharif Bukhash (1871–1946) came from the town of Bastak. He began trading in Dubai from the turn of the twentieth century... From 1913 until 1923 Mohamed Sharif lived in Bombay, a key port for the family's trade in garments, fabrics, rice and tea... Together the Fikree and Bukhash families had agencies in Lingeh, Karachi, Bombay, Aden and in Kalba and Buraimi... The Fikrees owned dhows which sailed as far as Zanzibar and Madagascar... Dhows from Lingeh would sail with various nuts, dried game meat and salt, to Bombay and Karachi. From there they would be loaded with timber, cloth, rice, sugar, spices and pepper destined for Dubai, Bahrain and Kuwait. From Dubai dried lemons were exported... [35]

Some of the original residents' stories offer a fascinating glimpse into the inner life of the district and its relation to the wider city – the nearby district of Shindaghah, across the Creek in Deira, or the remote settlement of Jumeirah. It is also interesting to observe that in these early days the district was considered to be at the edge of town, sea on one side and desert on the other. Known mainly for its Iranian community, other ethnic groups had their own areas. For instance, Bahrainis lived in an area between Bastakiy'ya and Shindagha. The district's relative isolation allowed women to swim in the Creek on certain days, which would be considered ladies' nights of sorts.[36] Also, the distinct nature of the place – emphasized by its architecture – intensified the sense of Bastakiy'ya as a self-contained unit. This notion of otherness is recounted by some residents. For instance Eesa Basataki, whose family owned a house in the district, recalls how it was defended by its youths from nearby residents who would come to 'flirt' with the girls. The Creek figures prominently in these stories. Located at the heart of the city many memories are recalled in relation to this waterway – crossing to the other side where there was a major *souq* as well as various commercial outlets, swimming if no other mode of transport was available. Many of these stories are told in an excellent ethnography titled *Telling Tales: An Oral History of Dubai* by Julia Wheeler and Paul Thuysbaert published in 2005.

The Decline of Bastakiy'ya

Given the historical significance of the area as well as its proximity to the ruler's house – the Sheikh Saeed residence – it was only natural that a palace for Sheikh Rashid as well as a customs house would be built to the north-west of Bastakiy'ya. Aerial photographs taken in the 1950s show close to fifty buildings with windtowers and around forty *areesh* compounds (houses built with temporary materials). According to Coles and Jackson (2007), the district reached its maximum size in the 1960s, covering an area of approximately 4 hectares (40,000 m²), with an east-west frontage of about 250 metres and 150 metres deep. At that time Dubai's ruler Sheikh Rashid commissioned London-based architect John Harris to prepare what would be considered the city's first master plan. Urban design guidelines were introduced in 1968 which included a 'prohibition on demolition in Shindagha or the Bastakiy'ya, or alterations other than for minor maintenance' (Coles and Jackson, 2007, p. 177). In 1978 Sheikh Rashid asked Iraqi architect Mohamed Makiya to restore the nearby Dubai Fort and to redesign it as a museum. Further expansion was carried out in 1988, leading to its current form (Frampton and Khan, 2000).

In spite of all these efforts at preserving the district and its historical significance, it is surprising that the 1970s witnessed what can only be described as a 'period of decline'. Many local residents left their homes for newly developed suburbs in Rashidiya, which offered greater space and more privacy from encroaching, low-income expatriates. Thus many of these historic buildings were left to deteriorate and crumble. Often they became residences for squatters and low-income labourers. Proposals for surveying the district and its preservation as a historical landmark were turned down by the authorities. Further accentuating its decline was a competition held in 1984 to extend the ruler's office, which resulted in the demolition of a large part, including some significant houses. This was anticipated since for many residents in Dubai Bastakiy'ya had become an eyesore which should be removed. Further accentuating this attitude was the extension of the ruler's palace and the construction of the Diwan complex, which resulted in the destruction of a large part of Bastakiy'ya.

In fact the area was largely perceived as a decaying slum. Buildings were in poor structural condition; they were being damaged by unauthorized changes and the sheer pressure of over-occupation by single labourers – sometimes well over fifty per house. Furthermore, the area was divorced from surrounding developments. Port activities were fenced off along the Creek to the north, the Diwan area was walled off to the west, and the cemetery to the east, and Al-Fahidi Road separates the area from the modern city to the south. Nevertheless, visually Bastakiy'ya was part of the wider city, the high-rise downtown of the Deira side of the Creek

4.5. The rooftop of one of the historic structures used for drying clothes (1997).

visually intrudes on the setting of the quarter, and the nearby neon advertisements are placed for maximum visibility from Deira. My own visit with a group of students in 1997 – when preservation efforts were well under way – shows some signs of this decay. A Filipino resident took us into a house occupied by labourers and this illustrated the extent of the damage to which these houses were subjected. The house was divided into partitions, which were occupied by a plethora of labourers engaging in different activities such as cooking and washing. Most of the second floor ceiling had been removed for some reason. Entering the house was like being in another, surreal, world. As we moved upward to the roof we found that it was being used as an area for drying clothes, next to imposing windcatchers! (figure 4.5).

As I noted earlier, a shift in attitude happened following a visit by the British crown prince. Subsequently, Dubai Municipality commissioned British planning and architectural consultants Llewelyn Davies to prepare a study on the district's conservation. This resulting report, 'Bastakiy'ya Conservation Preliminary Study', formed the basis for the restoration and reconstruction of fifty-five buildings in the area. Supervising these efforts was architect Rashad Bukhash from the Historical Section at the municipality, whose family used to occupy a large house in the district. Thanks to his efforts the district has been saved from complete eradication. Many of the demolished houses were reconstructed using historical photographs and remnants of building foundations. The result is a sanitized version of old Bastakiy'ya, yet it nevertheless represents for many the only trace of a historical Dubai.

The story of Bastakiy'ya is interesting in the sense that it illustrates a shift in attitude towards the preservation of this district. What was initially regarded as a decaying, perhaps even foreign (Persian, non-Arab), presence in the midst of a modernizing city suddenly became a symbol and a site of heritage that needed to be preserved. Echoing developments elsewhere in the region – the razing of Kuwait's old city (see Mahgoub, 2008) or the dismantling of Souq Waqif in Doha, only to be resurrected later as its touristic importance was recognized (Adham, 2008) – this could be seen as a late adaptation of a modernist ideology which views the past as something that needs to be forgotten. Yet the 1970s and 1980s witnessed the emergence of post-modernist ideologies which attempted to revive the past and recast it in more palatable ways. Thus buildings incorporated historical detailing and historic districts were revamped to cater for a growing tourism industry. Examples of this abound all over the world. It was only natural that the Gulf would be receptive to such ideas – albeit a bit late following the complete destruction of some of its historical monuments. Yet that did not prove to be a problem as many were reconstructed as noted earlier. But another explanation for this interest pertains to how the authorities are attempting to assert an 'Emirati' identity *vis-à-vis* a dominant expatriate population. Thus clinging to any historic symbols – the national dress (male and female), the presence of historic sculptures at traffic junctions, in addition to architectural signs – serves as a reminder for both

4.6. The Madinat Jumeirah roofscape dominated by non-functioning windcatchers. It is an upscale hotel/shopping centre located in new Dubai close to the Burj Al Arab Hotel.

residents and nationals about the city's 'projected' identity. Such efforts in some instances can truly reach bizarre proportions as can be seen in the massive Madinat Jumeirah complex modelled after the Bastakiy'ya district, where the monumental windcatchers have no functional purpose except to evoke a sense of history and heritage (figure 4.6).

Current Condition and Surroundings

Under the supervision of Dubai Municipality Historical Buildings Department the district has been carefully reconstructed. Demolished buildings were resurrected using authentic materials whenever feasible, coral stone for example. Architectural detailing evoking traditional Gulf architecture – which may not have existed in the original – is being used and documented. But, defying the original purpose of the windcatcher they are boarded and closed with wood planks and all buildings are air conditioned. Furthermore, the original function of these buildings – housing – has been supplanted by renting them as high end art galleries, restaurants and coffee shops. Furthermore the Historical Buildings Department occupies a house as well. Others remain empty.[37]

On any given day the area appears desolate except for the occasional wandering tourist(s). A fossilized version of what had been a vibrant district has thus been created (figure 4.7). The buildings cater for a very specific set of users – some upscale residents of Dubai but mostly well-off tourists. The ordinary, everyday and chaotic has no place in such a setting. In fact the owner of one particular establishment relishes in the fact that her 'bed & breakfast' does not cater for the everyday tourist trade. Or consider the conversion of the district on Saturdays during the Dubai Shopping Festival, to an outdoor market. The Souq Al Bastakiy'ya, organized by the recently formed Dubai Culture and Arts Authority, treats the historical setting in a manner that is evocative of a high-end shopping mall, even to the degree that visitors can use a valet car parking service! (figure 4.8). Thus the separation between the city and the district is done on purpose – creating a barrier of sorts to display the area as a precious object that should not be tainted by its surroundings. Only the initiated and the connoisseurs can have access to its hidden treasures. Yet it is precisely in these surroundings that a much more authentic city is found, whether in the Old Souq, the Hindu temple or intimate establishments considered among the oldest in the city such as the Special Ustadi Restaurant. The following are descriptions of these settings which are based on fieldwork and visits which I have conducted since 1997.

4.7. The desolate landscape of Bastakiy'ya as it appears on a typical day.

4.8. Carefully arranged stalls in the Souq Al Bastakiy'ya.

Souq Kabir

The Old Souq – also known as *Souq Kabir* – is located in an area roughly defined by Ali Ibn Abu Talib Road to the south and the Creek to the north. It is an area of traditional *souq* uses and still largely retains the old street and urban block layout, with narrow twisting *sikka's* (small alleys) and buildings which directly front the waterside. Official tourist guides suggest that the area gains much of its appeal from its overall townscape quality rather than from architectural set-pieces and that this quality is a combination of activity, urban form and pedestrian scale. It is seen at its best at the waterfront where the meaning of the place as a waterside trading town is apparent, and where the relationship between building plots, the *abra* station (small ferries carrying passengers to the other side of the Creek) and the Creek edge gives an urban quality which has been lost elsewhere in Dubai (figure 4.9). This is particularly apparent in one of the oldest structures in the area – standing since 1935 – currently housing the upscale al-Wakil restaurant.

My visit to the site in 2002 confirmed this carefully staged image of the market, a setting mostly geared to tourists. Yet the presence of the *abra* station, which is used by low-income workers, gives the setting a spontaneous character that is not found elsewhere in the city. What struck me most, however, were some gathering

4.9(*a*). Seating areas are provided along the *souq*'s edge which borders the waterfront.

4.9(*b*). The intersection of the *souq* and the Creek, a vibrant public space near the *abra* station.

places along the Creek which contained benches and seating areas, used by local elderly people as well as merchants from the district. Here perhaps more than anywhere else was a strong sense of urbanity and history. The mere presence of these elderly people offered some sort of refuge from the rampant consumerism dominating the city's official discourse and – in some way – suggested a level of authenticity. Yet, sadly, on subsequent visits these places were gone, closed off for construction of buildings and stores. Thus, it seems that these settings of 'last refuge' do not have a place in modern Dubai.

The Hindu Temple

Tucked behind the grand mosque of Dubai opposite the Fahidi Fort is the only Hindu temple in the city. Locally referred to as *Shiva and Krishna Mandir*, it is run in conjunction with the Indian consulate. The land was granted by Sheikh Rashid Al Maktoum, Dubai's previous ruler, to the city's sizeable Hindu community. Its location next to the city's religious, governmental and cultural symbols makes it all the more remarkable. The Bastakiy'ya district with its soaring windcatchers, the massive Diwan – a sprawling governmental complex housing government offices – and the Dubai Fort, its oldest surviving structure, are in close proximity – conspiring, it seems, to hide this symbol of diversity and tolerance.

My approach, when visiting the area in October 2008, was from the commercial district of Meena Bazaar where I had parked my car (see Chapter 7 for a detailed analysis of this area). Resembling parts of India, it was filled with visitors, shoppers and low-income labourers who use its various street corners, occasional open spaces and parking lots as meeting places. I passed next to an Indian restaurant called 'Vegetarian Restaurant'. It had a window opening to the street dispensing various food items; a family had gathered on the narrow sidewalk ordering sweets for their children (figure 4.10). I emerged from this rather lively part into a large open space containing the Dubai Fort (now the Dubai Museum). Behind the fort is a large mosque, the Dubai Grand mosque built in 1997, replacing a smaller version built in 1900. In order to reach the Hindu temple one has to pass next to this mosque and the imposing gates of the Diwan complex. The approach is rather modest as there is no indication that behind these structures is the only Hindu temple in the UAE and the region (with the exception of Muscat, Oman which has two). A small widening next to the mosque leads to a large open space, hidden, containing an outdoor lobby of sorts for the temple (figure 4.11). Slightly raised, it is surrounded by free standing iron gates marking an informal entrance to the complex. There are also a couple of shops selling items which are used by worshippers as offerings to the gods (sweets, flowers, and so on). One seller displayed his wares on a blanket (figure 4.12).

On this particular day the place was packed because it was a weekend and it followed Diwali, the Indian festival of light, marking the new year in the Hindu calendar.[38] This outdoor lobby of the temple contained various benches where

4.10. A popular Indian eatery in a road leading to the Hindu temple. A window serves passersby.

4.11. An outdoor space leading to the temple.

4.12. Opposite the temple informal activities take place such as the seller in the background displaying his wares on a blanket.

people were sitting and also an area where those entering the temple can remove their shoes and stack them in a special 'cupboard'. The atmosphere can be described as festive: families with children, couples, women in flowing saris, single men sitting on benches, all constituted a kaleidoscope of users.[39] There were also a few Western tourists, and I observed a group of three Iranian women. As I was busy photographing, a volunteer, who seemed to be organizing the crowd, approached me and suggested that I could enter the temple. Surprised, as I expected it to be

4.13. The temple's entrance has symbolic markings setting it apart from the surroundings.

only accessible to worshippers, he noted that it is open for everyone, 'It is our culture, please enter'. But he said that photography was not allowed and that I would have to remove my shoes (figure 4.13).

I did as told and soon found myself entering the temple. The building itself has no architectural distinction setting it apart from its surroundings. It appeared to be an existing structure adapted to suit the particular needs of religious activities. The main hall is accessed via an external staircase as it is located in the top floor. As I entered, the main hall appeared to me like a large living room in an apartment – not a soaring space one would expect in a more traditional temple. Nevertheless there was an aura of devotion and spirituality. Brightly lit, I found on one side of the space a group of elderly women sitting on the floor preparing various offerings and gifts. Ahead of me was a group of men sitting on the floor in various stages of meditation and prayer. But the focus was the front of the room which contained the main shrine, a large statue (Krishna) surrounded by flowers and photographs. A group of musicians and chanters were sitting in front – their music and chants dominated the setting and they were surrounded by onlookers. Their chants – devotions to the name of Lord Krishna – were derived from a large book, placed between them.

The way down is from another, internal staircase leading to a waiting and seating area which had a large plasma screen where some sort of speech was given by a preacher. There were also photographs of various gods' statues displayed on the wall. People would pass by these, offer words of prayer and kiss them. There was also a group of people, volunteers working for the temple, filling small plastic bags with sweets. As I went towards the exit and emerged into the outdoor space again, I was greeted by my 'friend' who asked if I had received *prasad*. I guessed he was referring to the sweets so I said that I had not. He insisted that I had to take it, took me by the hand and led me inside the temple again and asked those in charge of *prasad* to give me two bags. As I found out later these are offerings by the god in recognition of visiting the temple. He asked me where I was from and then his passing words were 'We all worship one God'.

As I lingered outside the temple for a while, I went behind the complex into a back alley which contained small shops selling items such as deity photographs, sweets, flowers and the ubiquitous clothing and fabric shops which seem to be everywhere. People were passing through this narrow alleyway, coming from the nearby *abra* station, which serves those visiting the place from the Deira side of the Creek. An accidentally open door showed stacks of some sort of blue deity – a religious storage room perhaps. On the alley's walls were Hindi magazines hanging from a clothes line. As one commentator noted the area 'looked and smelt India'.[40] It is in fact for many expatriates a place that is a reminder of home[41] – being hidden and tucked away from the city's main spaces highlights and accentuates that sense of 'foreignness' – being there is like observing an exotic locale, which has its own rules and rituals only known to insiders.[42] But it is also accessible – in fact the whole atmosphere was very friendly, no one was bothered by my picture taking and I was able to move freely (figure 4.14).

Looking at the surrounding context, one reason for its success as an urban node seems to be what environment-behaviour researcher Amos Rapoport (1990) refers to as a 'system of settings'. Basically a space 'works' if it is supported by settings that act in tandem with that space in terms of supporting activities. Thus one

4.14. A festive atmosphere as diverse users surround the temple.

could argue that the Hindu Temple works so well (aside from its strictly religious significance) because it is served by the nearby commercial centre of Meena Bazaar drawing people in as well as merging the secular with the religious (people exiting the temple were observed making their way towards the bazaar and vice versa). Also in terms of transport two significant stations are nearby: the *abra* or boat ferry, and the Ghubeiba bus stop – their close proximity is an important component in the temple's system of settings since these transport nodes serve low-income users and in turn their closeness enables them to access the temple easily.

On my way out of this rather remarkable place and passing next to the mosque, where the call to prayer was to be clearly heard, seeing Moslems entering their 'temple', observing the Dubai Fort in front of me, and on my left the entrance gate to the Diwan – I realized that there is perhaps no other city in the Middle East where the religious, the cultural and the political are so closely juxtaposed. It is a sign of tolerance, and it is in precisely such a setting that the multicultural nature of Dubai – dominated by the South Asian community – is clearly evident.[43] A microcosm of the city's attitude, its mantra perhaps – *live and let live*. Being there contrasted sharply with some of the sterile settings that we associate with Dubai: its megamalls and anonymous shopping centres, or lifeless streets and public spaces. Here was perhaps a level of authenticity, a sense of place, that I have not seen anywhere else. This feeling was further heightened by the modesty of its architecture – no elaborate decorations or monuments but a simple structure which was given meaning and relevance by its users. Yet there was also a sense of transience. Given the rapid changes taking place, the recently announced Creekfront Project by the commercial developer Sama Dubai, and the general attitude of relegating communities to their own enclaves, it is perhaps only a matter of time before this unique hybrid urban setting is moved to the city's surrounding desert.

Special Ustadi Restaurant

Special Ustadi Restaurant is owned by an Iranian immigrant – Mohamed Ali Ansari – who first came to Dubai in 1940 to work in his father's grocery store in Bur Dubai. He opened the restaurant in 1978 and it is considered to be one of the oldest in the city.[44] It quickly became a favourite among long-time residents of the city. It is located on Musalla Road, a busy commercial thoroughfare extending from the Bastakiy'ya district to Khaled ibn Walid Street (also known as Bank or Computer Street). My first visit to the restaurant in Spring 2008 showed a remarkable place, in spite of its small size alive with customers and offering a microcosm of the city. It displays in my view a greater sense of authenticity and history than the nearby elite establishments in Bastakiy'ya.

The restaurant seems lived in. An immediately noticeable characteristic are glass top tables underneath which are different banknotes. On the table in front of me were Iranian newspapers, showing without doubt the nationality of the owner.

Surrounding walls are covered with pictures and newspaper clippings anchoring the setting within the city's cultural and culinary scene. The interior space itself is quite small; there were about ten tables in an area of 8 x 8 m. Another room reserved for families is accessible from the outside. The menu is displayed in Arabic, Persian and English.

That sense of history and belonging is further accentuated by a large sign on the entrance door: 'Since 1978'. The clientele is a mix of different nationalities although there is a clear Iranian bias. During my initial visit I saw two Iranians wearing the *kandoura* – the traditional Arab dress. But there was also a bearded Egyptian sitting by himself in a far corner, who seemed to be a regular. He was joined by a compatriot – it appeared a chance encounter, but he expected him to be there since they had an extensive conversation. The table in front of me was occupied by two Iranians engaged in an animated conversation while enjoying the food. They were regulars talking to the waiters and overall feeling very comfortable. The staff were talking loudly in Persian and engaged the customers to varying degrees. I was treated as a newcomer which became evident since the waiter suggested modifying my order; in addition the owner's son asked me 'if everything was OK', which is unusual for such a restaurant. They gave the impression of being conscious of their significance in relation to the city – aware that they are in an historic landmark. Various events took place while I was in the restaurant, illustrating the extent to which the place is an integral part of the surrounding community, catering not just for Iranians. For instance, a Filipino woman walked in and ordered a 'take-away' – 'I always pass by here', she said. On another occasion a South Asian walked in and seemed puzzled by the place. The owner's son came up to him and said jokingly 'we have rice, kebab, what do you want'. He left without answering, but the son followed him outside. Locals also use the place; while I was there two young Arabs walked in and were greeted by the waiter in Arabic and, as I was told by one of my informants, the place is well known among Dubai residents.

The restaurant's location, the district of Hamriya, is one of the oldest areas in Dubai and borders Bastakiy'ya district. It is surrounded by *sikak* dirt roads. One particularly fascinating feature is that they are covered by carpets to make them walkable. There are also some – relatively speaking – very old buildings. The streets are irregular in layout, deviating from the straight patterns found in the main roads. They follow the original morphology, and buildings in turn are arranged in an irregular manner. Other restaurants in the street are mostly Indian. School buses were dropping off kids – all south Asian (Indian/Pakistani). Nearby is the Indian dominated market, Meena Bazaar, which I will discuss in more detail in Chapter 7.

It is interesting to contrast this informal, down-to-earth setting with the Basta Art Café in Bastakiy'ya, where the setting is more refined, centred around a shaded courtyard. Mostly occupied by Westerners and the occasional tourist it would fit perfectly beside similar establishments in Southern California, for example. The menu consists of health conscious items which reveals the clientele for which

4.15. Basta Art Cafe – contained within a traditional house.

it caters. It projects an aura of exclusivity, largely derived from the setting of Bastakiy'ya (figure 4.15). Thus within close proximity, almost overlapping, are two different versions of the city, catering for very distinct sub-groups. This enhances the sense of fragmentation and exclusion.

Baniyas Square

Most cities may be said to have a centre – a central square which lies at a city's heart. Dubai at first glance lacks such a centre. Yet there is one – known officially as Baniyas Square, but by long-time residents referred to as Nasser Square. The square was described in a newspaper article titled 'Baniyas Square – a testimony to early glory'.[45] In it is a description of the extent to which this space is still representative of an 'authentic' Dubai. It is contrasted with new developments – 'Manhattan-like' skyscrapers along Sheikh Zayed Road. Retaining its small-scale character, variety of shops and most importantly its cosmopolitan flavour, the square is seen as a snapshot of the city. According to the article, for many residents, changes within Baniyas express the changes which have happened in the city; they are representative of transformations which have moved Dubai from a small fishing village to a major global centre – an international city.

The square is in Deira, in what is now the city's central business district. While originally the commercial heart, this changed recently with the emergence of new high-tech shopping centres and it is now undergoing a major transformation to make way for a Dubai Metro stop. Prior to its closure for construction work, the square was a major hangout for the lower- to middle-class shoppers facilitated by its central location and proximity to the Creek. Also a number of key markets were

4.16. The vibrant character of Baniyas Square emerges at night.

within easy reach, such as Dubai's old *souq*, Naif Market (prior to its destruction in a fire, see chapter 7) and the Gold Souq. It is also surrounded by a variety of shops selling cheap merchandise, and a major bus stop (figure 4.16).

Dubai does contain other nodes, centres, and shopping areas. Within Deira are two major enclosed shopping centres: Ghurair City, one of the city's oldest shopping malls, and Deira City Center, a constantly growing shopping conglomeration. Both of these are, in addition to their retail function, considered a major hangout for city residents. Baniyas Square distinguished itself by being an outdoor setting and catering for a more low-income group than these two. This is evident in the presence of Asian labourers and East European tourists, for example.

The Origin of Baniyas Square

Baniyas Square was originally known as Jamal Abd El-Nasser Square, or as mentioned above, simply Nasser Square, after the late Egyptian president, considered at that time a hero in the Arab world. Leading a military overthrow in 1952 he became president in 1954. One can assume – no official accounts are available – that the name was given shortly afterwards (in the late 1950s or early 1960s). As noted above, the square does not appear as a clearly identifiable urban space except during that time, forming the centre of an expanding city. Historic photographs show that it was initially a cattle market with many images depicting cattle being led from the Creek. Small stores, constructed from fragile materials, appear at the square's edge. Also, water-carriers can be observed. In the 1960s the space became more defined; small scale stores appeared – among them Jashanmal, now a major department store in Dubai and elsewhere in the region – and high-rise concrete structures appear paving the way for a major transformation. I should also note that the area is bordered by a cemetery which at present is enclosed by a fence, rendering it invisible to passers-by. However the location is interesting because it demonstrates that the space was originally on the city's outskirts – a typical place for burial grounds.

It is worth noting that Baniyas was a major hangout for the engineers responsible for dredging the Creek in 1963. It also was the site of the first Arab Unity School founded in 1974. The association of the space with the city's growth and emergence as a modern metropolis (through the dredging of the Creek), while it retained its intimate, commercial character, led many to believe that it has 'essentially remained the same'. Yet with the city's expansion in the 1960s and 1970s, the Deira district where the square is located essentially became a centre, or a Central Business District, housing banks and various commercial establishments – even becoming a centre for the fur trade![46]

Transformation

An examination of the city's urban morphology using aerial photographs reveals some dramatic transformations. The earliest available photograph from 1935 shows a compact city consisting of three areas: Bur Dubai, Shindagha and Deira. The last being the largest. At the eastern edge of Deira appears a widening, bordering the Creek – which roughly marks the current location of Baniyas Square. The water there appears to be shallow as suggested by changes in colour. The southern and northern edges of this widening will eventually form the two streets bordering the square. A 1960 photograph shows some changes, with the 'widening' becoming more clearly defined, although still irregular in shape. Also, a small strip of land appears, reclaimed from the Creek. The space is still at the edge of the city, located next to the cemetery. In 1965 the area acquires a clearly identifiable character: more land is reclaimed thus moving the square further away from the Creek; the southern and northern streets clearly define the space. 1968 does not witness any major changes except for a road network appearing on the newly reclaimed land. In 1976 the 'modern' image of the square is complete, with a defined road network, recognizable structures and it now forms the heart of the city (Deira) having been at the edge from 1930 until 1960 (figure 4.17). A 2003 satellite image shows the setting prior to its closure due to construction. On its southern edge are large, high-rise buildings, consisting of commercial and office complexes. Its northern edge consists of low-rise structures. It is worth noting that buildings on the southern edge were all built on reclaimed land, whereas the northern edge and beyond was part of 'old' Dubai (figure 4.18).

Close-up aerial photographs illustrate how the square came to be associated with the growth of Dubai itself and its transformation into a modern city. As early as 1950, modern four-storey concrete buildings appear. Subsequent images

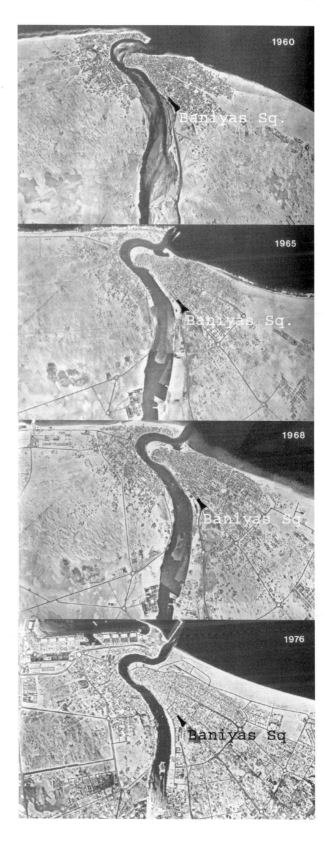

4.17. Morphological transformation of Baniyas Square and its surroundings. (*Source*: Based on aerial imagery by courtesy of Dubai Municipality)

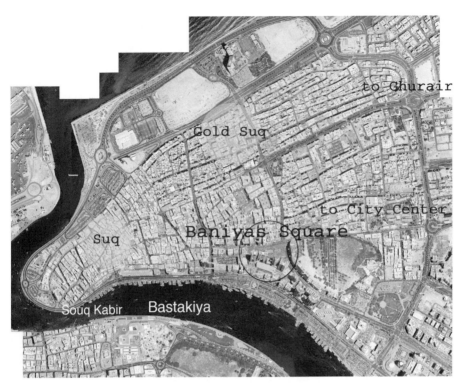

4.18. The square as it appeared prior to its closure due to construction (*Source*: Based on aerial imagery by courtesy of Dubai Municipality)

show a flurry of construction activities. Other images show clearances in which Baniyas as an empty space used primarily as a parking lot. Water fountains and landscaping elements begin to appear in the late 1960s. All existing structures, with a few exceptions, were eventually removed, and replaced by large office complexes (Baniyas Tower). The space itself retained some of its original character (the water fountains) while the eastern corner was occupied by a Tourist Information Center (replacing a Jashanmal store which had been there since the 1950s). In its current transformation it is set to morph into a new kind of centre anchored by a Metro Station – appropriately named Baniyas. At the time of writing the area is for the most part closed off; the green lawns and Tourist Information Center are gone and people are relegated to walking around its edges. Given its central location and the presence of large numbers of low-income workers it will be interesting to see how they will eventually interact with this newest addition.

A Great Centre Lost

For many people the essence of being Parisian is on the Left Bank, or the ultimate New York experience is in Times Square. London has Trafalgar Square (or Picadilly Circus), Rome the Spanish Steps, Berlin has the Gedächtnis-Kirche Plaza. The Middle East has its share of these centres as well such as the Tahrir

Square in Cairo, a vibrant urban space overlooked by the Egyptian Museum, the Hilton Hotel (Cairo's first modern 5-star hotel), and the Nasser era Stalinist-like 'Mogama' building – representing the quintessential Egyptian bureaucracy. It is telling that in an era of globalization in which the relevance of place is questioned, and in which such constructs as 'space of flows' are introduced signifying the linkages between global cities that such centres are becoming increasingly visible and acquire an almost mythical status – talked about in revered tones, signifying an authenticity which one can reclaim by simply 'being there'.[47]

Dubai has such places as well – although they are somewhat hidden. In support of this I would like to recall two encounters. One was with a taxi driver on my way to the square, and the other on a plane. Hailing a taxi, I asked the driver to take me to Maydan[48] Jamal Abd El-Nasser; he objected to the name noting that this is not how it is called, rather it is Baniyas. Then he said: 'Why do you want to go there? It's just a lot of Indians'. I then discovered that he was from Northern Yemen, and objected strongly to Nasser's policies in the 1960s vis-à-vis Yemen. The second encounter was on my way to the UAE in 1996 – my first visit to the country. On the plane a fellow Egyptian offered me a few tips and noted that if I were to look for some fun, I should go to Maydan Nasser, since 'this is where all the action happens'. The meaning was, of course, clear and confirmed by subsequent visits and observations in the square. The significance of these two encounters is that they highlight the extent to which a physical setting, the square, figures prominently in people's consciousness, whether in its association with Pan-Arab politics, ethnic views regarding Indians, or leisure and entertainment. In a discussion about a city's history – manifested in settings of memory – such spaces play an important role. Whether it is Nasser Square, Special Ustadi Restaurant, the Bastakiy'ya district or the *souq*, all are anchors for the city's long-time residents offering them a place of refuge from sweeping modernization encountered all over the city. And it is quite telling that in a city with seemingly marginal historical settings the removal of trivial items such as a long-standing TV antenna in Jumeirah, or the Hard Rock Café on Sheikh Zayed Road (about 10 years old), receives massive resistance from a transient population whose experience of the city is limited.[49] This shows the city's dilemma in articulating a clearly definable identity. Its multicultural character as well as the dominance of expatriates plays a large part in this as I will discuss in the concluding section of this chapter.

Inventing History and Creating Identity

I stated at the beginning of the chapter that my aim was to dispel the notion that Dubai fits the stereotype of an Arabian oil city with no significant history – essentially a *tabula rasa*. To that end I provided an overview of its history stretching back to the nineteenth century with the help of travellers' descriptions, as well as discussing some of its historical settings. Furthermore, the city has its share of centres and places that serve a mnemonic function, reminding its long-time residents of the city's progress, by being tied to significant social, political and even economic events. Yet one cannot dispute that in spite of this, there were efforts – particularly in the 1970s and 1980s – to simply start again and ignore this heritage. Recognizing that this would prove to be damaging to a city aiming to be a regional as well as global centre, a number of efforts were and are underway to establish, as well as strengthen, its identity. This can even reach a point of invention, manufacturing and borrowing as I will show in my discussion of the city's megaprojects (Chapter 6). But, to conclude this chapter I would like to mention two particularly significant developments. They are the recently announced Creekfront Project and the introduction of Heritage Protection laws.

The Creekfront Project is part of what has been called the 'Khor Dubai Cultural initiative', which is essentially a waterfront development along the two banks of Dubai Creek. The project, according to officials, aims at 'preserving and sustaining local heritage and values'. The newly formed Dubai Culture and Arts Authority will oversee the implementation of the project.[50] Specifically, it is envisioned as a 27 kilometre development which will include numerous museums and libraries as well as a Zaha Hadid designed opera. There will also be what is called 'Culture Village' – a project managed by Dubai Properties which is expected to cost about DH342 billion (about $1bn !). According to the developers the architecture will be traditional which means that there will be 'Arab' wind towers 'built on top of buildings' as well as 'cobbled walkways'. The CEO declares the following:

> The project is in the heart of Dubai looking over the legendary creek. This is where it all started, where the pearl divers maintained their boats. It has real sentimental and historical value in this part of the world. The aim of this project is to come up with something different that links back to our roots.

Heritage comes at a price: apartments range from DH13.57 million to a more affordable DH5.3 million ($4m to $1.5m). Given the obvious commercializing aspect of this, a Western real estate agent argues in all seriousness that projects such as these have noble objectives transcending commercialism, commodification and downright exploitation of other countries' heritage: 'One of the criticisms of the UAE is that it has forgotten its roots, and now this development is addressing that concern'.[51]

This emphasis on heritage – real or invented – is also of concern to Dubai Municipality which is considering introducing a set of laws and architectural regulations, which would ensure that buildings are 'in keeping with the culture of the region'. Thus buildings would be required to incorporate elements of Arab heritage in their design. According to Rashad Bukhash, head of the Department of Historic Preservation: 'Identity is something that is unfortunately lacking in Dubai … the worst type of feeling is that you are a stranger in your own country. We need to create an identity for Dubai that is related to Arabic heritage'.[52] Perhaps he is a lone crusader; Bukhash's family owned a house in a part of the Bastakiy'ya district which is now in the middle of the Diwan complex (see above). In a conversation with me, he talked nostalgically about the old houses. But he also noted that the city has various layers that need to be preserved as well. In response to this, a law has been introduced which would prevent destruction of buildings constructed before 1960 in addition to the preservation of the historic areas of Shindagha and Bastakiy'ya.[53] Thus economic, political and social factors play a role in forging the city's identity – yet it would perhaps be better to return to its origins, rather than simply evoking an illusive 'Arab' identity which was never really part of the city's heritage to begin with.

Notes

1. It is interesting to note that Aden, Yemen remained in Arab/Moslem hands throughout the entire Portuguese period.

2. Named after its founder Mohamed Ibn Abd Al-Wahab (1703–1791) who advocated a 'return' to pure Islamic values and an abolition of 'inventions'.

3. An interesting event known as 'The Hyacinth incident' occurred in 1910. The Sheikh of Dubai at that time, Butti Ibn Suhail, refused British demands for the installation of a British political officer, telegraph station and post office. In turn he was accused of hording 'illegal' arms, which led to an armed incursion into Dubai supported by the British warship, *The Hyacinth*, causing the death of thirty-seven locals. Interestingly, the charge of 'illegal' weapons was never proven (Kazim, 2000, p. 143).

4. Different identities were constructed among the various Trucial Oman sheikhdoms as evidenced in the use of currency. Between 1820 and 1945 all of Trucial Oman used the Indian Rupee because they were administered by the government of British India. After Indian Independence in 1947 all sheikhdoms adopted a special Gulf Rupee. In the 1960s separate currencies were adopted. Abu Dhabi used the Bahrain Dinar whereas Dubai used the Qatari Riyal (*Ibid.*, p. 224).

5. There is no consensus on how Dubai or *Dibai* as it was widely known until relatively recently was named. Of two theories widely espoused by historians, the possible favourite is that Dubai is drawn from *Dab,* the Arabic name for a spiny tailed lizard which was common in the desert of the Lower Gulf, although little known today because they avoid urban areas. Others believe that Dubai is a derivative from an Arabic word meaning 'land devastated by locusts'.

6. As further evidence of British dominance they argued in the 1960s that, given the various treaties signed with Trucial Oman, they have the 'right' to be their sole representative in the UN.

7. 'A group of men were constantly at work cleaning a sandbank in the creek and carrying the sand in baskets on their heads to build up one of the banks. This was a minor part of dredging operations intended to safeguard the trade of Dubai, but the new area of building land which was thus incidentally produced in the very centre of the town eventually made a profit for the present Ruler.' (Lienhardt, 2001, p. 122)

8. 'On the sea beaches, one saw again the fishing boats and great piles of tiny fish drying in the sun. A few people fished in the creek itself, but most people regarded such fish with distaste because the creek was the town's general sewer, being used like the seashore at Abu Dhabi.' (*Ibid.*)

9. 'Dubai suffered the same lack of public services as the other Trucial Coast towns. A few people had private electric generators, but most used pressure lamps or ordinary oil lamps, the latter being both cheaper and cooler. Some poor people had lamps made of old polish tins with wicks stuck into them. There was no cleaning of the streets or public refuse collection. Dirt and rubbish were thrown into the street unless people took the trouble to take their refuse down to the creek. Baluchi water carriers, poor immigrants who could not understand Arabic and so were treated more or less like imbeciles by their customers, sold water from door to door, carrying it in paraffin tins loaded in

panniers on the backs of donkeys. Dubai did have, however, a post office and a small hospital run mainly on British funds.' (*Ibid.*, p. 124)

10. 'It was a small room with whitewashed plaster walls, an exquisite Tabriz carpet on the floor, leather and fur cushions to sit on, a Zanzibar chest and, in one corner, a huge, white refrigerator, purring on power supplied from a specially imported generator. Next to an American car, the refrigerator seemed to the Eastern world to be a crowning symbol of power, prestige and wealth, an object worthy of the most prominent position in the household. Selim had thought fit to use it as a repository for a revolver, a tin of shoe polish and two saucepans full of yoghurt.' (Headley, 1958, p. 259)

11. 'In both main parts of the town of Dubai, on the two sides of the creek, were long and intricate markets roofed over with palm matting for shade. Only two shops in the whole town had glass windows. All the rest were open-fronted in the traditional way with the shopkeeper sitting with or behind his goods. At night, the shops were boarded up and padlocked, and the markets were dimly lit with oil lamps and guarded by night watchmen with daggers at their waists and rifles in their hands.' (Lienhardt, 2001, p. 123)

12. 'Shallow cubicles, cut into one of the lateral walls, served as shop booths. Their shuttered doors, instead of being flush with the level of the sand street, were a yard above it, broaching a long, wooden ledge on which the merchants squatted, everything in their dark dispensaries within arm's reach. An enterprising baker had used his cubicle for an oven and was shoveling large, flat pads of dough into its fiery maw, pulling them out again and spearing the baked *khubz* like quoits on a pole. Near him, in the aura of scalding heat, a public scribe sat sideways in a chair carefully inscribing Arabic calligraphy onto rough yellow paper with a ball-point pen.

The opposite wall had been partitioned off into open-fronted chambers, divided one from the other by wattle screens. Here the ironmonger, the butcher, the copper and brass smiths, the cabinetmaker with a display of nail-studded chests, and the chandlers had set up trade. Next to the brass smith was a clothier's stall with the only English sign in the souk: "DIAMOND TAILORS, Gent's Outfitter, Cutter and Dressmaker". Street sellers were stationed in front of most of the stalls and cubicles, sellers of camel bells and tomatoes and cheese and water pipes and dusty grapes and onions and tubs of dates. Frail-legged, creamy-furred donkeys twinkled by, laden with goatskin water bags.' (Headley, 1958, p. 255)

13. 'Dubai had one good-sized modern bank, and there would have been others, as there are now, had not the British Bank of the Middle East then held a monopoly. Also in Dubai was the main branch of the British shipping agents.' (Lienhardt, 2003; p. 123)

14. 'Dubai had numerous simple cafes in and around the market, but the more respectable people preferred to sit talking and drinking coffee or tea outside shops where not everyone had the right to sit down and make himself at ease. There was also an open air cinema owned by a merchant from Kuwait who had been living in Dubai for most of his life. This was before Kuwait itself had any cinemas at all, the shaikhs there having refused permission to build them on the grounds that they would corrupt morals. The Dubai cinema showed as many Indian films as Arab ones.' (Lienhardt, 2001, p. 123)

15. 'Baniyas square – a testimony to early glory', *Gulf News*, 29 March 2003, p. 6.

16. 'King Saud called patron of slavery', *The New York Times*, 26 February 1956, Archives.

17. Stelling, Marion (1961) 'Introduction to the Orient – The Persian Gulf', *The New York Times*, 8 January, Archives.

18. 'Intrigue and subversion in Arabia', *The New York Times*, 24 November 1968, Archive.

19. 'Gun running in the Persian Gulf', *The Times*, 9 June 1911.

20. 'Britain's burden in Arabia' *The Times*, 22 August 1956.

21. 'Journey by Dhow to Dubai', *The Times*, 22 May 1965, p. 10.

22. 'Now Dubai becomes an oil state', *The Times*, 7 June 1966, p. 16.

23. Thomas, Anthony (1969) 'Gold smuggling boosts Dubai economy', *The Times*, 3 March, p. 42.

24. 'The solid and prosperous base of trading gives the state a sense of identity lacking in some of the more financially fortunate countries farther north, whose identities seem to have been bought by a furious spending of money. One is never sure that, when the money has gone they will not simply disappear with a puff of smoke. There are no such doubts with Dubai.' (Roeber, Joe (1969) 'Better off than the fabulously rich', *The Times*, 30 May, p. 36)

25. 'Perhaps more than anything the dhow has become the symbol of Dubai. The Arabian Gulf is one of the last refuges of these colourful craft which once ranged from Africa to Indonesia and Dubai has become their last major port. On any day more than 50, their brightly coloured flags waving in the breeze, can be seen plying the blue waters of the creek or tied alongside the quay. It is a gay sight and the craft bear the marks of many ages.' (Ledger, David (1969) 'Boomtown growing pains', *The Times*, 30 May, p. 35)

26. 'Much of Dubai's phenomenal success has arisen from the cosmopolitan nature of the population and the good relations between the various communities. Of around 70,000 people only 25 per cent are native Dubaians, the rest being Indians, Persians, Pakistanis, northern Arabs and Europeans. The result has been a baffling profusion of languages. Although each race has been influenced by mixing with the others, each has succeeded in retaining its own individuality. A kaleidoscope of colour and people is the result. Arab women in deep black purdah, their faces disfigured by beaklike masks which give them the appearance of so many black crows, mingle with Indians in graceful saris. Persian girls in pyjama suits and Europeans in mini-skirts'. (*Ibid.*)

27. 'Dubai has exploited her geographical advantages as the nearest convenient smuggling port to Bombay. Dhows manned by Pakistanis and Indian sailors deliberately employed to blend into the Indian seascape, sail regularly across the Arabian sea carrying about $150m worth of gild to the Indian subcontinent every year… Most of the metal is loaded in the shape of 10-tola bars … and is handed over to Indian fishing boats off the coast of Bombay in exchange for silver, travellers' cheques, American dollars or other freely convertible payments, including Indian cloth.' (Thomas, Anthony (1969) 'When statistics lie', *The Times*, 30 May, p. 35)

28. Herbert, Nicholas (1969) 'Rivalry may mar friendly relations', *The Times*, 30 May, p. 33.

29. Izzard, Ralph (1974) 'Sights set on making Dubai a Free Port and business centre of Gulf', *The Times*, 23 May, p. 38.

30. 'No people have been rushed so ruthlessly into modern times as the inhabitants of the Arabian Gulf countries. Within a generation they have moved out of the mid-nineteenth century into the twentieth century… A mere 40 years ago it still seemed that nothing would ever disturb the tranquillity of the sun-scorched insanitary mud and rubble built villages scattered at intervals around the coastline.' (Izzard, Ralph (1975) 'The Gulf States', *The Times*, 20 March, p. 35)

31. 'Dubai's waterfront on the Deira side has been developed with multi-storey offices, hotels and flats of the faceless international type, while the absence of planning controls, or indeed any local authority structure that could enforce such controls, has resulted in chaotic sprawl on the outskirts.' (Cantacuzino, Sherban (1975) 'Western ideas clash with traditional architecture', *The Times*, 20 March, p. 30)

32. '… businessmen and their families are still arriving literally in their thousands. Hotel corridors and office block lifts are crammed with men in grey suits carrying Samsonites and the shops and restaurants are full of elegant Lebanese women in midi-length skirts buying couture clothes and accessories.' ('Dubai: Standing up well to the pressures of expanding and spending', *The Times*, 31 March 1976, p. 32)

33. 'In 1936 when the Shah abolished the traditional veil for women and required men to wear modern trousers, many Sunni families were appalled and many left for good.' (Coles and Jackson, 2007, p. 14)

34. Mohamed Abdul Razzaq Abdul Rahman Al Bastaki (pearl merchant) in Wheeler and Thuysbaert (2005).

35. *Ibid.*, pp. 68–69.

36. Ruqiya, a resident describing life in the 1940s (*Ibid.*).

37. At the moment the buildings contain the following: Sheikh Mohammad Centre for Cultural Understanding; Basta Art Cafe – a popular courtyard café; Majlis Gallery – which features the work of local and international artists; Ostra – a gallery specializing in contemporary art and sculpture; XVA – a small guesthouse and art gallery; Bastakiy'ya Art School; the Journalists Association; the Emirates Philatelic Association; WWF; the Association of Architectural Heritage Preservation (Landais, Emmanuelle (2008) 'Bastakiy'ya revamp to make area cultural nerve centre', *Gulf News*. 25 May, p. 2).

38. Diwali celebrates the return of the ancient King of Ayodhya, Rama, along with his wife Sita and brother Lakshman to his kingdom, ending 14 years of exile, after a war in which he killed the demon king, Ravana. The final day of the Hindu festival is marked by lighting earthen lamps to signify the journey from darkness and the triumph of good over evil.

39. In fact the entire city was transformed because of the festival: 'Hundreds of buildings in areas such as Al Karama, Bur Dubai and Deira were adorned with lights and lanterns, or kandils, which are made of colourful paper. Long queues have been forming outside the Hindu temple in Bur Dubai as Indians gathered to pray at their only temple in the country. Dressed in new clothes, young men and women and families queued up with flowers and sweets as offerings to the gods.' (Bhattacharya, Suryatapa and Menon, Praveen (2008) 'Let there be lights', *The National*, 28 October, p. 3; also: http://www.thenational.ae/article/20081027/PAGETHREE/946797193/1119)

40. http://hariwrite.blogspot.com/2007/10/dubai-temple-and-churches.html.

41. According to one resident: 'It is a very important religious week for us as it gives us an opportunity to connect with our roots' (Suryatapa and Praveen (2008)).

42. Witness the following account by an Indian visitor: 'The creek crossing wasn't very exciting for a Cochinite like me, but the dappling waves was green and clean. The bank on Deira side was filled with tall buildings and was a real sight in the rising sun. Soon I reached the other side and walked through a canopied market area with variety items for sale. The temple was a 10 minute walk along the creek and was more like a building in North Indian style. The entry to the temple was full of shops selling flowers and prasad items and looked and smelt India. Neatly dressed malayalee matrons in spotless white walked solemnly inside in no way different from their Keral routine, tall turbaned Sardars climbed up to the Gurdwara in the same building. I too climbed up to the Gurdwara with a kerchief covering my head. The Sangeet was melancholic and the place was peaceful and pleasant the temple was a bit crowded and as it was a weekend had a sprinkling of Indians of all states. Prasad was given and I walked out. Here religion is sacrosanct and personal, none can exploit it and abuse it like in India.' (*Ibid.*)

43. According to 2003 figures the UAE as a whole has 76 per cent Moslems, 9 per cent Christians, and 15 per cent classified as others. There are various missionary groups performing humanitarian work. There are about twenty-four churches in various parts of the country (Bathish, Hani (2004) 'UAE is an oasis of tolerance', *Khaleej Times*, 19 October; http://www.khaleejtimes.com/DisplayArticle.asp?xfile=data/theuae/2004/October/theuae_October415.xml&section=theuae. Accessed 1 November 2008).

44. Baldwin, Derek (2008) 'Seven decades in Dubai', *Xpress*, 11 April. http://www.xpress4me.com/articles/07/08/29/20002890.html. Accessed 27 June 2008.

45. Hilotin, Jay B. (2003) 'Baniyas Square – a testimony to early glory', *Gulf News*, 29 March. p. 6.

46. A recent media report notes: '… before the recent development boom, the Deira district was the centre of Dubai. When fur coat retailers arrived, they clustered around al Nasser square. Ten years ago, there were 18 fur coats stores there … today there are around 140… The area has acquired a bit of a Slavic accent. Local landmarks include the Moscow Hotel, Red Square Café, and Bolshoi Restaurant. Signs guiding buyers to fur stores are printed in Cyrillic as are most of the store managers' business cards. Almost all of the sales assistants are Russian. According to one sales assistant you cannot be considered for the job unless you are fluent in the language'. (Khourchid, Maya (2008). 'A fur deal', *The National*, 26 September, The Review, p. 2)

47. See, for example, James Traub (2004) *The Devil's Playground: A Century of Pleasure and Profit*

in Times Square; a place described in the book's blurb as being originally 'the whirling dynamo of American popular culture'.

48.   The Arabic word for square is *maydan*.

49.   For more on this see: Helmi, Ashraf (2008) 'A quick end without much ado in Jumeirah', *Gulf News*, 28 June; and Samaha, Nour (2008) 'Hard Rock Café to keep on rolling', *The National*, 12 September, p. 5.

50.   WAM (2008) 'Dubai Creek set to become world's comprehensive cultural destination', *Gulf News*, 16 May, p. 9.

51.   Hewitson, Jessie (2008) 'Century-old Dubai brought to life', *The National*, 19 August, p. 8.

52.   Grzesik, Monika (2007) 'DM laws to preserve culture', *Arabian Business*, 2 June. http://www.arabianbusiness.com, Accessed 6 June 2007.

53.   Grzesik, Monika (2007) 'New law will protect Dubai's old buildings', *Arabian Business*, 17 February. http://www.arabianbusiness.com, Accessed 19 February 2000.

Chapter 5

The Transformation of Dubai or Towards the Age of Megastructures

'Dubai, a new city every day'.
                    Government slogan, 2008

Approaching Dubai from Al-Ain highway in 1996 presented a memorable sight. In the midst of the desert a lone rising structure would signal impending arrival. This was the World Trade Center, at that time one of only a few high-rise buildings on Sheikh Zayed Road – a stark contrast to its current surroundings. The building seems to have been dwarfed, replaced first by the twin Emirates Towers and now by the tallest structure on earth, the Burj Dubai. Also, in 1996 a Hard Rock Café had opened in Dubai, as I and my friends were told. Assuming that it was not far off, we drove along Sheikh Zayed Road until we reached what was then the outskirts of the city. Assured that we were lost, we continued driving until we saw in the distance the familiar sight of the crossed guitars adjacent to an Empire State like building in miniature, which was the actual restaurant. Surrounding it was a vast, empty desertscape. Today it is still there but surrounded by Dubai Internet City, the American University and an assortment of high-rises constituting Dubai Marina, a luxurious water-front development – the restaurant which was so visible in its isolated existence has all but disappeared.

Now, if we consider that this has taken place within the last 10 years or so, the sheer scale of the city's development becomes clear. Countless media articles and commentators have noted the speed, and the increasingly spectacular nature of these developments. Headlines such as 'Skyline on Crack' or 'The Architectural Insanity of Dubai' were quite common.[1] Of particular interest was the increasingly spectacular nature of these designs, dubbed as 'iconic'. Emphasis was on what elsewhere I have termed 'superlatives' – the tallest, the highest, the biggest etc. (e.g. Elsheshtawy, 2004). From the sail-like Burj Al-Arab constructed in 1996 (figure 5.1), the sleek high-tech Emirates Towers built at the end of the 1990s (figure 5.2) to the development of the man-made Palm Islands, all employed the device of the spectacle by which the city was, according to one observer, 'trying to obsessively build itself into significance'.² This is of course a worldwide phenomenon: the employment of spectacularized urban forms as a sign of becoming global, in the process dramatically reshaping the skyline of cities as diverse as Los Angeles, Shanghai, Mumbai and Sao Paolo. These are, however, cities with history – developments occur within an established urban form. In the case of Dubai each announced or built project becomes an isolated icon set within the desert – an archipelago – thus drawing immediate attention.

Another distinction which needs to be made is that Dubai in its globalizing efforts is setting its sights on its neighbours, attempting to surpass, exceed, and

5.1. The ultra luxurious self-proclaimed, 7 star Burj Al Arab Hotel.

5.2. Dubai's ultimate symbol of luxury, the Emirates Towers Complex.

replace the traditional centres of the Middle East (Elsheshtawy, 2006). Here it is borrowing established traditional architectural forms and recasting them within a local context. The Jumeirah Mosque – a copy of an Egyptian model – is placed on the city's tourist trail and thus becomes part of its urban fabric (figure 5.3). On the other hand, its global credentials are established by constructing projects which symbolically evoke universal themes not specifically tied to a local or regional architectural language – the anonymous office blocks in Media City and Internet City, for example (figure 5.4).

5.3. The Jumeirah Mosque located in close proximity to luxurious shopping venues.

5.4. Dubai Media City while portions of it were still under construction in 2003.

My aim in this chapter is to continue the chronological narrative presented in Chapter 4. My focus, however, will be on the city's urban development, specifically discussing its Masterplan and the extent to which there is an underlying vision. Frequently observers have characterized Dubai's growth as being without a plan and this feeds into a larger narrative where Gulf cities are more or less shaped by the whims of their rulers, and are an artificial creation depending on oil money. Clearly such a view is incorrect, as I will try to illustrate. To that effect, I begin first by portraying the city's image in the 1970s – to situate its urban development. I then discuss the city's Masterplan and the degree to which it developed to adapt to changing requirements and circumstances. Having established the overall framework within which the city operates, my focus shifts to the urban level to look at the city's morphology and the resulting urban form. I conclude the chapter by focusing on real estate and architectural strategies and the extent to which they are playing a major role in establishing Dubai as a global city. The degree to which the global financial crisis, which began in 2008, has affected the city's ambition, causing a slowdown but not a complete stop, is also discussed. Thus this chapter should be read bearing in mind the crisis and that the seeds for the city's exposure to such financial turmoil have in fact been sown in its various plans, as I outline in the following sections.

Dubai in the 1970s: The Emergence of a Modern City

'A woman was walking across this grisly wasteland, balancing a rusty oil drum full of water on her head. She was lost to sight in the black shadow cast by the gables for a brand-new fake French chateau.'

Jonathan Raban describing the district of Jumeirah in the 1970s, in
Arabia: Journey through the Labyrinth (1979, p. 195)

Jonathan Raban, a British travel writer and journalist, wrote extensively on various cities in the Middle East in his book, *Arabia: A Journey through the Labyrinth*. His travels took place in the 1970s and, while based on brief stays, they offer an interesting glimpse into the life of some of those cities and the overall sense of adventure and of embarking on something new. Among his stops was Dubai, which he visited after a brief stay in Abu Dhabi. While his experience in Abu Dhabi is somewhat negative, his depiction of Dubai is quite different. After noting that he passed the tallest building in the Gulf (apparently he was referring to the World Trade Center which was at that time on the city's outskirts), he contrasts the liveliness of Dubai with the artificiality of Abu Dhabi:

A shanty town, a bridge, a glimpse of dhows and cargo steamers, and we were in the thick of the city. It swirled with acrid, chocolate-coloured dust of the kind that takes at least a century to accumulate. It had settled on the buildings, the streets, the people, and given Dubai, the instantly-recognizable gravity of a place with a history. There is something very reassuring and comfortable about old dirt. After the strain of living with the temporary and the brand-new in Abu Dhabi coming into Dubai was like easing oneself into a well worn tweed jacket. (Raban, 1979, pp. 163–164)

He was impressed by the cosmopolitan character of the city, the presence of multiple nationalities, which absorbs strangers easily and also the commanding presence of the Creek which gives the city 'a shape, a direction and a certainty of character which I have seen in no other town' (*Ibid.*, p. 164). Given these qualities he notes 'that I was going to like Dubai' (*Ibid.*). His depiction of the Bastakiy'ya district is particularly interesting as he points out its deteriorating character and that it has been taken over by labourers:

> We crossed the creek again … and nosed up along a decrepit street of ancient houses. Their rough mud stucco had cracked, and was falling away from their walls in jagged lumps, revealing the coral rocks from which they had been built. They had wind-towers on their roofs… The boatman pointed. He lived over there, behind those houses… From outside they were inscrutable – cubes of burned pastry without windows. But here and there a bit of wall had fallen out, and I caught passing glimpses of courtyards, vines, stairways, lattices, carved doors and hanging balconies … the houses had a sunken-jawed look, now just a storm or two away from collapsing into total ruin. Longshoremen, jobbing carpenters and small stallholders from the near-by souk had moved in… (*Ibid.*, p. 172)

Furthermore, he also devotes considerable time to describing the district of Jumeirah, at that time an outpost in the desert, 'Dubai's Los Angelean suburb' occupied by large houses separated by the desert. Armed private militia guarded the houses of some important expatriate officials. He observed that the district is divided in two parts: one occupied by rich and opulent palatial mansions and the other dominated by 'miserable shacks':

> Looking out of the window of one of those gimcrack Palladian villas, one's new view might never be checked by the miserable shacks of one's neighbours. They were barely even shacks. They were scoops in the sand with piles of junk for roofs: oil drums, car doors, bits of chicken wire, cardboard boxes, torn strips of rush matting. That they were human habitations at all, and not heaps of garbage from the surrounding houses, was only provided by the animals tethered round them – dogs, goats and camels. (*Ibid.*, p. 194)

Jumeirah is now an upscale residential district catering for Western expatriates and is an integral part of the city. Yet as these depictions show, it was until relatively recently considered a suburb. Historical photographs from that period confirm these impressions. Bearing in mind that this refers to the city as it appeared about 30 years ago, the speed of development becomes quite remarkable. I should also note that, based on these accounts, urban growth took place within an established urban fabric – consisting of old districts, suburban outposts, and landmarks. As such, the convenient scapegoat of the *tabula rasa* development is not applicable. In fact the city has an established history of urban development going back to the nineteenth century as I illustrate in the following sections.

From Masterplan to Structural Plan to Urban Development Framework

One could argue that Dubai's urban development – the first conscious efforts at controlling growth – began late in the nineteenth century. In 1894, Deira was ravaged by a fire leading to a new phase of development. Richer people began constructing their habitations from coral stone and gypsum, while the lower income inhabitants still lived in huts (*barastis*) constructed from palm fronds.[3] Dubai's population at the turn of the century was 10,000 centred in three areas: Deira which consisted of 1,600 houses and 350 shops whose population was primarily Arabs, Persians and Baluchis; Shindagha which had 250 houses and only Arab residents; and Bur Dubai which had only 200 houses and 50 shops, dominated by Persian and Indian merchants. There are no detailed data as to the character of these houses except that they were built of clay and coral fragments. In 1956 the first house using concrete blocks was built (Gabriel, 1987).

This first phase of urban development as it were, extended from 1900 to 1955. Dubai's urban growth in this period reflected a pattern of slow and limited physical expansion due to constrained economic activity and marginal growth in population. The entire population of the city was confined to three small enclaves located at the mouth of the Creek. Both the Creek and the Arabian Gulf were considered the main source of income for the local population, who were predominantly involved in fishing and pearl diving. Until 1955 the urban area did not exceed 320 hectares (3.2 km^2) and the land use was predominantly residential with extremely limited commercial space. The vast majority of the local inhabitants were living in extended families in *barasti* houses. Residential quarters were built in clusters to serve the purpose of privacy and collective tribal security. The internal parts of each enclave were connected by narrow walkways intended for pedestrians and domestic animals that were used for transport of goods and drinking water. The only source of drinking water was four public wells near the enclaves and water was carried directly by the families (Heards-Bey, 1982). Formal efforts at urban planning did, however. begin in the 1960s with what is known as the 'John Harris Masterplan'.

The John Harris Masterplan: The Second Development Phase

In 1960, British architect John Harris drew the first Masterplan for Dubai. He was introduced to Dubai's ruler, Sheikh Rashid bin Saeed Al Maktoum, in 1959 by the British Political Agent, Sir Donald Hawley. Harris rapidly won the ruler's trust and became the state's expert adviser on the new Masterplan. According to *The Times*, 'he developed a means of working that wedded Sheikh Rashid's ambitions with an architecture both respected and respectful'.[4]

The choice of Harris is an interesting one given that he was relatively unknown and had no large practice. In addition to economic reasons, it seems to suggest that Sheikh Rashid wanted an approach that was not based on a *grand vision* but one that is more modest. This was confirmed by his wife Jill Harris and his son Mark, both architects, in an interview at their London office on a cold, grey and rainy December 2008 (following his death in February that year). Their townhouse/ office in Marylebone had memories of Dubai – images and paintings of the World Trade Center in particular, which was designed by John Harris (as I discuss in the following chapter). Both had great regard for the previous ruler – Jill emphasizing his Bedouin origins, suggesting modesty and an approach to architecture and planning that is perhaps more wedded to the land and which takes into account the welfare of the city's residents. They also told me that John walked a great deal exploring the old city and this had a great impact on his subsequent plan. According to Mark, his father's approach was modernist (not surprising given that he and his wife were educated at the Architectural Association in London in 1948, then a bastion of modernity in architecture). Yet even with that in mind, his architecture and planning principles did in many ways respect the past – not a typical modernist attitude. With Sheikh Rashid growing increasingly ill, decision-making moved into the hands of his sons, which heralded a change in attitude – a move towards the monumental and the spectacular, perhaps necessitated by the conditions of the time.

As I noted in the previous chapter, the situation of Dubai in the 1960s was quite primitive. The city had no paved roads, no utility networks and no modern port facilities. Water was only available from cans brought into town by donkeys. Travelling to Dubai from London took several days in unreliable piston-engine planes with overnight stops. Communication was also difficult. There were few telephones and cables were sent by radio. The Masterplan developed by Harris aimed at rectifying this by addressing some fundamentals: a map, a road system and directions for growth. According to Mark Harris, his father's plan attempted to integrate the old town into the proposal for its growth and that he was in fact guided by Sheikh Rashid in not razing the old city as has happened elsewhere in the region. This initial plan (figure 5.5) would guide Dubai's development and be modified due to the discovery of oil in 1966.[5]

The second phase of Dubai's urban development can be characterized as compact growth, extending from 1955 to 1970. Developments followed the Harris Masterplan. It called for the provision of a road system; zoning of the town into areas marked for industry, commerce and public buildings; areas for new residential quarters and the creation of a new town centre. These rather modest goals were in line with the emirate's limited financial resources (oil had not yet been discovered in sufficient quantities). In 1971, due to the city's expansion and increased economic resources a new Masterplan by Harris was introduced. The plan called for the construction of a tunnel running beneath the Creek connecting Bur Dubai and Deira (the Shindagha Tunnel) and the construction of two bridges (Maktoum and Garhoud); in addition, the building of Port Rashid was also envisioned. A large area extending towards Jebel Ali was designated for residential use (now known as Jumeirah) and a further large area was reserved for industrial use; to the city's south additional areas were dedicated to health, education and leisure and recreation uses (Gabriel, 1987). This phase also saw the creation of a series of landmarks among them the Dubai World Trade Center, designed by John Harris.[6] The World Trade Center became Sheikh Rashid's final tribute to his state. At forty storeys it was the tallest building in the Arab world for the next 20 years and Dubai's first emblem. The presence of Queen Elizabeth II at the opening of the building in 1979 heralded the start of Dubai's global success — the city had finally been born. Given the significance of this building, I discuss it in more detail in the next chapter.

Some observers characterized the developments which followed in the late 1970s and early 1980s as 'planned suburban growth', a period of rapid expansion (AlShafeei, 1997). Of particular note was the emergence of the city's growth corridor along Sheikh Zayed Road towards Jebel Ali. Dubbed the 'new Dubai', this area emerged as the new commercial and financial centre of the city. Numerous projects were constructed along this stretch of highway and the skyline of the city changed as a result. These rapid developments have emerged both as

5.5(a). The city of Dubai in 1950. (*Source*: By courtesy of Dubai Municipality)

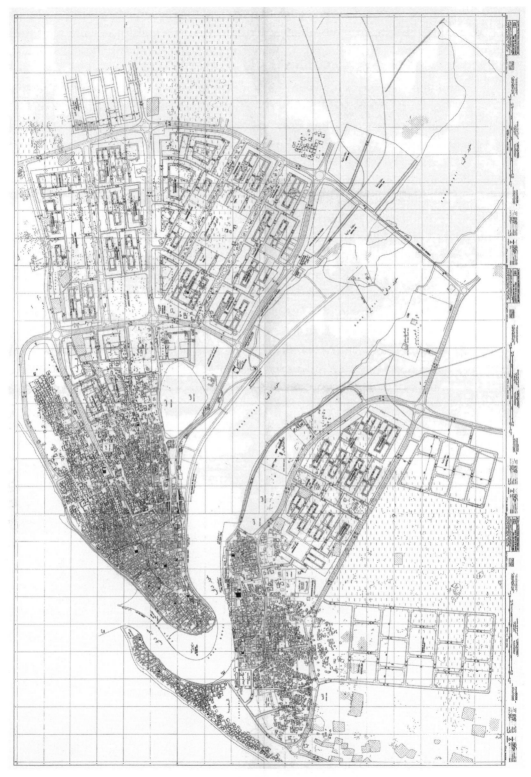

5.5(b). Dubai's first masterplan by John Harris, 1959 (1960 edition). (*Source*: By courtesy of Harris Architects)

a result of increased resources and an attempt to provide alternative sources for revenue. Yet the main problem which emerged due to these new axes of growth is fragmentation and the emergence of a city composed of disjointed archipelagos or islands – as has happened elsewhere in the world, particularly in rapidly urbanizing societies. Furthermore, the speed with which some of these projects emerged necessitated an approach that would not be based on a 'rigid' Masterplan – hence the development of the Dubai Structural Plan.

The Dubai Structural Plan

Given the rapid development taking place in Dubai, the old Masterplan proved to be insufficient in guiding its future urban development. Thus, in 1995 Dubai Municipality prepared a 20-year plan – also known as the Structural Plan – whose main aim was to be flexible enough to accommodate any changes. The Dubai Structural Plan forecasts that by 2015 the Dubai urban area will have the capacity for 2.7 million persons. Total land requirements for the future are: 30,912 ha (309 km^2) by 2010 and 38,669 ha (387 km^2) by 2015. By the target year, the total urban area to be developed, according to these official estimates, is 60,480 ha (about 605 km^2). Yet clearly if one measures the required land area for development based on various projections, the number increases substantially (in excess of 1,000 km^2). A significant factor in this massive increase in the city's urban area is the housing policy for citizens which envisages providing a land plot to all citizens of 21 years with a total area of 4,572 m^2 (figure 5.6).

According to Municipality officials this plan complements other strategic

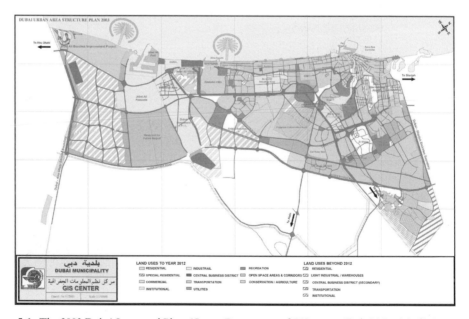

5.6. The 2003 Dubai Structural Plan. (*Source*: By courtesy of GIS center, Dubai Municipality)

initiatives such as the Comprehensive Development Plan 1985–2000, the Strategic Urban Growth Plan for the Emirate of Dubai (2000–2050), First Five Year Plan for Dubai Urban Area (2000–2005), and of course the Structural Plan for Dubai Urban Area (1993–2012).[7] In spite of these various plans it soon became clear that there is a need for a more comprehensive vision. Competing developments, matters related to sustainability, as well as growing social and economic problems due to the increased influx of foreign labourers, have all contributed to a realization that a new plan needs to be adopted – hence the emergence of what has become known as DUDF (Dubai Urban Development Framework). Before considering this latest promise of a plan I discuss the Structural Plan as it is responsible for, and anticipates some of, the city's current urban form.[8]

The report begins by situating the Structural Plan within a historical context, essentially describing the origins of the city's urban form. Thus, beginning in 1955 the urban area consisted of what are now the CBDs on either side of the Khor or Creek. The Deira side initially developed in a radial pattern as one would expect on a peninsular type of land area, but was constrained by the Dubai-Sharjah border and, later, by the airport. Due to these constraints, this radial pattern was transformed into a grid pattern as Deira developed beyond the CBD. In Bur Dubai, the initial street structure parallel to the coast established a linear urban form stretching to Jumeirah and beyond. As development progressed the location of the Khor, and particularly Ras Al Khor, forced roadways and utility corridors into a semi-circular pattern by-passing Ras Al Khor. Grid street patterns (and thus form) once again developed on both sides of the city as the road networks extended beyond the Khor. The grid network was the result of the traditional approach to the subdivision planning practiced by Dubai Municipality. This is the basic structure

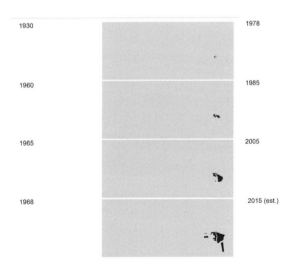
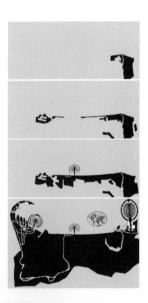

5.7(a). Urban development of Dubai from 1930–2015 (estimate). (*Source*: Author, based: on aerial photographs; Gabriel, 1987; Structural Plan, 2003, Dubai Municipality, GIS Center)

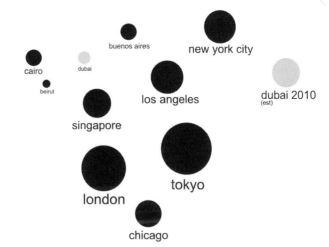

5.7(b). A comparative diagram showing the relative size of Dubai in relation to selected cities. (*Source*: Author, based: on estimates from Dubai Structural Plan; Wikipedia Encyclopedia for size of cities)

and form of the city today (Dubai Municipality, 1995, pp. 3–14). The report then goes on to develop a series of 'spatial growth alternatives' which include extensions to development along the Al Ain road; extensions to development parallel to the coast (what is now known as New Dubai), and concentrating development beyond Jebel Ali. These scenarios envision the construction of a major airport near Jebel Ali 'should it be required' (*Ibid.*) (figure 5.7).

Conceptually the Structural Plan is based on a series of nodes and axes of growth which, for the most part, account for the city's form as it appears today. In fact many of the major megaprojects (e.g. the Palm Islands) do to some extent follow this plan. The report proposes three new major recreational nodes: east of Mina Seyahi (which now contains Palm Jumeirah), in the area of Ras Al Khor, and south of Jebel Ali. According to the plan, Mina Seyahi and Ras Al Khor are to be multi-use areas which will combine institutional and cultural and other public uses, office parks, major educational and research facilities, along with recreational uses. Mina Seyahi, in particular, will focus more on 'tourism support', which is in fact currently taking place although the report suggested a 'magic world theme park'.[9] This project has actually been relocated to the Dubailand area along the outer bypass road (Emirates Road), a major artery that had been proposed in the Structural Plan. The report, however, fails to anticipate major developments which will occur in the Jebel Ali area, which had been planned as a 'public open space with limited tourism development'.

Some elements of the plan, however, were simply not realistic in anticipating the massive growth of the real estate business. For instance, one of the key conceptual tenets was a central civic spine, linking the CBD via 'the water elements of the sea and Khor, to the desert elements of the camel race track and desert/nature reserves beyond' thus 'greening this spine will provide an "oasis" linkage between the sea and the desert' (*Ibid.*, pp. 3–15). Along these same lines it was proposed that 'to break the continuity of the Jumeirah coastal corridor … a major space axis is proposed from the sea island to the desert' (*Ibid.*, pp. 3–18). The graphic representation of this idea envisions some sort of a park snaking its way through the city's urban area. Obviously this did not happen. In fact one could characterize the city's development as an attempt to overcome that desert image (which can only be experienced through special Safaris on its outskirts and beyond). Also the report did not anticipate the increased significance of Sheikh Zayed Road as a major artery effectively blocking any kind of sea-desert connection. The 'desert' discourse has simply disappeared from Dubai's urban narrative (it may have been an orientalist, romantic attempt at adding an Eastern touch to what is for the most part a typical Western Masterplan).

A significant amount of the report is devoted to housing policies and residential communities. Land plots allocated to nationals increased in size to between 12,000 and 15,000 ft^2 (1,100–1,400 m^2]; residential areas were to be allocated in a radial extension from the Ras Al Khor area and also along the coast in Bur Dubai (Jumeirah, Um Suqeim). Interestingly, it is suggested that there should be a 75: 25 local/expatriate mix in these areas (thus not becoming purely local) and there is also a suggestion that nationals should be encouraged to relocate to inner-city areas such as Satwa and Al Hamriya. The latter did not happen and these areas were left to decay and deteriorate. However, the complete razing of Satwa and the planning of Jumeirah Gardens in its place may fulfil this vision at a scale that no one could have ever anticipated.

Commercial development was envisioned correctly along the CBD area with its traditional markets and banking district. Outside the CBD, the areas of Wafi, Burjuman, City Center and Port Saeed were all identified as major centres of commerce, given that they all house major shopping malls. This also included Sheikh Zayed Road, planned as a major node for office development, although the report notes that the area has been 'up zoned to 30 storeys' – which did not take into account that it would eventually house the tallest building on earth, at more than 160 storeys! Also, regarding commercial development, the area next to Garhoud was planned as a 'central park' for Dubai – which would eventually be realized but in a commercial form through Festival City – a mixed-use commercial development which includes a waterfront promenade, but little in the way of any green areas.

The Structural Plan report relied to a large extent on the Comprehensive Development Plan (CDP) prepared between 1985 and 1988. The establishment of the urban area boundary for Dubai in the 1985 CDP was based on the objective of containing urban growth within a predefined limit, primarily as a means of implementing the policy of encouraging 'infill of vacant, serviced inner land areas'. A related policy was to retain flexibility for planning, so the urban area boundary was extended to include designation of 'areas which could reasonably be assumed to become a part of the urban area after the planning target of 2005'. The boundary target to accomplish this latter policy incorporated large vacant tracts. The extension was contrary to the policy to promote infilling, since it allocated land for development outside 'the serviced inner land areas'. The demand for developable land has been such that both infilling and low density contributed to 'scattered site', or 'sprawl'.

The plan estimated that the residential holding capacity of the Dubai urban area would be approximately 1.7 million persons, given prevalent land-use development and population trends and excluding communities which were yet to be planned and approved. The remaining residential capacity of the urban area was estimated to be 1.07 million, based on an approximate population of 637,800 (in 1985). Provisional population projections prepared for the Structural Plan report indicated that this residential holding capacity figure might be surpassed within fifteen years or by 2008 (Dubai Municipality, 1995, pp. 4–11).

Policies pertaining to land distribution policies to nationals had a significant impact on the city's urban area. These call for the allocation of land, as mentioned earlier, of 15,000 ft^2: (1,400 m^2) to nationals above the age of 20; 'certain categories of females' receive a plot of 10,000 ft^2 (930 m^2). The report notes that this would result in a 'dramatic' increase in the number of plots, and thus land areas since these policies provide plots to individuals rather than families/households. Plot requirements were actually double what actual housing requirements would be. Another anticipated impact was a deteriorating housing condition in older nationals' housing areas, which were being vacated in favour of the new, larger plot areas (Satwa, for example, or Bastakiy'ya). Furthermore, through such policies large subdivisions were created with 'low livability quotient'. And in an insightful comment the report states that nationals were moving to suburban locations away from the major employment, shopping and recreational opportunities. This would lead to 'suburbanization of nationals' and is considered by the report as an 'unhealthy trend which alienates nationals from their own city'(*Ibid*., pp. 5–3).

The report discusses housing needs for expatriates and particularly notes the immigration policy which stipulates that low-income earners cannot bring their families.[10] As a result, there will be a reduction in households which will lead to a reduction in the need for family type accommodation and thus there will be a demand for single-person accommodation, which is a major problem plaguing the city's low-income housing sector. The report does not make any specific recommendations for dealing with this problem, leaving it mostly in the hands of the private sector. It is clear that this 'hands off' approach has led to what can only be described as a housing crisis which the city is currently experiencing (discussed in Chapter 8).

Clearly, the criticism levelled at Dubai that it is a city growing without a clear plan, or what some remarkably decry as an absence of a 'Masterplan', reveals a lack of knowledge concerning some of the work that has been done in this regard. The Structural Plan reviewed here offers a detailed 'vision' of the city, supported by statistics and research. Yet it also shows that there is great discrepancy between what has been proposed/envisioned and what actually took place. And the question one needs to ask is: has the plan been responsible for the city's current lack of urban form?

To some degree the answer is yes. The report lacks a general overarching vision, and seems to be dominated by generic clichés. Written in the 1990s, when issues of sustainable development were being discussed, no mention at all is made of sustainable urbanism, with its emphasis on social sustainability and creating an open and accessible city. This is not just a question of rhetoric, but by de-emphasizing issues of social justice, the city left itself open to real estate speculation leading to the current trend of exclusivity (encouraged by the government). The report also does not include any visual analysis, guiding the city's three-dimensional development; this would have included: 3D massing studies; perspectives; and desired visual patterns. Again, due to this negligence the city appears without any unifying visual character and more like a generic twenty-first century metropolis.

Of course the report was written prior to the city's remarkable real estate boom and the emergence of numerous players impacting its urban environment. Developers such as Nakheel, Emaar and many others are now crucial in determining the city's growth. The current speed of development supersedes the Structural Plan which has become outdated. The Dubai Urban Development Framework currently being prepared should, hopefully, rectify the present 'chaotic' situation. Although this may seem to be difficult since it is being prepared 'after the fact' and will be based on realities on the ground that have taken on a life of their own. The global financial crisis impacting the city's urban growth is just one reality that the city has to grapple with.

The Dubai Urban Development Framework

In August 2007, amid wide media fanfare, it was announced that the Dubai Urban Development framework had been awarded to consultancy firm URBIS from Australia as well as the WSP group.[11] According to reports the plan 'seeks to create an innovative, flexible and fully integrated development planning and management framework for Dubai to the year 2020 and beyond'. The plan is a direct outcome of the Dubai Strategic Plan 2015 (DSP) which focuses on economic development, social development, security, justice and safety, infrastructure, land and environment and public sector excellence.[12] The project falls under the auspices of the Urban Planning Committee (UPC) of Dubai Government. The UPC has key stakeholders including Dubai Municipality, the Road and Transport Authority (RTA), Dubai Electricity and Water Authority (DEWA), Dubai Land Department, and the Executive Office, as well as such developers as Dubai Holdings, Emaar and Nakheel. Technical experts from each of these organizations will be part of a Task Force which will help prepare the DUDF. The project will be administered by the Executive Council Secretariat and managed and directed by the Dubai office of the multi-disciplinary consultant, Halcrow Group.

The plan is based on what has been widely characterized as explosive growth. For instance the emirate's GDP has been growing at rates close to 16 per cent, while foreign trade increased as well. More than 80 per cent of the UAE's Dh510 billion (US$139 billion) merchandise trade is conducted through Dubai, while the city's attractive hard infrastructure is attracting massive investments that are putting further pressure on its capacity, pushing the property and rent prices higher, beyond the reach of the middle-income group. Furthermore, traffic and skyrocketing rents have been identified by the city's residents as the major causes for concern. Thus, according to an official:

> In 14 months time, the consortium will offer an integrated master-plan that will be based on the future needs of Dubai's growing population, in terms of land use, traffic impact, water and electricity consumption requirement... The government has not yet re-calculated the population growth projections... The consortium, in its master-plan, will suggest that and the plan will be based on those calculations.

Yet I should note that at the time of writing (Spring, 2009) no announcements have been made concerning the plan or its details which are being developed in complete secrecy without apparent input from key stakeholders (namely city residents). This contrasts sharply with the Abu Dhabi Plan 2030 which was announced in 2007 and made available to the general public for review and comment. But a few details have been announced in the media concerning DUDF. According to official reports the plan will have three key modules:

1. A Vision for Dubai;
2. An Integrated City and Regional Development Planning Framework; and
3. A Legal and Institutional Framework.

This 'vision' seeks to improve 'environmental, economic and social sustainability and business conditions in the city' and it also aims to develop 'quality of life targets, seeking to firmly position Dubai within the short list of the world's most "livable" places'. There is also a realization that some form of coordination is necessary for the various agencies operating within the city. Furthermore, key elements of the framework will include: 'integrated land use and mobility, housing provision, economic and demographic growth, urban character and design, heritage management, integrated community facilities provision, civic harmony and sustainability strategy'. Various legal strategies and frameworks are being worked out to cater for these ambitions. Given the city's seemingly haphazard mode of development it remains to be seen if this plan moves beyond lofty rhetoric to actually fixing conditions on the ground. Otherwise it simply becomes an afterthought, used as a tool to justify existing developments.

Public-Private Relationship

To understand better the conditions within which these developments are taking place I would like briefly to discuss the nature of the public/private relationship – the city has been sometimes referred to as 'Dubai Inc.', with its ruler frequently referring to himself as the CEO of Dubai.[13] This does of course highlight the rather unique situation of the city.

The government continues to be the driving force behind developments, despite efforts to establish a more traditional private sector removed from government financing. The largest development projects, mostly in the real estate sector, also fall under a government umbrella. Dubai has consolidated most of its local and foreign projects in two holding companies, Dubai World and Dubai Holding (with approximately one hundred and five and twenty-six different companies respectively). These holding companies will continue to finance and execute large-scale development projects, such as Dubailand and the offshore Palm Jumeirah and the World Islands. Emaar, a publicly-traded real estate firm building the Burj Dubai, at one time contributed the largest share volume to the limited Dubai stock market. But Emaar recently announced a land-for-shares deal with Dubai Holding, increasing the government control as a majority shareholder.

Further complicating the picture are the presence of multiple agencies responsible for implementing development strategies such as the Dubai Municipality, the Road and Transport Authority (RTA), the Federal Environment Agency, and the Ministries of Economy, Environment and Water, Health, Education, and Energy. Each autonomously plans, invests in, and executes activities in its specialty area. While all of these agencies are more or less controlled by the government, the private sector plays a large role as well. Historically, Dubai has been referred to as a city of merchants, exemplified by the well known statement 'What is good for the merchants is good for Dubai' made by its late ruler, Sheikh Rashid.[14] They continue to play a major role in the city's growth; for instance the Al-Futaim group is responsible for some of the major projects such as Deira City Center, Festival City and the massive Mall of the Emirates. But, as I noted earlier, one of the main objectives of DUDF is the coordination between these different agencies, so ensuring that there is some sort of harmonious vision, which at present seems to be lacking resulting in the city's fragmented and splintered appearance.

Challenges

Some of the major challenges which need to be addressed by the development plan involve the following:[15]

- Inefficient transportation, road congestion, and traffic accidents.
- Housing affordability, infrastructure needs, and a rising cost of living.
- A need to integrate different cultures and lifestyles.
- Pollution and waste management problems.

I discuss these briefly in the following sections.

Transportation

One of the main problems facing Dubai is traffic, which involves endemic queues, air pollution, noise and accidents. Many of its major thoroughfares are in a constant state of gridlock, particularly the central area in Deira and Bur Dubai. Based on Dubai Municipality estimates some numbers are quite staggering: 470,000 vehicles are registered in Dubai; furthermore additional vehicles arrive from the nearby emirates of Sharjah and Abu Dhabi, which is equivalent to almost 1 million vehicles on the road (based on two trips per day) which is roughly the equivalent of Dubai's population.

It is estimated that by 2020 the city's population will reach 4 million, and the number of car trips 13.1 million per day (Pandey, 2008). The rate of growth in the number of cars is rising at an average of 10 per cent per year, which far exceeds the world average of 2–3 per cent. Such staggering rates can be attributed to the relative affordability of cars and cheap fuel. Furthermore, public transport – while increasingly being expanded – is not as ubiquitous as it should be.

To combat these problems and to develop a transport strategy Dubai Government formed the Road and Transportation Authority (or RTA), which was formerly a department integrated with Dubai Municipality. One of the major objectives of the RTA is to integrate the various transportation modes currently in operation – bus, water and light rail (under construction). To understand the extent of the problem, buses carry about 240,000 people daily, representing 20 per cent of the city's population.

One of the major projects currently under construction is Dubai Metro at an estimated cost of $4.2 billion. The project consists of several lines which will begin operating in phases with the first set to open in 2009. It is expected that the system once in operation will transport 1.85 million passengers daily. Another strategy is to prevent people from driving on certain roads through the implementation of a toll system – also known as *Salik*. Initially installed along the city's main artery, Sheikh Zayed Road, it is currently being expanded and will eventually cover other parts of the city.

Housing and Infrastructure

Increasing rents and availability of proper housing arrangements represents one of the main problems facing the city's low-income expatriate population. Over 2005 and 2006 rents sometimes increased by as much as 100 per cent leading the government to impose rent restrictions, preventing landowners from increasing rents for existing residents. Also, recently, the government began a crackdown on what has been referred to as apartment or villa sharing by bachelors and families – a major problem which I address further in Chapter 8.

With regard to infrastructure, there is continued and increased spending on major projects: $2 billion for roads and bridges, including a new 12-lane bridge across Dubai Creek; $300 million for drainage and irrigation projects; and $700 million for public projects. Yet increasingly the city is reeling under an expanding population which is straining some infrastructure elements.

Cultural Integration

An often cited number is that Dubai is home to residents from about 200 countries. Yet the city is not a melting pot. There are strict lines of segregation among various nationalities, but particularly between local and expatriate. This becomes particularly evident in the city's housing policy whereby a distinction is made between local – *muwatin* – and expatriate – *wafid*, resulting in ethnically homogeneous districts (unlike the 75:25 per cent mix proposed in the Structural Plan). However, new developments are catering for both categories. This does, however, raise another line of demarcation – an economic one. Current policies emphasize this distinction through a variety of measures: raising rents in low-income areas thus driving poorer residents away; demolition of poor areas; and so on. Thus one of the major challenges facing planners is integration between these various sub-groups to avoid turning Dubai into a 'city of walls' as has happened in other cities throughout the world.

Pollution and Waste Management

While not having reached pollution levels encountered in some world cities, current developments are an indicator that it is moving towards unacceptable levels. Data indicate that the increasing number of vehicles is contributing to 80 per cent of pollution levels. In fact vehicle emissions in the city exceed UAE government limitations by between 13 to 25 per cent.

Regarding the issue of waste, the UAE has one of the world's highest levels of domestic waste. Per capita household waste has reached an annual average of 1,598 pounds (725 kg) in Dubai and 1,609 pounds (730 kg) in Abu Dhabi. In the United States, the average is 1,565 pounds (710 kg); in Australia, 1,521 pounds (690 kg); and in the UK 661 pounds (300 kg) (Pandey, 2008). Additional refuse comes from street litter, gardens, and from the waste dumped on beaches and in the sea.

The last problem can be attributed to a lack of proper sewage treatment facilities. Trucks unloading sewage obtained from some areas in the city lacking a proper sewage drainage system can go to only one treatment centre where waiting times can reach 10 hours or more. Thus, some drivers in an effort to maximize the number of trips they make, resort to dumping sewage in the city's storm drain network which feeds into the sea. As a result a major problem of coastal pollution occurred in September 2008, with some beach areas closed for clean-up operations.

Due to the various coastal developments taking place in the city, there is a danger of disturbing the very delicate marine ecosystem. There have been efforts by both governmental and non-governmental organizations to deal with this yet clearly more needs to be done – particularly as the city is embarking on more massive developments which will result in a substantive change to its coastline. Also, while many studies are initiated by developers to investigate the effect of their interventions (Nakheel's Blue Communities initiative, for instance), independent bodies need to be set up to ensure objective assessment.

Towards Sustainable Development

The challenges which I have discussed in the previous sections pertain to issues related to sustainable development. This has become a major goal for countries all over the world. Dubai began to address this by issuing a law in 2008 which stipulates that all buildings need to follow green design standards. Clearly, simply addressing this issue at the level of individual buildings is not enough. A comprehensive sustainable development strategy entails an improvement in city planning; increasing social cohesion among various social, cultural and economic groups; provision of an efficient and affordable public transit system; and the availability of affordable housing. Various assurances have been made by officials that the, yet to be announced DUDF, will deal with these issues in a comprehensive manner.

As I have tried to show in this section, the city is seemingly being developed without a clear vision or framework – or at least this is the popular view. But, since the 1960s a series of Masterplans and various revisions have contributed to guiding the city's growth. Yet as a result of these changes, and the rapid urbanization, a certain morphology was 'created' – which I discuss in the following section.

Dubai's Urban Morphology: Transient Urbanism

One of the first impressions of the city is its fragmentary nature and the reliance on cars as the primary means of circulation. Dubai is composed of multiple, disconnected centres, which are separated by multi-lane highways. This precludes any meaningful pedestrian circulation or, for that matter, a conventional urban fabric which can only be found in the 'traditional' areas of Bur Dubai/Shindagha and Deira. Because of this, it is compared with Los Angeles and other US cities; furthermore it is cited as a prime example of what is termed 'splintering urbanism', thus placing it squarely within worldwide urban trends (Graham and Marvin, 2001). Yet there are certain aspects of its development which are unique. They pertain to the city's rapid urban development and its land-use and land distribution policy.

First, its rapid expansion has been widely noted. Up until 2008 roughly 25 per cent of all construction cranes operating worldwide were in Dubai. Using historical and contemporary aerial photography it is possible to estimate that the city expanded from a mere 2 km^2 in 1950 to approximately 140 km^2 in 2005. At the current rate of expansion and taking into account future planned projects, the financial crisis notwithstanding, the area may, by 2015, reach more than 1000 km^2, putting it close to major world cities such as London, New York and Tokyo and well above Singapore (see figure 5.7(b)). While these world cities have populations between 4 and 12 million, Dubai's population at the present is roughly 1.4 million, mostly transient residents. Furthermore, it is expected that the current number of visitors will increase from 3 million to 15 million, thus justifying this expansion. However, while the city is rapidly 'building itself into significance', it should be noted that all of this is taking place within a desert. This *tabula rasa* type development has resulted in large gaps or patches between developments; vast expanses of sand which need to be filled. Thus the general feeling of the city in its present state is that of a construction site – it is still a work in progress. Furthermore, lacking the high population density that would sustain such a momentous rate of building, many areas appear empty without a sign of life. Its neighbourhoods lack a sense of community – they have a transitory feeling.

Second, the city's land development policy with regard to its native population, as outlined in the Structural Plan, is another factor causing the rapid increase in the built-up area which is also directly linked to its housing policy. A clear distinction is made between housing for expatriates (*wafidoon*) and locals (*mowatinoon*), with each allocated certain distinct and separate spaces within the city. This policy still persists although there have been changes in ownership laws allowing expatriates to own property in specially designated zones. However, of more significance is the land grant policy. Every citizen in Dubai (as well as the UAE) has a right to land given by the government, free of charge – as well as access to a loan to build a house. This has caused a massive increase in the city's urban area. However, many plots remain undeveloped due to the high cost of construction, and the delay in loan disbursal, which in some cases can take more than seven years.[16] In addition, some of the older sites in Satwa, for example, which were owned and occupied by locals, have now been turned over to low-income workers, while locals have moved to outlying suburban areas. These older sites had a small plot area and higher densities. New regulations have increased the allotted plot area which in turn has resulted in much lower densities.[17]

As I indicated in the previous section, further compounding the problem of unchecked growth is the seeming absence of a masterplan. Also, the existence of multiple agents and real estate agencies – all owned by the Dubai government – such as Nakheel, Emaar, Dubai Properties, as well as private enterprises such as Futaim, is another factor causing this uneven, and sometimes conflicting development. Thus, while Dubai Municipality is nominally in charge of coordination, developments are many times given the go-ahead, and approval is obtained after the fact, and then incorporated into the Structural Plan.[18]

To get a clearer sense of the city's urban morphology figure 5.8 shows a figure-ground analysis of the city as a whole (up to Defense Roundabout on Sheikh Zayed Road) as well as select areas: the central, historical part; the extension along the Sheikh Zayed Road spine; and some of the newer parts. The analysis clearly reveals its disjointed appearance – there is no integration between these various parts. They do not add up to a coherent whole. And while some areas display a typical, traditional urban fabric, such as the spaces surrounding the Shindagha district as well as Deira, the appearance of a traditional morphology – narrow and twisted alleyways – is deceiving since the majority of the buildings are 4–5 storey concrete structures built in the 1960s and 1970s. Others simply exist as isolated islands – archipelagos, as some urbanists have indicated. Also, there are large undeveloped areas contributing to a general sense of discontinuity in the

5.8(b). Figure-ground diagram of Dubai's central area.

5.8(a). Figure-ground diagram of Dubai.

5.8(c). Figure-ground diagram of New Dubai – Sheikh Zayed Road and Satwa.

'urban fabric'. In general there is an absence of a genuine 'urban realm' in the conventional sense.

The Creation of a Global Image

My discussion so far has centred on the city's urban development framework – or lack thereof – as well as the resulting splintered and fragmented urban form. While there is a seeming absence of a general vision guiding all these developments, one cannot discount that there is in fact a shrewd strategy at work aiming to establish Dubai as a global centre. Through the development of iconic landmarks, for instance, the city is placing itself on the map of significant urban centres. Its splintered urban fabric does in some way cater for the 'space of flows' and the movement of transnational workers. Thus the city has become, or is on its way to becoming, a perfect embodiment of this new transnational urban space within which the new nomads operate. While my previous discussion centred on Dubai's urban strategy I now shift the discussion to the various projects currently underway in different sectors.

This involves increasingly 'bold' architectural projects: the Palm Islands, Burj Al-Arab Hotel, Dubai Marina, and the twin Emirates Towers. Other projects are geared to the global economic infrastructure of media and the internet: Dubai Media City, Dubai Internet City (DIC) and Dubai International Financial Center (DIFC). Other cities are in the making: Healthcare City, Textile City and International City.

Described by some officials as 'megaprojects', they distinguish themselves by using superlatives to ascertain their uniqueness. Furthermore, these projects are seen as a continuation of major developments which have taken place in the city, contributing to its rapid urbanization, such as the dredging of the Creek thus facilitating commerce, and the creation of the largest man-made artificial port, Jebel Ali, a free-zone and industrial area located north of Dubai. In the following sections, I make the argument that this is part of a larger strategy whereby Dubai is asserting itself as a major global player – and it is utilizing well-established real estate and architectural tactics to achieve this larger goal.

Real Estate Strategies

Real estate has become 'one of the cornerstones of Dubai's economy', according to a report by the Oxford Business Group, a research consultancy.[19] As evidence in excess of $20bn worth of projects were being built or actively planned. In 2005 real estate accounted for 24.2 per cent of the emirate's GDP (oil represented only 4.9 per cent). The driving force behind this growth is the government which controls to varying degrees three major developers – Nakheel, Emaar and Dubai Properties as I noted earlier.

Nakheel (fully government owned) is responsible for the three iconic Palm Islands as well as the World Island. Among its major ambitions is the Waterfront project – a massive offshore development on reclaimed land which will surpass Manhattan in size. Masterplanned by Rem Koolhaas, it was expected to be completed between 2010 and 2015 (but is currently on hold) and, according to the developer, should be the last coastal development in Dubai. Emaar is 32 per cent government owned and is responsible for a variety of residential projects such as Dubai Marina in the 1990s, and has increasingly focused on gated, suburban communities such as the Springs, Meadows and Emirates Hills. Its most significant project to date is the Burj Dubai. The third is Dubai Properties responsible for the massive Jumeirah Beach Residence (or JBR) which consists of 40 towers forming a massive wall-like enclave facing the Gulf waters and is said to be the 'largest single-phase project ever attempted'.

A question that immediately arises in examining these developments is whether there are enough people to occupy the buildings. Looking at population growth figures, developers assume, based on supplied government estimates (which I discussed earlier), that the population will reach 2 million by 2010 and 4 million by 2020. Furthermore, the number of tourists is expected to reach 15 million by 2010.

Clearly, the real estate sector is planning for a future population – not the current one. And given the current global financial crisis these numbers may change even further.

Prior to 2002 the concept of real estate was non-existent. Expatriates rented apartments and locals were allocated land by the government (which they were not allowed to resell). This is due to a large extent to the visions and policies of the UAE's late ruler Sheikh Zayed, who was aiming to counterbalance three hegemonic powers surrounding the country – Oman, Saudi Arabia, and Iran – by preserving the united federation of the emirates. According to the Oxford Business Group (2006): 'The UAE's tradition of centralist land policy went hand-in-hand with the drive for unitary federal self-preservation'. Other factors include Sheikh Zayed's image as a benefactor, granting land to his people; and demographics which were not in favour of locals, thus restricting ownership would ensure that land remains firmly in their hands.

In spite of these factors there was a realization in the mid 1990s that real estate represented an opportunity for diversifying an economy too reliant on oil. This was particularly the case for Dubai which had limited oil supplies (unlike its neighbour Abu Dhabi which was virtually sitting on a sea of oil and gas ensuring supplies for the foreseeable future, leading to a more measured approach to city planning and growth). One of the main challenges for Dubai, in attracting more tourists, was its limited coastline, hence the decision to increase this by developing the three Palm Islands as well as a plethora of other sea related projects, dredging of canals etc. Furthermore, a major stumbling block was the legal definition of ownership for expatriates, significantly limiting investment. In 2002 the Dubai government declared – after much anticipation – that 'freehold' property would be available to foreigners in the city. Yet the rule contradicted federal law which does not allow foreign ownership. A 'one country two systems' formula was adopted in 2006, effectively creating special zones within the city (free zones) where exceptional rules would apply.

A common criticism directed at the city's real estate sector is its exclusive focus on luxurious, high-end development while ignoring the majority of the population who are crammed into small apartments and rooms in the city's centre and downtown area. This focus is justified on the grounds that low-income housing is not spectacular enough to 'brand the country'. They cannot be the tallest, nor can they be built on reclaimed land. According to the chairman of Nakheel – Sultan bin Sulayem: 'You can't do low cost housing on reclaimed land'.[20] Recent developments have been correcting this imbalance in two ways: demolishing existing housing stock for low-income people in the city's centre; and the creation of workers cities and camps on outskirts in the desert thus sanitizing the city in a way by displacing its poor who should be kept out of sight for fear of spoiling the carefully crafted ultra-luxurious cityscape.

For example, the low-income district of Satwa, wedged between the 'uber-luxurious' Sheikh Zayed Road and the multi-million dollar villas in Jumeirah and

5.9. The towers of Sheikh Zayed Road as they appear from Satwa's bus stop.

Um Suqeim, began to be demolished in 2008, thus potentially displacing more than 150,000 residents. In its place a government owned developer, Meraas, aims to construct a mixed-use high-end development. Similar demolitions are taking place in other parts of the city as I discuss in Chapter 8. To compensate for these displacements, in 2005 Dubai Municipality announced plans to construct low-cost housing meant especially for expatriate workers in the Al-Quoz and Al-Ghusais areas of the emirate. These units will eventually house more than 100,000 workers (figure 5.9).

Another criticism directed at Dubai's real estate development is that it is a bubble which will eventually burst or, at the very least, that a correction will take place which will limit the phenomenal growth which has taken place so far. This prescient prediction proved to be correct in 2009, but the full extent of this is yet to be assessed. According to the Oxford Business Group (2006) one of the factors which has created a volatile market is the close interconnection between the stock and real estate market. For example Emaar and its home financing arm Amlak dominate the Dubai stock market, and fluctuation in their stock value can impact financial trade to a large degree. Also, the role of speculators has driven prices upward – yet in the absence of any reliable statistics about buyers,[21] it is difficult to assess the exact impact. Anecdotal evidence suggests that many units remain empty or at the very least are bought by investors residing outside the UAE who in turn lease their units to a transient expatriate population.[22] In some cases they are vacation homes for wealthy Western expatriates.[23]

Yet in spite of some of these misgivings, there are signs that the real estate market is maturing, which would enable the city to weather the global financial downturn. For example, rent capping introduced by the government to mitigate excessive rises has stabilized the market to some extent. Also the introduction of a real estate regulatory authority (RERA) and the use of a consultancy firm to do market research for the Dubai Department of Land and Properties are seen by some as signs that the market is moving beyond excessive, unregulated speculation.[24]

Others factors contributing to a favourable outlook are 'the edge' which the city maintains over its neighbours. For example, it has an unprecedented degree of economic freedom, a streamlined bureaucracy, full ownership possibilities and, most significantly, political stability. Furthermore, social freedom and tolerance have made the UAE and particularly Dubai an attractive place for businesses. This is particularly evident in the repatriation of Arab capital following the events of 9/11; the city has effectively become a main centre for these funds, reaching billions of dollars which have found their way into the real estate market.

Given the political situation of the emirate, whereby the lines between the public and private sector are blurred and where most developments are effectively controlled by the state and a few wealthy 'merchant' families, there is widespread belief that these constitute an effective mechanism to counteract any financial downturns. Furthermore, a steady supply of cheap labour, the absence of any effective non-governmental organizations which would challenge some of these developments, and the absence of environmental and labour policies which would slow this growth ensures that it would continue unabated. And perhaps most significantly, the presence of Abu Dhabi emirate with its massive wealth almost guarantees that any dramatic fluctuations would be immediately corrected. According to the Oxford Business Group (2006) it would 'come to the aid of the sector rather than see the reputation of the entire country damaged'.

The Megaprojects

Dubai has been marketing itself in a number of ways – specifically as the region's capital of 'glitz and glamour' or 'the Monaco of the Middle East'. Representing this trend towards exclusivity is the Burj Al Arab – a self proclaimed seven star hotel which spawned numerous other buildings – with the Burj Dubai representing perhaps the ultimate in luxury. These projects cater mostly for an elite clientele made up of wealthy GCC nationals and Indians, Iranians, Russians and others. In order to attract such a clientele, a strategy of spectacular architecture has been adopted which has become one of Dubai's trademarks, focusing specifically on superlatives. For instance, Dubai World Central, a major airport area under construction in Jebel Ali, will be larger than London's Heathrow and Chicago's O'Hare combined and there are many others (see Chapter 6). Furthermore, sea dredging is being undertaken to create 1,500 km of coastline resulting in cities which will house more than 1.3 million people. Some estimates suggest that 70–80 per cent of the world's sea dredgers will eventually be working just on the Palm Deira (the third Palm Island; ten times larger than the original Palm Jumeirah).

All of this comes at a massive cost. Combining all the public and private sector projects now underway and planned, the UAE has invested more than $1trillion. But it should be noted that a recent report by research house Proleads has shown that about $582 billion of civil construction projects in the UAE are now on hold which represents 52.8 per cent of the total civil construction portfolio.[24]

Dubai's Architectural Strategy

Looking at Dubai's approach to architectural styles – or lack thereof – is revealing. More than any other city in the region, and perhaps in the world, it has made the notion of branding, i.e. developing icons which capture attention through superlatives (the tallest, biggest, etc.) or the borrowing of styles from other regions and cultures and rebranding them as its own, a key ingredient in pursuing global city status. The sheer scale with which this strategy is pursued has been the subject of countless media articles which does, of course, underscore the larger purpose behind this seeming explosion of styles: placing Dubai on the map of significant world cities. Yet until recently those responsible for the city's architectural character were corporate architectural offices and developers. Interestingly, signature or star architects were lacking (unlike other cities in the region such as Riyadh or Kuwait which attracted well known architects such as Norman Foster). This has changed recently, but for a long time commercial interests dominated the architectural discourse – there was simply no time to contemplate the conceptual musings of a Jean Nouvel, or the sculptural acrobatics of a Frank Gehry. For instance, Burj Al Arab was designed by an architect named Tom Wright from Atkins – a largely unknown figure. There are exceptions to this of course – the sail shaped National Bank of Dubai designed by Argentian Carl Ott, or the elegant Emirates Towers, designed by Hong Kong architect Hazel Wong. The city's seeming lack of context – what I have called the seductive allure of the *tabula rasa* – did however provide an opportunity for architects all over the world to reinvent the architectural wheel as it were – resulting in an abundance of mutually exclusive styles (Elsheshtawy, 2009, forthcoming).

The Oxford Business Group report on Dubai's real estate and construction industry devoted a large section to the city's architectural character, noting that the emergence of iconic (i.e. quirky) buildings began in the 1990s. The report is based on interviews with a number of architects practising in the city. There is a general consensus that the sail shaped Burj Al Arab has 'served to accelerate the recognition of Dubai as a regional modernizer'. The architects' statements reveal a mindset that is opportunistic in a way, recognizing the relative aesthetic inexperience of the local population which in turn they are using to advance their own commercial interests. In explaining their stylistic choices, terms are invented that have no existence in common architectural discourse – e.g. *futurisms*, i.e. twenty-first century futuristic buildings. Or consider the following statement: 'In Dubai we generally follow a style known as interpretive modernism … an international, modern style in which the functional meets the decorative' (Oxford Business Group, 2006). Aside from these theoretical musings, the following statement shows the degree of freedom architects enjoy (which is similar to other experiences in newly emerging economies such as China): 'Aesthetically speaking, there are some height limitations… But aside from this, there are very few limitations to what we can do' (*Ibid.*).

With these statements in mind it is no surprise that there would be proposals for an underwater hotel; or that there would be serious consideration given to a proposal by an obscure Italian architect for a rotating tower. Or consider the Palm Islands – a marvellous engineering feat no doubt, but whose 'thousand and one nights' architectural fantasy – manifested in the Atlantis Hotel, seems to underscore the tasteless image of the city and its architects (figure 5.10). Further accentuating this problem is the absence of local architects. There are a few exceptions, but most commissions are in the hands of Western architects. There is no inspiring local role model. Even among the talented younger generation, their educational background precludes them from developing an assertive Emirati identity (as arguable as the existence of such an identity may be; or whether this is desirable in the first place).

5.10. The spectacle of the Atlantis hotel located on Palm Jumeirah.

Exclusive City

My aim in this chapter was to provide an overview of Dubai's urban development. The city, unlike many other centres in the region, developed around a historical core or focal point – namely the Khor or Creek and the centres of Bur Dubai and Deira. Its various planning strategies attempted both to cope with rapid growth and to preserve this centre. While the initial Masterplan was quite specific in trying to integrate new developments with the historic centre, the Structural Plan which would guide the city into the twenty-first century was much more flexible and open-ended. As a result the city developed in a manner that resulted in a splintered urban fabric – isolated islands connected by highways (figure 5.11). I have discussed the various factors that have led to this situation – the political context as well as the increasing role of developers in shaping the city's built environment. The emphasis on exclusivity – and in turn matters related to social exclusion – will lead to an environment that is non-egalitarian. And while one could argue that these developments follow what has happened elsewhere – Los Angeles for instance, which lacks a centre and where planning revolves around car traffic – one cannot discount the fact that there are certain aspects to Dubai's growth that are unique. Chief among them is its land distribution policy which allocates land to its nationals. The result is a sprawling urban conglomerate, dominated by suburban centres – where these plots are distributed – consisting of villas with little community life, and a complete absence of social interaction among the city's various groups. With that in mind, the following chapters will take us closer

5.11. The envisioned, sprawling metropolis of Dubai. (*Source*: By courtesy of Nakheel)

to the city as 'lived space' – to use a 'Lefebvrian' term – by discussing some of its megaprojects and also by looking at some of its less spectacular spaces inhabited by the 'forgotten' low-income inhabitants.

Notes

1. These are headlines and quotes from *The New Yorker* and *Vanity Fair*. See: Parker, I. (2005) 'The mirage: the architectural insanity of Dubai', *The New Yorker*, 17 October, pp. 128–143; and the skyline on crack quote is from Nick Toshes writing in the June 2006 issue of *Vanity Fair* and this is worth quoting in its entirety: 'The Dubai skyline is like no other. Silhouettes of cities come into being over the course of centuries. Here, where a few buildings rose from the dirt 15 years ago, countless structures now crowd the land and gasp for what space remains. Here there is no sense of accrued form, no sense of architectural strategy, no sense of past becomes present. Here, there is no sense, period. It changes every day, every night. Looking out one evening, I see Manhattan. The next night, it's a boundless industrial fantasia, a ten-fold Newark-by-the-sea. Then, another night, it is what it is: Dubai, shape-shifting, hammering and grinding madly and somehow silently, toward the sun and the stars. There is no architectural rhyme, no cohesion of design, no defining style. It is the visual equivalent of a bunch of speed freaks babbling incoherently to one another. Las Vegas is a sputtering 20-watt bulb compared with this fire in the desert. Forget about babbling speed freaks. Forget about everything. *This is a skyline on crack*.'

2. Rose, S. (2005) 'Sand and freedom', *The Guardian,* 28 November. *http://arts.guardian.co.uk/features/story/0,11710,1652149,00.html*. Accessed 8 May 2006.

3. http://www.sheikhmohammed.co.ae/vgn-ext-templating/v/index.jsp?vgnextoid=6abc4c8631c b4110VgnVCM100000b0140a0aRCRD

4. *The Times* (2008) 'Obituary, John Harris', 21 March.

5. 'When oil was found in August 1966 Harris witnessed the presentation of a "jam jar" full of oil to Sheikh Rashid in the Majlis. Sheikh Rashid told Harris to progress with plans for the Rashid Hospital and subsequently other hospitals, a modern school, banks and commercial buildings. The development plan was also updated'. ('John Harris, Obituary', *The Times*, 21 March 2008)

6. Harris recalls how he was introduced to Dubai's important project: 'I was leaving Dubai and flying back to London. My suitcase had been placed on the new hoist at Dubai's international airport and sent down to the loader below. At that moment a hand rested on my shoulder and a voice said, "Sheikh Rashid wants to see you". I explained about my luggage, but of course my suitcase went one way and I went the other'. ('John Harris, Obituary', *The Times*, 21 March 2008)

7. AME Info (2006) 'Dubai forum on sustainable urban development opens', *AME Info*, 18 March. http://www.ameinfo.com/80724.html. Accessed October 4, 2008.

8. Dubai Municipality (1995) *Structure Plan for the Dubai Urban Area (1993–2012)*. Report prepared by Parsons Harland Bartholomew & Associates, Inc.

9. The notion that this growth-recreation axis anticipated the Palm Jumeirah was suggested to me by Egyptian planner, Maher Stino, during a conference in 2003 at Harvard Graduate School of Design. He was one of the major figures from Dubai Municipality, responsible for formulating the Structural Plan. In response to criticism about the lack of planning in Dubai he pointed out emphatically that the location of the first Palm Island is along this axis and that it did follow the Structural Plan.

10. As of 2008, individuals earning less than DH4000 per month are not permitted to bring their families.

11. AME Info (2007) 'Government of Dubai awards major contract for 'Urban Development Framework Project', *AME Info*, 26 August. http://www.ameinfo.com/130017.html. Accessed 7 October 2008.

12. According to officials: 'The DUDF is an ambitious plan and places particular emphasis on

the need for innovative thinking, while leading to the creation of new and exciting approaches to Dubai's city planning. The Framework will also serve as the vehicle for translating DSP into an appropriate set of strategies, special plans, policies and guidelines'.

13. For further elaboration on the ruler's vision see his biography published in Arabic (Al-Maktoum, 2006) as well as an article published in the *Wall Street Journal* (Al-Maktoum, 2008).

14. For more on this see the study by local historian Fatma Al-Sayegh (1998) on the role of merchants in Dubai's growth.

15. These are based on a recent Report by Vishai Pandey (2008) for the Urban Land Institute.

16. A recent change in the regulations governing the disbursal of land/loans to locals stipulates that only those who are married, and in possession of DH 500,000 ($150,000) are eligible.

17. This information is from Khaled, one of my informants, a former employee at Dubai Municipality, as well as former resident of Satwa. In addition I also obtained a report titled, 'Planning study for the development of the Satwa area', *Dubai Municipality*, 1995.

18. *Abu Dhabi City Planning Conference*; 10–12 April 2005; presentation given by Dr. Hamid Hattal, Head of Comprehensive Planning and Studies Unit, Dubai Municipality.

19. Oxford Business Group (2006) *Real Estate and Construction*.

20. *Ibid.*, p. 154.

21. Some reports indicate that for the Palm Jumeirah, for example, UK nationals account for 25 per cent of buyers – the rest are from 75 different nationalities. Calderwood, James (2007) 'Investing in Dubai's Palms', *Gulf News*, 27 June, p. 57.

22. A colleague residing in Jumeirah Beach residence has leased his units from Dubai Properties who are acting on behalf of a Russian owner, living outside the UAE.

23. See: Richardson, A. (2007) 'Dubai's real estate market matures', *Emirates Today*, 1 February, p. 16; and Bowman, D. (2007) 'Dubai to set up real estate watchdog.', *Arabian Business*, 31 July. http://www.arabianbusiness.com. Accessed 6 August 2007.

24. *Gulf News*, 5 February 2009. http://www.gulfnews.com/BUSINESS/Construction/10282633.html. Accessed 10 February 2009.

Chapter 6

Spectacular Architecture and Urbanism

'The biblical story of Babel takes up a handful of verses in the 11th chapter of Genesis, and it illustrates, among other things, the terrible consequences of unchecked ambition. As punishment for trying to build a tower that would reach the heavens, the human race was scattered over the face of the earth in a state of confusion – divided, dislocated and unable to communicate. More or less as we find ourselves today.'

A.O. Scott (from a review of the movie *Babel* in the *New York Times*, 2006)

A recent Deutsche Bank advertisement in a local newspaper showed the symbols of various Middle Eastern cities and countries as a way to establish its transnational credentials. Egypt's Sphinx, Jordan's Petra and Lebanon's Baalbek represented the 'old' or traditional Middle East. Appropriately, all its symbols are historic. But when it came to the 'new Middle East', the choice of imagery changed. Cities and countries were represented by modern buildings – the Faisaliah Tower in Riyadh and Kuwait's Water Towers. The focus of the advertisement, however, was Bahrain's Financial Harbour and Dubai's Emirates Towers. A clear distinction was drawn between the past and the future – and it was quite clear where a transnational financial institution sees the future. Aside from the political and financial implications of this, it is telling that architecture is used to communicate these meanings. And not just any architecture – it has to be spectacular, unique – in short iconic.

This notion of using iconic buildings to suggest significance is a global strategy adopted to enhance the appeal of cities and make them attractive to investors, tourists and visitors. Sometimes described as the 'Guggenheim effect', named after the success of Frank Gehry's museum in attracting people to the once obscure city of Bilbao (figure 6.1), this phenomena is also referred to as the 'spectacularization' of urban space in the global city literature. Anne Haila (1997) argues that in order to attract foreign investment cities engage in image creation. Thus global cities encourage new developments, resulting in an increased importance of real estate and investors. She ties this to the work of Lefebvre (1972) who noted that real estate has supplanted industrial production, or Baudrillard (1972) who argued that the laws of production have become obsolete. Consumption, symbolic exchange, simulations and signs are what is important. Harvey (1989), in his examination of entrepreneurialism and urban

6.1. The spectacular architecture of the Bilbao Guggenheim Museum by Frank Gehry.

governance which favours entrepreneurs at the expense of inhabitants, adopts a similar thought.

In some instances the process is as important as the building itself. Ute Lehrer (2006) discusses strategies for globalizing cities – specifically what she calls the 'spectacularizing' of the building process. According to Lehrer it is not just the end product which is important but also the process – the production of images accompanying the project. Her analysis focuses on the Potsdamer Platz project in Berlin. She points out their use of superlatives such as 'The largest construction site in Europe'.

Dubai is no stranger to this and has in fact built its entire image on the notion of megaprojects, distinguished by superlatives – the tallest, the highest, etc. My aim in this chapter is to present three cases, which I believe represent the degree to which Dubai is using the 'spectacle' as a way of placing itself on the map of globally significant cities. I begin by briefly discussing the Burj Al Arab Hotel, the first iconic building in the city; the second project (actually a series of projects) is the Palm Island which to a degree created a logo for the city. I conclude by focusing on the ultimate icon – the world's tallest building, Burj Dubai. Here the notion of 'hegemonic Dubai', a city that asserts itself both regionally and globally, is evident. There are, of course, many other projects that have been built, planned or envisioned, but these three are major milestones in the city's attempt to draw the attention of the world. Prior to this review, however, I discuss the theory of the spectacle, to show the degree to which Dubai is becoming a fulfilment of this vision, focusing on the work of French situationist Guy Debord whose name has become synonymous with 'spectacular' urbanism.

The Theory of the Spectacle

While the construction of gigantic buildings and monuments has been a defining characteristic of human civilization it is only recently, through the proliferation of mass media, that they have acquired the status of a 'spectacle'. Guy Debord, in his widely read 1967 polemic *The Society of the Spectacle* and subsequently in *Comments on the Society of the Spectacle*, published in 1988, as well as a movie bearing the same title, offers a damning vision of a consumerist society. He notes that in societies where modern modes of consumption prevail, life becomes an 'immense accumulation of spectacles'. It can come in many forms, such as information, propaganda, and advertisement, and it permeates all types of social relations and perceptions. He further defines the spectacle as a world vision that has become objectified, splitting up the world into 'reality and image'. Within this discourse, such constructs as commodification become ways to show the disconnectedness between lived reality and what is being communicated, thereby contributing to a general sense of alienation. What Debord suggests, and this is crucial, is that the society of the spectacle demands an attitude of 'passive acceptance', a passivity that is triggered by the spectacle's 'manner of appearing without reply, by its monopoly of appearance'. Furthermore:

> The spectacle's externality with respect to the acting subject is demonstrated by the fact that the individual's own gestures are no longer his own, but rather those of someone else who represents them to him. The spectator feels at home nowhere, for the spectacle is everywhere. (Debord, 1967, 1995, p. 23)

Thus the spectacle can contribute to a general sense of alienation by emphasizing the disconnectedness between observers and the material object. It is the only thing that matters. He sets out this construct as a means of inducing passivity in the mass population. This argument is compatible with that of Adorno (1991), who argued that real life becomes more and more like the movies under the spell of what he called 'the culture industry'. The spectacle is, therefore, the product of a system of alienation which produces it. This can also be tied to Walter Benjamin's idea of phantasmagoria and commodity consumption in the arcades of nineteenth-century Paris (Benjamin, 1999).

Debord's focus is on the mass media, but he also extends this to the built environment. Linking 'spectacular developments' to fakeness, he argues that this is a natural outcome of capitalism, which 'builds a fake version of everything'. He cites as examples for this what he calls 'museum districts' (historically preserved neighbourhoods, for example); also his movie is frequently sprinkled with images of identical housing blocks. Ultimately, Debord informs us, such fossilization and conformity will lead to a 'loss of individuality'. Urbanism becomes a tool of domination by capitalism. The notion of fakeness becomes particularly poignant in a city such as Dubai whose very name evokes artificiality.[1] Of course, the objective here is establishing relevance by 'obsessively building itself into significance', as one observer put it.[2] The only way it can create this significance is by exaggeration, focusing on superlatives (the tallest, the biggest, etc.) irrespective of any relation to local context. The seeming absence of a 'substantive history' led to the proliferation of museum districts and themed developments. The result is a fragmented, splintered urban fabric. Its widely discussed megaprojects seem to exist in a parallel universe within an endless desertscape.

Debord adopts a Marxist perspective, criticizing contemporary modes of production. He was a proponent of the situationist movement, prominent in the 1960s, so his writings are related to a context that is very different from a Gulf city-state. Yet it is interesting to note that such viewpoints are echoed – although not necessarily in the same terms – by contemporary leftist thinkers such as David Harvey (2006) in his discussion of the geography of uneven development, and by Mike Davis (2005). Echoes of the Debordian perspective can also be found among post-structuralist thinkers such as Baudrillard (1995, p. 11) who, in describing Los Angeles, notes that it is composed of 'imaginary stations' which feed reality 'to a town whose mystery is precisely that it is nothing more than a network of endless, unreal circulation: a town of fabulous proportions, but without space or dimensions'; it is nothing more than 'an immense script and a perpetual motion picture' which needs an imaginary that is, in turn, based on 'faked phantasm'. Applying this to architecture and urbanism, buildings become the means through which nations, cities and communities mediate 'meaning'. Through them various notions of power and identity are represented. It is here that one can begin to understand the role of 'tall' buildings. In most cases they are functionally unnecessary but they become the means through which an announcement is made of the transformation of a second-rate city into one of 'global stature'. King (2004, p. 5), in an insightful analysis on the discourse of tall buildings (influenced by Debord), introduces the term 'architectural spectacle', in which buildings '… mediate the meaning of the nation to the gazes of the world'.

This notion of the spectacle has become wildly popular in contemporary architectural theory. William Saunders in a 2005 book titled *Commodification and Spectacle in Architecture* – a collection of studies examining the effect of spectacular architecture/urbanism – notes that the design of the built environment has been 'increasingly engulfed in and made subservient to the goals of the capitalist economy' by luring consumers for the purpose of gaining their money. Thus 'design is … a means to an end rather than end in itself' (Saunders, 2005, p. vii). Further, he defines the spectacle as follows:

> *Spectacle* is the primary manifestation of the commodification of commercialization of design: design that is intended to seduce consumers will likely be more or less spectacular, more or less a matter of flashy, stimulating, quickly experienced gratification, more or less essentially like a television ad. The stimulation that leads to 'Wow!' or to immediate sensual pleasure is more prominent than any implicit invitation to slow savoring and reflection. (*Ibid.*, p. viii)

And because spectacle 'discourages independent thought' there is only one way out for most architectural theorists and sophisticated practitioners – resistance. Yet Saunders shrewdly asks: 'what is so bad about commercial culture? Its many pleasures are harmless' (*Ibid.*). To answer this question we need to examine a few case studies that deal with the spectacular. Such an inquiry is particularly relevant in Dubai which has, almost more than any other city, made the spectacular its *raison d'être*!

The Burj Al Arab or Tower of the Arabs

I begin my examination of the spectacular in Dubai's architecture with the building that started this trend: the Burj Al Arab Hotel. Construction started in 1994, was completed in 1999, and is considered the city's first truly iconic building. It revels in superlatives: the tallest hotel in the world; a self proclaimed seven-star hotel; as well as the home of the most expensive cognac. But perhaps most tellingly, its entire allure is based on its seeming inaccessibility. It seems to exist as a remote object to be admired from afar (figure 6.2).

6.2. The Burj Al Arab Hotel as it appears from a residential neighbourhood.

Description and Conceptual Origins

The Burj Al-Arab, or Tower of the Arabs, is a fifty-six storey, 'seven' star hotel with 202 suites, three restaurants, a conference centre and health spa. It is built 290 metres out to sea on a man-made, landscaped island and at 321 metres is one of the tallest hotels in the world. The accommodation wings enclose two sides of a triangular atrium which rises to the full height of the building. The hotel whose tower is topped by a 60 metre mast, has a cantilevered restaurant 27 metres long and 200 metres above sea level. Access is through a heavily controlled bridge and only hotel guests and those with reservations at the hotel's upscale outlets are allowed entry. A helipad located at the top of the tower, and 212 metres above the sea is for those arriving from Dubai Airport – as an alternative guests are whisked away in Bentleys (figure 6.3).

6.3. Guests are transported to the Burj Al Arab by helicopter.

Stepping into the hotel atrium, one is confronted by gold coated pillars, extravagant fountains, and brightly coloured furnishings – in fact a one-thousand-and-one nights atmosphere. The sheer extravagance and scale is unprecedented and comes with a steep price tag (US$2,000–5,000 per night).[3] This opulence is justified by being cast as a form of traditional Arab hospitality.[4]

The hotel was designed by British firm W.S. Atkins and its chief architect Tom Wright. The company claims that the hotel is the 'ultimate landmark of Dubai and indeed the region'. Furthermore, the project had to be 'Arabic, extravagant and super-luxurious and – most importantly – become a symbol for Dubai'. The architect looked at:

> … historical Arabian themes like wind-towers before realizing the potential of the seafaring theme. But instead of picking on the time-honored shape of the dhow sail, as many expected, he fine-tuned the design to incorporate the profile of a J-Class Racing Yacht, itself a symbol of opulence and technology. Eventually he had a design which would be easily recognizable worldwide as Dubai's Burj Al Arab – Tower of the Arab – a balance of east and west.[5]

In describing the design process he notes that his main aim was to find an 'iconic form'. His search eventually led him to discover that an easily, instantly recognizable form would be the proper approach.[6] Regarding the issue of culture, having noted that he did not know the location of Dubai, he argues that its people were forward looking, aiming at the future, hence his decision to move away from the 'limiting' historical context.[7]

The Building as Symbol

The hotel, after it opened, became, for a while, the 'official' symbol of Dubai. Its image was used extensively by the advertising industry and replaced the 'old' symbol of Dubai – the Fahidi Fort and the Shaikh Saeed House – on car licence plates (in 2005 a decision was taken to have no images on licence plates). The project has not been without its critics, however. While some have noted its extravagance, others have pointed out that the project displays a schism in its dealing with local culture by trying to 'have it both ways', suggesting 'deep cultural roots' even though the real point is to show the city's sophistication and modernity.[8]

Others have decried its lack of contextual attachment. Thus, in official publications the surrounding area is never clearly shown. The hotel appears isolated in the midst of a wide expanse of water – somehow hiding the inescapable and harsh reality of the surrounding desertscape. Edward McBride (2000), expressing the official architectural reaction to this project, noted that the hotel is symptomatic of an era where 'the medium is the message' although unlike in Las Vegas, where one has roulette wheels, magic shows or night clubs, here the 'spectacle' is the structure itself. He further noted the project's exclusiveness '… the management has tried to heighten the hotel's allure by preventing people from visiting it' (McBride, 2000, p. 118). He describes it as a 'ritzy haven from Arabia's sandstorm' and that the hotel has become a symbol for 'the triumph of money over practicality' by 'elevating style over substance' (Ibid., p. 125). The project thus was designed from the top down, going from a desired image to its physical manifestation. Such a reaction is typical of professional 'sophisticated' architectural circles. One critic describes it as follows: 'It's fabulous, hideous, and the very pinnacle of tackiness – like Vegas after a serious, no-expense-spared, sheik-over'.[9]

Most residents of Dubai or the UAE have never, nor will ever, set foot in the Burj. Yet it has become a symbol of sorts for the city. It is well known and its ubiquitous presence in the media has made it a highly recognizable icon.[10] I have on many occasions observed low-income workers on their day off, taking pictures alongside the tower – without entering, of course. Its seeming exclusivity is somewhat diminished given the prevalence of luxury hotels which have opened in the city since 1999. Unlike the Emirates Palace Hotel – its Abu Dhabi equivalent, which has become a cultural centre, accessible to anyone – the Burj still caters for the ultra rich and regular folk are simply discouraged from entering. Stand and admire at a distance!

The Hospitality Sector

Since the Burj opened numerous hotels have followed suit. In close proximity are the wave shaped Jumeirah Beach Hotel, the Bastakiy'ya inspired Mina Salam and Qasr, and the Arabian themed Royal Mirage (figure 6.4). But perhaps the one that may overtake the Burj as an iconic destination is the Atlantis Hotel, located on Palm Jumeirah (figure 6.5) and managed by Kerzner International, which has brought its Bahamas Atlantis concept to Dubai. It features a huge water park, shark lagoon and dolphinarium – in addition to 1,539 rooms and seventeen restaurants, including the famed Japanese eatery, Nobu. Its managing director observes that

6.4. The Entrance to the Royal Mirage Hotel is guarded by golden camel statues.

'like the Burj Al Arab hotel, this is another icon for Dubai ... we are planning to become one of the landmarks in the emirate that people from all over the world would come to see'.[11] This point is of particular importance since the Burj Al Arab is part of a wider trend within the hospitality industry worldwide whereby hotels become destinations in themselves. For Dubai, lacking any significant cultural features, this is quite significant and is reflected in the various ultra luxurious hotels which are being planned.

One major project representative of this trend is Dubailand, a spread of forty-five gigantic mixed-used projects with a total investment of Dh235bn ($64bn). The project's master developer, Tatweer, believes that it will attract 40,000 visitors a day. Dubailand's largest project will be Bawadi, which is to include one of the world's largest hotels, the Asia-Asia, with 6,500 rooms covering more than 55 hectares, which will overtake the Las Vegas based MGM as the largest hotel in the world. According to the developer, many worldwide destinations will be placed

6.5. Approaching the Atlantis Hotel on Palm Jumeirah; to the left is the island's monorail.

inside the hotel itself thus it 'will have an Asian theme, which means there will be Asian shops, a floating market like the one in Thailand, and a "Great Wall of China" roller-coaster ride'.[12] Asia-Asia will employ about 12,000 people, compared to a standard 250-room hotel that employs about 400 staff. The Bawadi masterplan for the surrounding area aims to make it the longest hospitality and retail strip in the world, a 10 km stretch that will add fifty-one hotels, 60,000 rooms and 370 hectares of retail space to Dubai at a total investment of Dh200bn ($54bn). I should note that these numbers were announced prior to the 2008/2009 financial crisis and, while there has been no official announcement about its cancellation, some scaling down should be expected.

This trend for the spectacular is not restricted to size or design features. Another strategy is to tie the hotel to a brand: whether it is an iconic fashion brand or a celebrity. Representative of this is the Tiger Woods Dubai Hotel. Also, a Palazzo Versace is planned for the city, to be built on the shores of the Creek. The only one in existence, on the Gold Coast in Queensland, is said to be the most expensive hotel in Australia and a 'favourite haunt of Hollywood stars'. Also planned is an Armani Hotel, the designer's first foray into hotel design anywhere in the world. It will be located in the Burj Dubai, spread over seven floors.[13] These hotels are part of a much larger drive aiming at turning the Gulf region into a major tourist destination. To put this into economic perspective, Dubai and its Gulf Arab neighbours are hoping to develop hotels worth about $18 billion. The UAE is leading the drive, building or planning hotels worth about $12.7 billion. About 100 hotels will eventually open in the UAE, adding 30,000 rooms.[14] In such a market, the adoption of theming and branding strategies seems to make perfect sense – for the hoteliers and their exclusive clientele, of course.

The Palm Island(s)

Sheikh Faisal speaking to Lawrence

'... the English have a great hunger for desolate places. I fear they hunger for Arabia ...
you must be another of those 'desert loving Englishmen' ... no Arab loves the desert. We love
water and green trees... There is nothing in the desert... But you know, in the Arab city of
Cordova were two miles of public lighting in the streets – when London was a village!...
I long for the vanished gardens of Cordova.'

From the 1962 movie *Lawrence of Arabia*

For many observers urban developments in the Gulf region are synonymous with island reclamation, which is not surprising given the media attention devoted to Dubai's Palm Islands. Two major factors drive these developments: first, counteracting the cliché of the Arabian desert; and second, investment of capital in preparation for a post-oil economy. Regarding the first, our perception of the Arabian Peninsula is one that is dominated by images of the desert, camels majestically roaming its endless horizons, and oases miraculously appearing within desolate landscapes. Inhabitants of this region are acutely aware of this perception and in their drive to attract tourists have embarked on these developments as a way to provide an alternative. Rather than just the dryness and heat of the desert there is also the richness of waterfronts, lush gardens, and luxurious beaches. This is not only seen in these coastal developments but also in efforts to 'green the desert' by planting trees or maintaining gardens and trees in metropolitan areas – at huge cost. The second factor is economic. Due to the events of 9/11 there has been a repatriation of Arab capital which, in addition to the massive increase in oil price in 2007–2008, has led to surplus capital being invested in massive real estate and infrastructure projects. The development of the islands represents one particularly visible manifestation of this.

Dubai's Reclaimed Islands

Dubai is no stranger to reclamation and expansion of its coastline. In the 1960s, under the rule of Sheikh Rashid, it embarked on two major projects which transformed the city from what was more or less a small fishing village into a major metropolis. First was the dredging of the Creek which divides the city into two parts, thus enabling boats and dhows to enter the waterway unimpeded. In the process significant amounts of land were added to its central area (see Chapter 5). Second, the creation of the Jebel Ali Port near the border with Abu Dhabi established its status as a major centre for trade and commerce. These were all precursors to major coastal development projects which began in earnest in the late 1990s with two projects, as noted before, the Burj Al Arab Hotel, built on an artificial island and the Palm Jumeirah Island, the first in the series of reclaimed islands.

Nakheel, a fully government owned developer, is responsible for most of what are called 'Dubai's coastline enhancement projects'. After Nakheel began building Palm Jumeirah in 2001, it went on to develop the bigger Palm Jebel Ali in 2002, and in 2004 Palm Deira, which is seven and a half times the size of Palm Jumeirah, and five times larger than Palm Jebel Ali, with an estimated surface area of 46 million square metres. In addition to this 'Palm trilogy', in 2003 Nakheel introduced the exclusive 'The World', a set of islands whose overall layout resembles a map of the world, which was followed by 'The Waterfront', claimed by Nakheel to be 'one of the biggest offshore projects ever attempted' and 'the largest urban development project in the world'. The development is expected to be completed by 2015 and represents, according to Nakheel, the last coastal development in Dubai. Although another project was recently announced called 'The Universe', located between The World and Dubai's coastline it resembles the planetary system. Work has not yet commenced on these islands. Their general character in terms of land use differs. Jumeirah is a resort/residential development, Jebel Ali has a commercial orientation, while Deira is envisioned as a complete city – these are the characterizations of the developer.[15]

Some numbers illustrate the enormity of the developments and their unprecedented scale. Nakheel estimates that the cost of the projects is of the order of $60bn. More than 1,500 km of coastline will be added to the city's original 67 km. The expected number of inhabitants in these 'cities' is 80,000 for Palm Jumeirah, 300,000 for Palm Jebel Ali, and The Waterfront will eventually house 1.5 million people. It is estimated that 70–80 per cent of the world's sea dredgers will eventually be working on Palm Deira alone. Once completed all projects – according to the developer – will be visible from space. For the most part these projects, the parts that have been completed, have been financially successful. More than 40,000 properties had been sold since 2002, although only at the end of 2005 did Nakheel deliver its first 850 units. I should note that these developments were expected to be completed by 2015, however the recent financial downturn caused Nakheel to halt dredging operations on Palm Deira as well as the Waterfront project.

Located near the Burj Al-Arab Hotel, Palm Jumeirah is the only fully completed island in the series. The island is built in the shape of seventeen huge fronds surrounded by 12 km of protective barrier reef, extending 5 km into the sea south of Dubai city. It is accessible by 300-metre bridges from the mainland or by boat to two marinas, while the main causeway will also have a monorail system.

When the project was first announced it was claimed that it was the biggest man-made island, and '… like the great wall of China it will be visible from the moon'. The original Palm was the brainchild of Dubai's then crown prince Sheikh Mohamed bin Rashid al-Maktoum, essentially responding to the expected increase in tourists. To cater for them additional shoreline was needed and the island, measuring 5 km by 5 km would give Dubai 120 km of new, sandy coastline.[16] The date palm design was chosen because it is '… one of Dubai's most enduring symbols of life and abundance'.[17]

The project was managed by Dubai Palm Developers and dredging work was undertaken by a Dutch firm (Van Oord ACZ). Some of the statistics associated with this construction are quite impressive. Palm Jumeirah has been built using 95 million cubic metres of sand and rock. Rocks for the foundations were, according to official records, taken from quarries around the UAE. Special barges were used to dredge sand from the sea and, with the help of satellite GPS technology. The sand was then deposited to create the crescent shaped fronds (figures 6.6. and 6.7).

6.6. The outer crescent of Palm Jumeirah as it appeared in 2004 while the island was still being reclaimed.

6.7. Palm Jumeirah nearing completion. (*Source*: By courtesy of Nakheel)

Legend has it that the project was based on a sketch by Sheikh Mohamed. Officially, however, it owes its conceptual origins to a New Zealand architect based in Australia, Warren Pickering. He was asked in 1995 to create a design for an island. His proposal for an island shaped like a palm was eventually adopted. During three years of planning the project 'involved a total of forty-two consulting firms and more than fifty studies, all especially commissioned to include key aspects such as marine ecology, human population and the business development of the islands'.[18] While the need for additional shoreline is understandable, the various implications of this project were not quite clear, specifically the ecological ones– even if claims to the contrary were (and are) made. In fact according to one official at the time, these were all details that would eventually be worked out, what mattered was the 'right attitude'.[19]

As a developer, Nakheel did not allow for the purchase of plots and design of individual villas, but customers were given a range of pre-designed housing styles and configurations. It was envisioned as a masterplanned community and thus to reflect the 'global outlook' of Dubai. The development company offered thirty-two architectural styles ranging from Islamic to Mediterranean to modern. These were shown to potential buyers as perspective images. The sale was accompanied by typical 'developer speak'. According to architects involved in the project, the villas represent a new approach in residential architecture in Dubai. Rather than being enclosed on all four sides by a wall, as one may find elsewhere, only three walls are built and the fourth side will face the waters of the Gulf so that 'people … enjoy the benefits of living by the sea' – hardly a revolutionary concept but nevertheless offered as an incentive for buying.

In addition to the residential units, fifty 'boutique' hotels will also be constructed. These will offer different themes and will be built on the 'crescent', an 11 km long crescent-shaped breakwater protecting the residential fronds from the seaward side of the island. All hotels on the crescent were to be low-rise, not exceeding three storeys. At the time of writing the first of these has opened – the Atlantis – although, clearly, it did not follow the initially set height limit!

The project was marketed as a means for individuals to realize a dream of owning property.[20] Yet at an initial price tag of $500,000 plus, that dream is not within everyone's reach. Aware of criticism that the island caters for the super-rich or will become a 'rich man's retirement colony' an official noted: 'I don't think it is only for retired people and it is not only for the rich either. The rates are very reasonable and many will be able to afford them'.[21] According to sales records, when the project was introduced all villas had been sold and there was a long waiting list of potential buyers.[22] Initially offered on a 99-year lease basis, authorities decided to sell the units as freehold. Thus buyers would own their property and to encourage sales further, they would also be given unlimited residency visas. The latter fact is of particular importance since Dubai consists mainly of a transient population, hence having the option of unlimited stay is particularly attractive – conditioned of course by job stability and the ability to pay the high mortgage rates.[23]

Architectural Style

The architectural style of some of the buildings is described as 'Arab eclectic'. According to one of the architects associated with the project, US based Larry Ziebarth (whose clients include Disney, Universal Studios and Sea World), this style offers a 'sensitive blend of Islamic tradition with new architectural elements'. His company HHCP Design International had been asked to inscribe this style on some of the developments taking place on the Palm. Describing the 'style', he notes that: 'We have sought to create a building style that is deeply rooted and borrows from regional Islamic traditions, but with a strong dash of fantasy – which will become synonymous with the entire project'.[24] The result as can be seen in the Palm Sales Center located on the shore and facing the island, is a 'Disneyesque' creation – not surprising given the architect's clientele. The Atlantis Hotel as well as the residential towers located along the Palm's main axis are also an adaptation of this style (figure 6.8).

It is interesting that what is in essence described as Arab eclectic is nothing but a reminder of post-modern excesses of the 1970s and 1980s which are finding a re-affirmation in Dubai. That description, however, has been adopted by officials and is being used extensively in the media. Also, the literal and figurative are used not only in the site plan of the islands but extend to the design of some of the major buildings such as the Palm Centers – which will include retail outlets and a transport interchange for boats – in that the design is 'inspired by the Nymphea or Water Lily and resembles a large flower on a reflecting pool'.[25]

6.8. The Disneyesque details of the Atlantis Hotel which are referred to as Arab eclectic style.

Criticism

Nakheel has been criticized by international marine biologist Peter Linley,[26] other biologists and environmental monitoring groups such as mongabay.com[27] for the environmental impact these projects will have on the region. One concern, for example, is how marine life will be affected by changing the coastline and the ocean floor. According to Tina Butler writing for mongabay.com, construction activity is damaging the marine habitat, burying coral reefs, oyster beds and subterranean fields of sea grass, and threatening local marine species. Oyster beds have been covered in as much as two inches of sediment, while above water, beaches are eroding with the disruption of natural currents. Citing a number of ecologists she notes that 'standardizing' the marine environment will alienate native marine species, and is likely to encourage the introduction of new, foreign and possibly destructive species.[28]

In response, Nakheel's environmental manager, Shaun Lenehan says that after the conduct of fifty-five separate environmental studies, it was found that little coral and few fish exist in the Gulf in the first place;[29] some environmental scientists at Nakheel have also argued that marine life has flourished due to the construction of these islands. For instance, one scientist notes:

> Just recently we discovered that the channels between the fronds of the Palm projects seem to be ideal habitat for seagrass meadows. We've discovered large tracts of two species of seagrasses establishing in these areas. The protection offered by the crescent offers a sheltered environment favourable to seagrasses. The Palm Jumeirah crescent itself represents about 40 hectares of rocky reef. I dive on it every week and it is flourishing with invertebrate and vertebrate fauna. We've recorded dolphins, manta rays, sharks, trevally and more within the waters of Palm Jumeirah.[30]

In general, Nakheel's response centres on the notion that their interventions are localized, small in scale and will thus not affect the larger marine ecosystem in the Gulf. And that any criticism of their efforts is largely 'philsophical' since any man made activity will have an environmental impact, and that their projects' impact is minor compared with most residential developments.

Another problem pertains to water circulation in the island's fronds (elongated earth shapes on which the residences are located, and that, together, resemble palm fronds from the air). The management of sewage and garbage may cause excessive pollution among the fronds. To deal with these problems, the developer has created mechanical systems using pipes to channel seawater and ensure a steady, continuous flow that prevents the water from stagnating.

Nevertheless, as Peter Linley pointed out, the real problem starts when thousands of people move in and their waste is not managed effectively. Some criticism has also been levelled at the high density of the houses built on the frond-shaped areas of the island. Specifically, critics say that the space between residential units is too small at only about 4 to 5 metres;[31] recent aerial photographs confirm the limited space available between units. According to Nakheel, however, this distance is standard for beachfront development, as the main focus is the water. The location of the newer islands can also block views from the older ones. For example, buyers of property on Palm Jebel Ali, who initially thought they had an unimpeded view of the Gulf, have voiced concern that they now face the massive Waterfront development. In short, there is the danger of saturation, which could bring down the iconic status of some of the islands. (figure 6.9)

Another area of concern is the degree to which these projects are integrated with the city of Dubai. Nakheel officials note that agreements have been signed with RTA (Road and Transportation Authority) and DEWA (Dubai Water Authority) to facilitate extension of infrastructure to these islands. Yet this does not dispel the fact that these are exclusive developments – in essence gated communities which are not accessible for a large majority of Dubai's residents. The planned monorail – which will link with Dubai Metro system – may help in overcoming this aura of exclusivity and facilitating access to regular visitors.

In response to this, and in an attempt to deflect increasing criticism, Nakheel recently announced a 'Blue Community' initiative which supposedly makes its projects more environmentally conscious. Thus the Waterfront project, for example, is described as being the 'world's first ecopolis' relying on an extensive network of pedestrian circulation and public transport, effective water management and reliance of renewable energy sources. Whether these are sincere attempts at sustainability or merely a sales tool to attract buyers, or a response to Abu Dhabi's foray into green building remains to be seen.

Another area of concern relates to the question of who actually lives in these villas. A popular view is that many are empty. Yet some people have already moved in. An Associated Press report notes that British people account for 25 per cent of buyers – the rest are from seventy-five different nationalities. Furthermore, buyers are speculators, long-term residents, and people looking for a vacation home. In a rare insight into who actually lives there, a local English newspaper – *Gulf News* – in a 2007 article profiled one resident described as a 43 year old Englishman, who was a former executive with a London-based Internet company. The article is topped with a large picture of him tanned and barefoot dragging a small boat from the beach – houses appear in close proximity to each other and the view is the back of villas on the opposing frond. There is no one else in sight. The beach is shared with all the other villas – and houses are directly facing the sand. Regarding plot size our 'token' resident is more than happy, using European standards as a comparative measure.[32]

Another newspaper article on that same resident observes that his villa is on Frond E which is known as 'the Party frond'.[33] Furthermore, after a year living on Palm Jumeirah, he bought another villa on Frond P 'dubbed the second-best party frond' which is rented to holiday makers. Another frond is called VIP, which is where David Beckham supposedly bought a home. Our resident was drawn

6.9. The high density of villas on one of the Palm's fronds. (*Source*: By courtesy of Naheel)

to the Palm project because of the close affinity to the sea. He spends his days 'swimming, kayaking, entertaining guests and dealing with enquiries from fashion directors and the like keen to use his bright, airy and luxurious – an overused tag for new homes in Dubai, but applicable in this case – homes for photo shoots'. There are of course other occupants; in Fall 2008 the island was home to about 4,000 people. One interesting observation pertains to the lack of basic amenities such as a supermarket but 'for frond villa owners, who are predominantly expatriates, there's a simple solution to fetching a pint of milk: send the maid, while those living in the Shoreline Apartments have a mini-market'. Even our resident is not immune from the perils of daily living as he 'makes coffee at his home, he runs out of milk', he then notes that the 'reality for people living in the villas is that you have someone to do the grocery shopping for you, that is part of the lifestyle'.

It is ironic that even within such an exclusive community one can find social divisions and distinctions. I noted the categorization of the fronds, but close to the entrance are the Shoreline Apartments, where residents have shared access to a beach and pool, and this is somehow viewed as being less prestigious than the frond villas. An interpreter from Kazakhstan rented a holiday home there for a week, and her biggest dream is to one day own a home on Palm Jumeirah. But the article makes an interesting observation, highlighting the social problems that exist in such a place. According to one visitor – and he deserves to be quoted in full:

> It seems as if the best parts are 'gated' and reserved for the lucky few. It is a wonderful piece of civil engineering, but I think the entrance is uninspiring and the building density is too high, which doesn't do justice to the 'island' brand. As you drive in, you can't even see that you are

coming on to an island – a place that is supposed to be about access to the sea… The potential was there to create a slower paced and less dense oasis within a thrusting city. Dubai has a lot going for it, but if it's to be a sustainable city where people of differing tastes put down social and economic roots, then it needs to diversify in terms of what it offers as a place to live – and I don't mean offering towers that rotate or reach closer to the stars, I'm talking about environments and neighbourhoods.[34]

Such pointed criticisms are rare, but this does highlight one of the many problems of such mega developments in that they are not geared to fostering a sense of community. This can be observed throughout the city's various luxurious residential districts. That sense of neighbourhood, a place where one can walk and where children can play safely, does not enter into the equation of real estate developers.

Another criticism is directed at the uninspiring architecture of these islands as well as their 'quirky' shape – regarded with derision by some observers. However, the recent commission of Dutch superstar architect Rem Koolhaas may go some way in alleviating the impoverished aesthetic character of these islands. He has been asked to develop a masterplan for Waterfront City – located within the massive Waterfront development (figure 6.10). Known for his experimental architecture, and fondness for what he calls 'the generic city', the island represents a perfect laboratory for experimenting and testing his ideas. According to *The New York Times*, the project consists of 'a mix of nondescript towers and occasional bold architectural statements, [and] it would establish Dubai as a center of urban experimentation as well as one of the world's fastest growing metropolises'.[35] Furthermore, the article observes that this project represents a growing trend in which high-end architecture is used as a tool for self-promotion. Thus, cities

6.10. The Waterfront project by Rem Koolhaas, designed to resemble a mini-Manhattan.

are reduced to theme parks of 'architectural tchotchkes that mask an underlying homogeneity'. But in an insightful social critique, it is noted that the 'boardwalks framing the project lack the intricate layering of public and private spaces found, say, on the Corniche in Beirut' and 'Mr. Koolhaas will have little control over the makeup of this community, which, if current development in waterfront Dubai is any indication, is still likely to serve a small wealthy elite'. I return to these social observations in my general assessment of all the case studies.

Finally, regarding the 'funny' shape of these islands – palm trees and the world map – they do serve one specific purpose: creating an instantly recognizable symbol for Dubai! By propagating such a heightened awareness of 'Brand Dubai' – one can think of these islands as company logos – they direct attention to the various projects that are being carried out and thus increase sales and profits. This particular approach represents a major point of departure from the development direction taken by its neighbour Abu Dhabi, for instance, and elsewhere in the Gulf (see Elsheshtawy, 2008).

The Tallest Building in the World: Burj Dubai or Tower of Dubai

In striving to become a global centre, Dubai has embarked on a series of high profile projects designed to signify its achievement of global city status. As I noted in the previous section, from the largest fabricated island to the tallest hotel, these projects seem to be dwarfed next to what is being planned – the world's 'tallest' building. The project's height was initially a closely guarded secret, but at the time of writing reports have indicated that it will reach 818 m including the recently mounted antenna – thus exceeding all tall buildings constructed to date.[36]

The accompanying discourse of Burj Dubai suggests an 'arrival' on the world stage and the emergence of Dubai as a world city and financial centre. The metaphor of 'arrival' has positive connotations: the act of arrival evokes a new beginning, the dawn of a 'new age'. On the other hand, the project could also be construed as a departure, which begins to evoke negative connotations. The aim now is to mark the arrival of Dubai on the world stage and its departure from regional influences. Using the metaphor of arrival and departure is suggestive of a paradox characterizing emerging global cities. To resist homogenizing influences, a discourse is created which attempts to provide an alternative to the Western modernization project. Moving away from the traditionalism of the past, the notion of hybrid identities, in which certain cultural traditions are merged with modern ideals resulting in a 'new' identity offering some kind of resistance (in-between spaces), has become quite common among many scholars. Certainly, the work of Jacobs (1996) and AlSayyad (2001) highlights such an approach, while the concept of hybridity itself is based on the work of Bhabha (2004).

While such optimistic conceptualizations may lead one to consider the benign side of globalization – a happy blending of cultures – there is also a downside. Opponents of globalization argue that nations and cities may be exploited to further the aims and objectives of the modern Western project – with hybridity being just another code word for imperialism – thus '… the hybrid viewpoint belongs to the West' (Cheah, 1998, p. 301). Such a view assumes that globalization is a process activated from the outside (exogenous) yet, as Sassen (2001) pointed out in many instances, globalizing processes are instigated from the inside (endogenous), with governments and local agents initiating many of these projects.

Furthermore, in cities where there is no deep tradition to begin with, as is the case in Dubai which only began to engage actively with modernization in the 1960s, the notions of multiple modernities and hybrid identities need to be re-thought. Here, a city is being modelled after the latest urban fads, catering for multi-national corporations and a transient population. As King (2004) noted, buildings embody and mediate meanings. Thus, it would be helpful to examine one particular building typology – the high-rise building in Dubai – so as to establish the extent to which the city responds to, and engages with, the modern (Western) project, or, alternatively, has been able to establish an alternative discourse.

With that in mind, I will explore the construction of the Burj Dubai, but first I consider the development of skyscrapers worldwide to contextualize the efforts currently underway in Dubai. Second, I investigate the emergence of high-rise buildings in Dubai, explaining how they were a key to modernization. Finally, my discussion shifts to the development of Burj Dubai within the context of these developments where I rely primarily on a 'view from above' to explore these issues. However, an attempt to deal with the 'view from below' is made by examining the discursive representation of the project in the media, the building's visitors' centre, and reactions from locals. Within the framework of Middle Eastern urbanism, where Dubai has become a centre of influence, such developments need to be examined carefully for both their positive and negative repercussions.

Height as a Symbol of Power

Historically, the use of 'height' as a statement of power was first limited to religious buildings – perhaps Egypt's great pyramids were the first physical manifestation of this. Churches in medieval Europe competed to achieve the highest spire. The world of Islam, while originally not concerned with size as an expression of religious hegemony, gradually began to use buildings as a means of representing power both to its populace and to the world beyond. This is the case of the Sultan Hassan Madrassa built in fourteenth-century Cairo during the Mameluk rule, but also in later epochs (figure 6.11). In Istanbul, the famous Ottoman architect, Sinan, attempted with his mosques to surpass the height and dimensions of the city's churches, the tallest of which was the Hagia Sophia. It is only in late nineteenth century, however, that the skyscraper emerged as a building type – a symbol of (American) capitalism – aided by the invention of the elevator. This raises the question of why, particularly in the US, there was such an obsession with height. According to van Leeuwen (1988), this was primarily a way to establish

6.11. The monumental Sultan Hassan Madrassa in Cairo.

a distinctive American style, a characteristic of its emerging civilization and the triumph of capitalism.

For most of the twentieth century, the skyscraper remained a distinctly American phenomenon with a few exceptions, such as the construction of Manhattan-style skyscrapers along Shanghai's Bund, the first tall buildings outside the United States and in Asia (Ali and Moon, 2007; Lee, 1999). It was only in the 1980s, however, that the proliferation of skyscrapers began in Asia (King, 2004; Zukin, 1991).

China, in its desire to represent its emerging economic power and to transform Shanghai into a centre for global capitalism, turned towards the construction of gigantic towers and buildings. In this drive, the country was using an 'image' of what a central business district should look like – New York's Manhattan, Hong Kong's Central, Tokyo's Shinjuku, London's Canary Wharf and Paris's La Défense – all of which are defined and represented by a skyline of high-rise buildings.

Such developments have not been restricted to China. The Petronas Twin Towers in Kuala Lumpur, for example, or Taipei 101 in ROC Taiwan, are both imbued with symbolism meant to communicate – each is in essence a giant billboard. In the case of the Petronas Towers (designed by American architect Cesar Pelli and recently awarded the Aga Khan Award for Islamic architecture), the meanings invested in its structure (based on an Islamic geometric pattern) are '… bound up with rivalries between the Chinese and non-Chinese business class, between Muslim and non-Muslim' (King, 2004, p. 19). Taipei 101, while using Chinese motifs in its overall form as well as in its details, is aimed at establishing Taiwanese independence *vis-à-vis* mainland China (Bunnell, 1999).

While King (2004) argues that the use of symbolism had become a strictly Asian phenomenon, it should be noted that the Freedom Tower in New York is using height as a symbolic gesture, a way to communicate a political message, its height corresponding to the year of American Independence (1,776 ft [540 m]) – a gesture, however, that will only be comprehended through pamphlets and media accounts. This is a prime example of an 'architectural spectacle' existing in an imaginary world. It is within this context that one can begin to understand the 'Dubai phenomenon' and the city's efforts to be placed among the rank of world cities. In the following sections, I examine Dubai's attempts to embrace modernity using 'spectacular' architecture as a primary means of achieving this.

The Skyscraper Index

One particularly interesting way of looking at skyscrapers is as predictors for economic downturns. Based on an apparent relationship between the construction of tall buildings in the twentieth century and the onset of financial crises, economists developed what has been called 'The Skyscraper Index'. In 1999, economist Andrew Lawrence created this indicator which purported to show that the building of the tallest skyscrapers is coincidental with business cycles. He found that the building of the world's tallest building is a good proxy for dating the onset of major economic downturns. Lawrence (1999) described his index as an 'unhealthy 100 year correlation'. The ability of the index to predict economic collapse is surprising. For example, the Panic of 1907 was presaged by the building of the Singer Building (completed in 1908) and the Metropolitan Life Building (completed in 1909). The skyscraper index also accurately predicted the Great Depression with the completion of 40 Wall Tower in 1929, the Chrysler Building in 1930, and the Empire State Building in 1931. Lawrence noted overinvestment, monetary expansion, and speculation as possible foundations for the index.

Economist Thornton (2005), in an analysis of Lawrence's theory, discusses the various stages which precede economic collapse. Thus, the skyscraper project is announced and construction is begun during the late phase of the boom in the business cycle, when the economy is growing and unemployment is low. This is then followed by a sharp downturn in financial markets, economic recession or depression, and significant increases in unemployment. The skyscraper is then completed during the early phase of the economic correction, unless that correction was revealed early enough to delay or scrap plans for construction. For example, Thornton notes, the Chrysler Building in New York was conceived and designed in 1928 and the groundbreaking ceremony was conducted on 19 September 1928. 'Black Tuesday' occurred on 29 October 1929, marking the beginning of the Great Depression. Opening ceremonies for the Chrysler Building took place on 28 May 1930, when it became the tallest building in the world.

Thornton's analysis of the Asian financial crises in the 1990s is particularly relevant for the current discussion on skyscraper development in Dubai as well as in the wider Middle East. The Pacific Rim countries such as Hong Kong, Malaysia, Singapore, Vietnam, and South Korea experienced significant economic growth during the 1980s and 1990s. With the region's leading economy, Japan, in recession and stagnation for much of the 1990s, the 'Asian Tigers' were considered miracle economies because they were strong and durable despite being small and vulnerable. The Petronas Towers were completed in Kuala Lumpur, Malaysia in 1997 setting a new record for the world's tallest building at 1,483 feet (452 m) beating the old record by 33 feet (10 m) (the two towers were only eighty-eight storeys compared with the 110 storey giants built in the early 1970s). It marked the beginning of the extreme drop in Malaysia's stock market, rapid depreciation of its currency, and widespread social unrest. Financial and economic problems spread to economies throughout the region, a phenomenon known as the 'Asian Contagion'.[37]

Thornton's discussion leaves out the construction of skyscrapers in the Middle East and it is here that the index may have found confirmation in the financial crisis of 2008. During the Dubai Cityscape exhibition in October 2008, developer Nakheel announced the construction of a more than 1 km tall skyscraper; similar projects were also announced in Saudi Arabia and Kuwait; and this was preceded, of course, by the ongoing construction of the Burj Dubai. No sooner was Nakheel's announcement made than the financial markets throughout the world witnessed a decline described by some as the greatest financial crisis since the Great Depression. Dubai, because of its reliance on real estate as well as bank loans, was particularly hard hit. The index – it seems – accurately predicted this crisis (see Chapter 1 for a more thorough discussion on the impact of the financial crisis on Dubai). Yet it also shows the extent to which Dubai is integrated into the global financial system. According to Carol Willis (1995, p. 181) 'Skyscrapers are the ultimate architecture of capitalism', and as such their construction in Dubai is the ultimate triumph, and supposed downfall, of capitalism.

Tall Buildings in Dubai

One of the first architectural manifestations of modernization was the construction of the Dubai World Trade Center, located at what was then the outskirts of the city. According to Mark Harris, the son of the building's architect, John Harris, the building was initially envisioned to be located at the top of the Creek – the city's geographical centre at the time – and it was also designed as a low-rise structure.[38] But changes in location and height were greeted by local residents with scepticism, questioning the need for a thirty-nine storey office building in the desert. The project nevertheless went ahead and was completed in 1979. For many years thereafter, indeed until the 1990s, the building was considered a major landmark in the city. The tower is even now known as Burj Rashid or Rashid's tower among locals, acknowledging the former ruler who initiated the project. The building itself addressed some regional concerns, its architecture responding to the harsh climate by the construction of a deep outer skin that moderates the intensity of light from the outside (figure 6.12). In addition, the external features use triangular arches evoking 'Islamic' or 'Arab' elements.

6.12. The World Trade Center designed by British architect John Harris.

The next building to emerge on the scene was the Burj Al-Arab discussed above. Another pair of buildings using height to imply significance is the twin Emirates Towers (figure 6.13). An office/hotel complex with fifty-one storeys and a height of 350 m, officials like to describe it as the tallest in the Middle East and Europe. Designed by Hong Kong based architect, Hazel Wong, who argues that the building is inspired by Islamic geometry and certain mythological constructs related to the sun, earth and moon, the towers' footprints consist of two triangles placed on a circular base. However, the buildings convey a high-tech, ultra-modern image, their sleek atria and speedy elevators visible from the main highway.

This highway – Sheikh Zayed Road – also contains the World Trade Center and passes close to the Burj Dubai. The main corridor along which the city is currently expanding has numerous high-rise buildings and is overlooked by Dubai's financial centre. There is no doubt that the city aims to construct a

6.13. The Emirates Towers as they appeared in 2004, prior to the construction of the Dubai Financial Center and other high-rises.

business district where the height of buildings plays a major role – inspired by similar centres, as King (2004) has observed elsewhere (figure 6.14).

The buildings are used by the State to represent the city and to advocate its progress, and are thus extensively promoted. For example, the World Trade Center appears on the 100Dh (approximately US$30) bank note. In addition, the hotel's

6.14. The 'Gate' Dubai's landmark building in its financial district. In the background is 'The Index', a skyscraper designed by Foster Architects.

image is used in various advertisements figuring next to TV sets, newspapers, radio stations, and banks, thus situating these brands and organizations squarely within the city of Dubai.

The Burj Dubai: 'History Rising'

The site of the Burj Dubai is a decommissioned military base, a location that used to be considered at the edge of the city. The project's developer is Emaar Properties and the design was awarded to the Chicago-based Skidmore, Owings and Merrill (SOM). Official statements describe the design as inspired by 'the cultural and historical influences of the GCC [Gulf Cooperative Council]', achieved in the tower's base where the 'geometry reflects the six petal desert flower of the region'. This building, according to Emaar's chairperson, Alabbar, will 'create a new architectural landmark'.[39]

Mark Amirault, a Canadian and group senior director for development at Emaar Properties, says the company had considered a tall tower as early as 2000, but in a different location, a few miles down the coast at the Dubai Marina. As Dan Halpern writes, it was in February 2003 that the concept for the Burj Dubai – and its enormous attendant development – came into being.[40] According to Amirault (as quoted by Halpern), 'We looked at the success of KLCC [Kuala Lumpur City Centre] … not only did they build the Petronas Towers, but they added in a major shopping centre, a large man-made lake and park, [and] a hotel, and created the new centre of Kuala Lumpur'. Thus, Emaar hired the master planner who had designed the Malaysia project, David Klages of RNL, and began to envision a new city centre for Dubai on essentially the same model. The cost is projected at US$20 billion.

A competition was held in which a number of firms were invited including Kohn Pedersen Fox, Cesar Pelli and Associates, Carlos Ott, Denton Corker Marshall, and SOM Chicago. The SOM design was the favourite because, according to Amirault, 'It had the heroic, romantic massing qualities of the great New York skyscrapers, but had a modern skin and was technically state of the art. They also picked up subtle references to Islamic architecture in the arched plan shapes, which appealed to our Emirati staff [who] worried that the building would look like it could belong anywhere'.[41]

While the developers claim that the design is inspired by a desert flower (prominently highlighted in the project's website), it is of interest to observe the process itself. According to an architect working with Dubai Municipality and responsible for granting building permission, the tower initially had a pseudo-Arab design evocative of an incense box. Rejected due to its naïve imagery, the architects returned with the current design (in many ways similar to Chicago's Sears Tower). Municipality officials, wanting a more authentic expression, asked for a conceptual statement contextualizing the tower's form. The architects returned a few days later with the same design but arguing this time that it was derived from the desert flower, and this proved sufficient and became the official justification for the building's footprint.[42]

The project's website now claims that the architect 'drew inspiration from a flower. The *Hymenocallis* is a plant that is widely cultivated in Dubai, in India and throughout this region. The flower's harmonious structure is one of the organizing principles in the tower's design'.[43] This flower is certainly not unique to Dubai, nor was it a direct inspiration, but these conceptual musings were added after the design was submitted as indicated above. The real value of the project, however, is in its height, which, it is believed, on completion will hold the record in all categories recognized by the New York-based Council on Tall Buildings and Urban Habitat – highest structure, roof, antenna, and occupied floor. According to Faridooni, a leading Dubai based architect, 'Whatever I presented to the sheik,

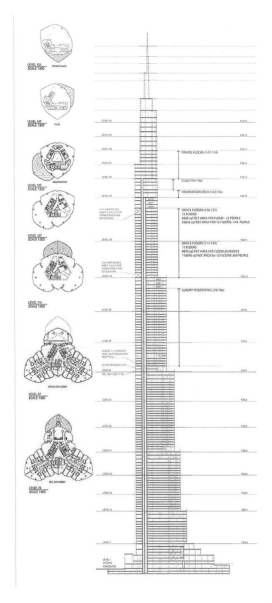

6.15. Floorplans and section of the Burj Dubai Tower. (*Source*: By courtesy of SOM)

he said to make it bigger… When Alabbar was negotiating with SOM, the sheik made sure Alabbar kept him informed. What he wanted to know above all, again and again, was: Is it the tallest?'[44] A major factor enabling this height is, of course, that the top floors – as the tower grows narrower – are not filled with a substantive amount of office space (figure 6.15).[45]

The development will include, in addition to the tower, the world's largest mall and a low-rise residential development called 'Old Town' (figure 6.16). All the buildings will be located around an artificial lake. Advertisements for the project invariably draw comparisons with existing 'famous downtowns' such as Manhattan, Paris, and London. One could argue that this is a perfect example of a 'Debordian' spectacle in a desert context – remote from any contextual relevance! Comparisons with existing record holders illustrate the sheer magnitude of the development and that the Burj will surpass all of them.

Aside from the sheer physical feat of this building it is of interest to examine the discourse created around its construction. Advertisements display a depiction of the tower with the words 'History Rising' indicating that the construction of this tower heralds the dawn of a new era for Dubai. Official announcements proclaim

6.16. The Burj Dubai surrounded by the pseudo-Arabian architecture of Souq Bahar.

that this 'iconic' building symbolizes 'modernity and engineering prowess' and that it will make 'the surrounding district the most prestigious square kilometre in the world'. Furthermore, the developer's Executive Director notes:

> We now embark on the exciting part of the development where the world can witness our promise of 'History Rising' coming to fruition… [The towers design] combines … historical and cultural influences with cutting edge technology to achieve a high performance building which will set new standards for development in the Middle East and become the model for the future of the city of Dubai.[46]

In addition, the project is intended to be 'a symbol of human endeavour and success that makes Dubai one of the finest cities in the world that believes in excellence and a desirable quality of life'. Furthermore, '… skyscrapers have historically represented our quest for bettering our urban centers and have created some of the world's most desirable and admirable places. Burj Dubai will do the same for the city of Dubai'.

These official proclamations lead to a series of observations. The modernity discourse plays a prominent part in justifying the construction of such a gigantic building. Simply by placing this tower in Dubai, the city could proclaim itself to be truly modern, irrespective of the fact that it is designed by an American firm (SOM), built by a Korean construction company (Samsung), worked on by a plethora of Asian labourers, and that most of the apartments and hotels are purchased by an expatriate clientele. Regardless of this, the developers felt the need to contextualize the project and give it an 'Arabian' touch, whether through some imaginary conceptual directions (a desert flower) or the creation of pseudo-Arabian districts, which are part of the overall development.

Urban geographer Tim Bunnell, in his paper dealing with the Petronas Twin Towers of Malaysia, argued that their 'role in national development is not merely aesthetic, envisioning a state conception of Malaysian urbanity; the building also promotes new "ways of seeing" among citizens' (Bunnell, 1999, p. 6). In an insightful analysis, he presents both a view from above – the extent to which the state uses the tower to further modernization objectives and establish a Malay identity – and a view from 'below' – how citizens' perception of, and reaction to, the towers plays a role in their representation. Clear differences exist between Dubai and Kuala Lumpur: for one, Malaysian identity is defined according to its various ethnic groups, unlike Dubai, with its large expatriate, transient population and small, local minority. As such, the towers do not address contesting identity visions. However, the analysis is useful in that it attempts to reconstruct the towers' representation through the eyes of the city's citizens, a micro-view, rather than the more typical macro approach common in urban studies related to the Gulf region (Fuccaro, 2001). Clearly, such an approach is needed to provide a more accurate representation of newly emerging cities such as Dubai.

Media coverage for the Burj has been intense. In 2006, the tower was mentioned in more than 200 articles,[47] local newspapers presenting the project's progress, highlighting that the building is going up at the rate of one floor a week. Advertisements for the tower occur frequently; gigantic billboards placed throughout the city announce the emergence of a 'new downtown' (figure 6.17). Various events such as the annual Cityscape extravaganza prominently display the

6.17. A billboard for the Burj placed on Sheikh Zayed Road.

6.18. Visitors admiring the Burj Dubai at the Cityscape 2007 exhibition.

project's model, showing officials and foreign dignitaries admiring the construction of such an icon (figure 6.18). Of particular interest was the now closed visitors centre. Here visitors would enter a bunker-like structure, move through a series of dark spaces, carefully illuminated to show text, images, and models and then slide through a door and move into another space at the end of which was a gigantic model of the entire development. The centre was only accessible by appointment and was meant to entice potential investors, but two days a week were reserved for the public – to enhance the project's perception among the general population.

Unlike the Petronas Towers, there is no need to ascertain the prominence of one local identity over another. Instead, the project is meant to show the emergence of Dubai as a regional powerhouse and to enable it to become a global city. Some local reactions do in fact suggest that the tower is a source of pride – both among Arab and local Emirati citizens – suggesting that 'Arabs' do have the potential to develop such a project similar to others (the 'West'). Such reactions – based on those of students in a class that I taught – are quite typical of those to other projects – inaccessible to most residents, they are nevertheless a source of pride.

It remains to be seen whether such feelings of pride will remain after the tower's completion. Even at this stage, however, there are some voices of dissent. In particular with regard to the city's attempt to highlight its cultural roots – for example, the desert flower footprint of the tower – with one of my local Emirati students suggesting that the city is merely trying to project an image of historical and cultural identity, while they are clearly embracing a modern, Western image ('They just want to show that they have history!'). Cultural sensitivities prevent many from voicing such views, yet they clearly exist.

However, as Philip Nobel poignantly observed, the lack of any NIMBY industry – preservationists, public intellectuals, and grassroots local groups – prevents the proliferation of any kind of resistance.[48] In fact, local media act as a deterrent to any voices of dissent and criticism. A 2007 article by David Westley in a local business publication responds to a criticism by a New York University professor, who ridiculed the building of super tall buildings ('We no longer have to prove our mettle by bragging about the length of our edifices'). The writer argues that because Dubai is young it should aim at building higher; reflecting an official view, he noted, that the city 'has achieved in 50 years what European and American cities took centuries to do'.[49] Examples are cited, such as the Burj Al Arab that 'gave the emirate a face to the world'. Through these projects, 'Dubai is showing the world how to build real estate in people's minds'. He then argues, in all seriousness, that irrespective of cost and environmental concerns, such projects would thus have achieved their 'real' purpose.

That real purpose is regional hegemony. By claiming that its developments are derived from local and regional influences, the city is obviously looking beyond its borders to become a source of influence. Regional centres such as Cairo are in fact regarding Dubai as a model (Elsheshtawy, 2006; also see Chapter 9). The Burj Dubai is thus the ultimate symbol of the city's dominance.

Assessing the Burj

An interesting lesson from the Burj Dubai project is its affirmation of the relevance of constructing tall buildings as a sign of power and progress. King (2004) noted that this has become an outmoded form of urban development occurring primarily in Asian cities aspiring to become world-class centres. Yet developments throughout the world disconfirm such a view – the Freedom Tower in New York, Foster's Gherkin building in London, and elsewhere. Efforts in Dubai are thus an essential part of this global phenomenon and are not merely a 'megalomaniacal' outcome of its rulers' aspirations as described by some critics (e.g. Davis, 2005). Recent research has also confirmed the prevalence and viability of the tall building discourse; calls for the death of the skyscraper following the 9/11 events are, it seems, exaggerated (e.g. Charney, 2005). Within the Gulf region, and Dubai itself, the project has spurred intense competition. For example, Nakheel announced the construction of a tower simply called 'Nakheel Harbour and Tower' set to exceed 1 km in height. In Kuwait, a 1 km skyscraper is planned which will form the centrepiece to the proposed City of Silk.[50]

Furthermore, by examining the naming of the high-rise building, one can gain significant insights. It changed from an international, generic term (World Trade Center) to one emphasizing pan-Arab idealistic tendencies (Burj Al-Arab) and then to one suggesting inter-emirate unity (Emirates Towers) and finally to Burj Dubai – Tower of Dubai. It is as if by naming the tower in such a way, and giving it global significance by making it the highest, it will place the city in a global network – the building as sign and spectacle belonging only to Dubai! In such a manner, the city is trying to distance itself from its Middle Eastern context. By employing global devices of urban capitalism, a new global urbanity is created.

Conclusion: Perpetuating an Illusion

'As the plane slowly banks toward the desert mainland, you gasp at the even more improbable vision ahead. Out of a chrome forest of skyscrapers (nearly a dozen taller than 300 meters) soars a new Tower of Babel. It is an impossible one-half-mile high: the equivalent of the Empire State Building stacked on top of itself.'

Mike Davis (2005) Dubai: Sinister Paradise

The above quote is part of a larger narrative in which well-known urban critic, Mike Davis, imagines Dubai in the year 2010.

[Dubai] has become a huge circuit board into which the elite of transnational engineering firms and retail developers are invited to plug in high-tech clusters, entertainment zones, artificial islands, 'cities within cities' – whatever is the latest fad in urban capitalism. The same phantasmagoric but generic Lego blocks, of course, can be found in dozens of aspiring cities these days. (Davis, 2005)

Urban capitalism is an apt term to describe the vast developments taking place in Dubai. In addition, in order for the city to be noticed, it is employing the device of the spectacle. Yet as Debord (1967, 1995) has pointed out, the spectacle can contribute to a general sense of alienation by emphasizing the disconnectedness between observers and the material, physical object. The creation of these fragments within the desert, objects that are inaccessible except for the very wealthy, may eventually lead to dissatisfaction and various social problems. This situation is further highlighted by the plight of labourers who construct these projects. Viewed as a cheap, easily deportable workforce, they are generally kept out of sight by housing them in work camps located on the outskirts of the city, in conditions sometimes described as 'squalid'.[51] Social exclusion is, of course, not a phenomenon restricted to Dubai, but is a characteristic of global cities; indeed it has been argued that it is a defining element of cities in general (e.g. Madanipour, 1998). And it is, of course, significant that the site of Burj Dubai has been associated with riots which took place in 2006 and were reported extensively in the international media, highlighting the plight of labourers (figure 6.19).

The three projects described here have a number of commonalities. First is the use of superlatives to describe them: whether it is the 'tallest' hotel or the 'largest' man-made island, or the tallest building in the world.[52] In using such attributes, the distinctiveness of these developments is ascertained, thus setting them apart. Their exclusive nature is further highlighted by locating them offshore, for example, and controlling access by a variety of means: security guards, entrance fees, and by their sheer extravagance, prohibiting (or inhibiting) ordinary folk from entering. In that same vein, the projects are located outside the relatively dense urban context of

6.19 Workers taking a break at the Burj Dubai complex.

Dubai – thus playing a major role in the development of 'new Dubai' which will supposedly replace Singapore or Hong Kong as the financial and leisure hub of Asia.[53] In terms of imagery, the hotel, the islands and the Burj are using easily recognizable symbols – the sail, the palm or a desert flower. While the sail can be seen from ground level, the palm and the flower are essentially a planning device meant to be seen from the air, not an everyday occurrence. Thus, the purpose is for these 'images' to be used as a marketing ploy – blatantly clear in the desert flower analogy for the Burj Dubai – but also to become a symbol for Dubai. In the case of the hotel, the sail shaped image temporarily replaced the traditional Shaikh Saeed House on all Dubai license plates. The Palm aerial view is used in advertising and media campaigns by a variety of companies and financial institutions. While it is claimed that these 'symbols' are inspired by local and traditional elements, they acquire a more universal character: the sail and the palm, are associated with many places throughout the world and are not necessarily exclusively linked to Dubai or the UAE.

The use of direct symbols such as can be found at various roundabouts and other public spaces (the 'coffee pot' or *dal'la* appearing periodically in towns throughout the UAE) reflects a desire to connect with the past and to construct an identity *vis-à-vis* a predominantly migrant population.[54] The Palm island, Burj Al-Arab and Burj Dubai could be comprehended as a continuation of such thinking, albeit on a gigantic, i.e. global, scale. In such a way the stage is set for Dubai as a global entity. Simple, humble developments will not achieve such an effect. Projects will have to be big, unprecedented, and constructed quickly. Issues of scale (large) and aestheticism/symbolism (easily understood and quickly communicated, no time for abstract reflections) are becoming paramount!

Furthermore the perpetuation of 'mythical environments' is another feature shared by these developments. The Burj Al-Arab reflects an aura of one-thousand-and-one nights opulence and decadence (for example a simulation of a submarine ride to reach a seafood restaurant is one of its dominant features). However, the Palm in particular has taken this concept to new levels. The residences being sold are distinguished by created stylistic forms (Mediterranean, Islamic, Asian, etc.) thus offering buyers a 'created' environment catering for their desire – the formal language for establishing stylistic links is, of course, purely personal (effectively mythical); furthermore, the propagation of these mythical environments is taken below water in developing coral reef landscapes based on different regions in the world (the Red Sea, for example); visitors may thus move from one submarine environment to another without leaving Dubai. Burj Dubai is surrounded by imaginary Arabian residential districts and a shopping centre resembling a Mamluk citadel – Souq Bahar. It will also contain the largest fountain in the world set within a vast artificial lake, in what is basically a pure desert environment, far removed from the sea.

The water theme is particularly significant. Arabs have, traditionally, shunned the sea in favour of the endless horizons of the desertscape – yet they have always been fascinated by water. In many respects the Palm, the Burj Al Arab and Burj Dubai are attempts to connect with the sea and to move away from the desert thus becoming 'modern' and 'advanced' by overcoming the perceived image of a nomadic people confined to the desert – similar to Abdelrahman, Munif's fictional settlement in *Cities of Salt*. Here, however, the settlement is initiated by the colonial power and Munif's nomads have to go to incredible lengths to overcome their fear from building and living near water!

Notes

1. *The Economist* (2006) 'Dubai in America: fake parks', 13 July, p. 44. An interesting article about the trend of building fake parks and resorts in the US which is compared to Dubai: 'Is America catching up with Dubai, home of desert skiing, the world's only seven-star hotel and other outlandish attractions? Nature, clearly, is too inconvenient to fit the modern lifestyle. Ray Petro, who started an indoor mountain-bike park in Cleveland (the world's first, of course), boasts of being able to "beat Mother Nature"'.

2. Rose, S. (2005) 'Sand and freedom', *The Guardian*, 28 November. *http://arts.guardian.co.uk/features/story/0,11710,1652149,00.html*. Accessed 8 May 2006.

3. An article describes the hotel as follows: '... the Burj Al Arab, where Russian gangsters with suitcases of cash and Saudi sheiks vie to occupy palatial suites with gold-plated taps, gold-leaf banisters and screaming colour schemes of crimson, citrus and carrot. The exterior of the Burj Al Arab is shaped like a full-blown spinnaker, and its outside walls are covered with a milky Teflon-coated fabric as protection from the searing sun ... the hotel consists of 202 duplex suites. The two royal suites, which rent for $8,000 a night, are occupied only occasionally. The basement seafood restaurant, enveloped by walls of an aquarium and reached by an elevator designed as a faux submarine, is not always full either. But who cares? The hotel, with its revolving bed in the royal suite, is more talking point than hostelry. Nelson Mandela is said to have been dismayed by the opulence. But Bill Clinton, twice a guest, talks up Dubai as an exemplar of the possible marriage between Islam and the modern world. Perlez, Jane (2002) 'Dubai journal; living high and aiming higher, come war or peace', *The New York Times*, 4 October. http://query.nytimes.com/gst/fullpage.html?res=9906EED71F38F937A35753C1A9649C8B63. Accessed 3 November 2008.

4. An official promotional publication notes the following: 'In designing the Burj Al Arab one had to have an understanding of the location; its culture, people, climate and future. Equally important is Arab hospitality, which is recognizably second to none. In Arabic tradition, each visitor to one's home should be received and welcomed as if he or she was a manifestation of the Prophet. In its recent times the older generations can still recall the nomadic Bedouin tribes that roamed the stark desert, graciously offering food and shelter to passing caravans. Here at the Burj Al Arab this tradition is being followed by its seven star service ...' (Chew and Schmitt, 2000)

5. In 'Atkins wins world's 'best new building award' (www.atkingsglobal.com). Also the architect describes the process as follows: 'We were seeking an image that was evocative, recognisable, and expressed these desires. The Arabian Gulf had always been a major focus for the city and now with the fast emerging tourist trade reinforcing the maritime association it seemed reasonable to design the tower hotel in the form of a giant sail. Not the shape of the historic dhow but the shape of a modern high tech sail, the type of sail that would be found on a yacht in St. Tropez. The type of sail that has always evoked a sense of luxury, excitement, sophistication and adventure. To complete the design, we would build the sail on an island offshore creating a building that we hoped would instantly be recognisable the world over'.

6. It is of interest to quote the architect's description of, and in turn the significance placed upon, the icon: 'The tower was to become an icon for the developing Dubai, as Sydney has its opera house and Paris the Eiffel Tower, so Dubai was to have a similar landmark. It was soon realised that to

create a building that would become iconic was the most difficult aspect of the conceptual design. A list was drawn up of instantly recognisable buildings that had become synonymous with a city or country. The prerequisite of the list was if the form of the building could be drawn and recognised within 10 seconds, Pictorial style. The list was surprisingly small and most of the buildings were historical. Try it for yourself, you will be lucky to find 10 buildings in the world that fall within the category. You will find that each of the buildings has one thing in common, an economy and uniqueness of form' (Chew and Schmitt, 2000).

7.   The architect described this as follows: 'It didn't take long to realise that the people of Dubai were enjoying their newly found freedom and wanted to be seen as a fast developing forward looking "first world" culture. This being the case we decided to look at the future aspirations of the people for our ideas rather than basing them on the limited historical cultural context' (Chew & Schmitt, 2000).

8.   Sudjic, D. (2000) 'Is that room service? Where am I?', *The Observer*, 20 August. http://www.guardian.co.uk/theobserver/2000/aug/20/2. Accessed 3 November 2008.

9.   Wollaston, Sam (2007) *The Guardian*, 10 July. http://www.guardian.co.uk/culture/tvandradioblog/2007/jul/10/lastnightstvindianfoodmad. Accessed 23 October, 2008.

10.   This has not always been positive however. For many local residents the hotel is known as 'the one with a cross'. Approaching the hotel from the sea its structure does indeed resemble a cross from a head-on angle. A rumour circulated that the architect intentionally placed this symbol on the shores of Arabia. For a while – based on anecdotes – cars displaying the Burj Al Arab on their license plates were turned back from the borders of Saudi Arabia. For more on this read the following blog: Burj Al Arab – The world's largest Christian cross. http://blog.miragestudio7.com/2007/09/burj-al-arab-world-largest-christian-cross/. There also is a YouTube video about this: http://www.youtube.com/watch?v=cQrNoaH3Ssc.

11.   Bakr, Amena (2008) 'Destinations with a difference', *The National*, 6 August, p. 8.

12.   *Ibid*.

13.   Yacoob, Tahira (2008) 'Labelling the luxury of Dubai', *The National*, 22 June, p. 24.

14.   Cordahi, James (2007) 'Gulf in $18bn hotel blitz', *Arabian Business*, 3 December. http://www.arabianbusiness.com/505486-gulf-in-18bn-hotel-blitz?ln=en. Accessed 23 October 2008.

15.   See Mishra, Shiha (2008) 'The final frontier: Palm Deira', *Arabian Business*, 11–17 October, p. 21; quoting Abduallah bin Sulayem, operations director.

16.   A Palm official notes that 'this is definitely the most exciting time ever in Dubai's real estate history; for the first time expatriates can buy their own property and really feel a part of this boom … the increased demand for property has been a major boost to the economy. It is creating thousands of new jobs in the construction sector as well as other professions such as architecture and interior design, and, of course, the hospitality industry' (Belbin, (2002) 'A personal piece of paradise', *Identity*, November/December).

17.   *The Times* (2002) 'Biggest man-made isles rise from the Gulf', 5 January.

18.   Belbin, C. (2002) 'A personal piece of paradise', *Identity*, November/December, p. 30.

19.   'Our problem was that Dubai had run out of beach', Mr. Gergawi said. 'We were brainstorming one day. Someone said, "Why don't we make an island".' But just one blob in the sea was insufficient. The plan for a series of finger islands arranged in the shape of palm trees evolved as the best way to maximise the amount of beach front, he said… Environmental concerns? Mr. Gergawi said they had been taken into account. Even if every detail of how so many people and structures would exist on slender slivers of sand is not quite clear, it is the attitude that matters'. Perlez, Jane (2002) 'Dubai journal; living high and aiming higher, come war or peace', *New York Times*, 4 October. http://query.nytimes.com/gst/fullpage.html?res=9906EED71F38F937A35753C1 A9649C8B63. Accessed 3 November 2008.

20.   According to officials UAE nationals account for 75 per cent of buyers while 5 per cent constitutes other Gulf nationals. Of the remaining, 15 per cent comprises long-time UAE

expatriate residents and 5 per cent is from overseas. Other estimates place nationals at a much lower percentage.

21. *Khaleej Times* (2002) 'Paradise regained', 11 May.

22. In a 2002 newspaper article a sales agent notes: '"There is so much demand from buyers, it is hard to meet the requirement with one island. Palm office currently has a waiting list of over 800 firm orders. With almost 90 per cent of the units put on sale already sold, they believe the 1,100 units on the nine fronds will be sold out in the next 10 days", said Zubair S. Mostafa, marketing manager of Al Khayat Real Estate. Buyers comprise mostly Arab nationals, Europeans and people from the subcontinent who apparently prefer the Palm island to other beachfront properties in Cyprus and Greece. Some 70 per cent of the buyers are UAE nationals' (*Khaleej Times* (2002) 'Palm project records biggest-ever booking wait list', 21 May).

23. *Ibid.*

24. Belbin, C. (2002) 'A personal piece of paradise', *Identity*, November/December, p. 30.

25. 'RMJM to design Palm centers; firm is selected from short-list of 11 architects', *Gulf News*, 10 May 2003.

26. TimeOut Dubai, 17 May 2007.

27. In an article titled: 'Dubai's artificial islands have high environmental cost'; http://news.mongabay.com/2005/0823-tina_butler_dubai.html.

28. *Ibid.*

29. Slater, Matt (2007) 'Sand castles', *TimeOut, Dubai*, May. http://www.timeoutdubai.com/dubai. Accessed 17 May 2009.

30. *Ibid.*

31. See, for example, Catherine Moyer writing in *The Daily Telegraph* ('Palm before a storm?', 18 August 2005).

32. Calderwood, James (2007) 'Investing in Dubai's Palms', *Gulf News*, 27 June, p. 57.

33. Giuffrida, Angela (2008) 'All in the Palm of his hands', *The National*, 27 October. http://www.thenational.ae/article/20081027/BUSINESS/626458820/1051. Accessed 3 November 2008.

34. *Ibid.*

35. Ourussoff, Nicolai (2008) 'City on the Gulf: Koolhaas lays out a grand urban experiment in Dubai', *The New York Times*, 3 March. http://www.nytimes.com/2008/03/03/arts/design/03kool.html. Accessed 21 October 2008.

36. *The National*, 13 February 2009; p. B1.

37. The economic explanation for this is as follows: 'The common pattern in these four historical episodes contains the following features. First, a period of "easy money" leads to a rapid expansion of the economy and a boom in the stock market. In particular, the relatively easy availability of credit fuels a substantial increase in capital expenditures. Capital expenditures flow in the direction of new technologies which in turn creates new industries and transforms some existing industries in terms of their structure and technology. This is when the world's tallest buildings are begun. At some point thereafter negative information ignites panicky behavior in financial markets and there is a decline in the relative price of fixed capital goods. Finally, unemployment increases, particularly in capital and technology-intensive industries. While this analysis concentrates on the U.S. economy, the impact of these crises was often felt outside the domestic economy' (Thornton, 2005, p. 58).

38. Mark Harris (2009) personal communication.

39. AME Info, 2003. Emaar is a government-owned real estate company based in Dubai and is considered the largest in the world in terms of capital investment. Its projects have become synonymous with Dubai's recent development and are characterized by being 'exclusive' and 'luxurious' catering for a high-end clientele. Among its achievements are the introduction of gated

communities ('Emirates Hills') and waterfront developments (Dubai Marina). It recently began to expand into other markets in the Middle East such as Egypt, Syria, and Morocco.

40.   Halpern, Dan (2007) Arabian heights: how does an emerging global power announce itself? With the world's tallest building. *Architect Magazine*, May. Available at http://www.architectmagazine .com/industry-news-print.asp?sectionID=1006&articleID=492847. Accessed 27 February 2009.

41.   *Ibid.*

42.   Khaled A. (2003) personal communication,

43.   http://www.burjdubai.com.

44.   Quoted in Halpern (2007).

45.   Nobel, P. (2007) 'Lust for height', *The American*, January/February. http://www.american.com. Accessed 27 February 2009.

46.   Emaar website; http://www.emaar.com/MediaCenter/PressReleases, 2006.

47.   Nobel (2007).

48.   *Ibid.*

49.   Westley, David (2007) 'Dubai: a city on a high', *Arabian Business*, 17 July.

http://www.arabianbusiness.com/496348?tmpl=print&page=. Accessed 27 February 2009.

50.   Media reports accompanying the Cityscape 2008 exhibition in Dubai note: 'Yesterday [Nakheel] announced plans to build a skyscraper more than a kilometre high, hundreds of metres more than the world's tallest building, the Burj Dubai, which is just 10 minutes down the road... The structure, which has been on the drawing board for more than three years, is to be the centrepiece the Nakheel Harbour and Tower development. It will be built near the Ibn Battuta Mall on Sheikh Zayed Road... [The project is] designed by the Australian architects Woods Bagot... Work on the tower's foundations is already under way and is expected to take three years... Despite the global credit crunch and a slowdown in financing for construction projects, Mr O'Donnell [CEO of Nakheel] said Tall Tower would proceed because it was being developed over a decade' (Giuffrida, Angela (2008) 'Dubai skyscraper will be top of the world'. *The National*, 6 October, p. 4).

51.   Ahmed, Ashfaq (2007) 'Drive against illegal housing intensifies', *Gulf News*, 13 August, p. 2.

52.   A distinct Dubai characteristic. A 2001 newspaper account notes that 'It rejoices in superlatives. The Guinness Book of Records is on permanent stand-by to record them. Normally they apply to the biggest and best of everything that "Maktum Inc", as some call it, can boast. It may be the tallest and most luxurious hotel in the world, like the phantasmagoric Borj al-Arab, recently completed on a man-made island in the Gulf, the world's largest man-made port at the Jebel Ali free zone, or the largest-ever wedding cake' (Hirst, D. (2001) 'The emirs in the internet era: Dubai, a sheikhdom happy to embrace globalization', *Le Monde Diplomatique*, February. www.mondediplo.com).

53.   A 2001 local newspaper article cites a British academic study which claims that '... the rise of UAE's profile in the international arena is challenging Singapore's stature as a premier "global city"' (Hilotin, Jay (2001) 'Rise of UAE profile worries Singaporeans', *Gulf News*, 1 February). http://archive.gulfnews.com/articles/02/02/01/39628.html. Accessed 3 November 2008.

54.   The persistence of the national dress – a free flowing robe – called *dishdasha* for males and 'abaya for females, as well as the pre-dominance of certain forms of dialect and the discouragement of intermarriages (specifically between female locals and foreign males) are symptomatic of this phenomenon.

Chapter 7

The Spectacular
and the Everyday:
Dubai's Retail Landscape

As I indicated in the previous chapter globalizing cities throughout the world are using the spectacular as a strategy to achieve their objective. My discussion centred on examining megaprojects – the tallest building, the largest man-made island and so on. I have tied these projects to notions of a 'Debordian spectacle' because of the degree to which they contribute to a general sense of alienation among citizens. This is being used by many critics to dismiss urban developments such as those occurring in Dubai as mere fantasy. Yet this reveals only a partial picture, based on the notion that people are 'cultural dupes' and are passively accepting what is on offer. If the focus begins to shift to the everyday practices of city residents we see that the actions of ordinary citizens and civic groups in some way provide a counterpoint to the dominating, hegemonic quality of the 'spectacle'. People are, in fact, not passive and within the 'spectacular' spaces of global capital an alternative order asserts itself – an informal mode of urbanism. It is interesting that in an effort to combat the perception of Dubai as the land of spectacle some media observers have tried going 'beyond the spectacle' to portray the city as a 'unique' model of urbanism, and a successful example of state controlled intervention – which is more or less a strengthening of the spectacle model without really going 'beyond' anything.[1]

To that end, I am contextualizing the developments taking place in Dubai, by looking at the city's less spectacular spaces – those that have escaped the critical gaze of urbanists. My focus is on two particular aspects: its retail landscape which is the subject of this chapter, and its 'forgotten' urban spaces, gathering places of its migrant, low-income population, which I discuss in the following chapter. Both should be seen as a counterpoint to the previous chapters, so as to give a balanced portrayal of the city.

The city is seemingly defined by its commercial character – as can be seen in the proliferation of themed shopping malls and the staging of 'spectacular' events such as the Dubai Shopping Festival. Yet alternative spaces of consumption do exist and, while not part of the city's official image, they slip between the cracks of its carefully maintained portrayal of itself.

The purpose of this chapter is to uncover these hidden spaces of consumption and contrast them with the city's spectacular retail spaces. By juxtaposing the spectacular and the everyday I hope to offer a more balanced view of a globalizing city and also to illustrate that in many instances citizens are not passive recipients of 'spectacular images', but actively seek alternatives – in essence moderating these spectacular developments. As in the previous chapter where I discussed the Debordian theory of the spectacle, here I briefly establish the degree to which this could be applied to the city's retail environment. My objective is to problematize the construct and the extent of its applicability within the retail environment of a modern metropolis. Following this my focus shifts to Dubai's retail landscape, examining both its 'spectacular' and 'non-spectacular' components.

Problematizing the Retail Experience

Examining Dubai from the perspective of the spectacle is based on the assumption that it has power over how people think and behave – a form of environmental determinism. Particularly from a retail perspective, the use of advertisements would be a perfect example of how using the spectacle can goad people into a mindset that leads them to perceive certain needs which in reality do not exist. This viewpoint has been articulated by Margaret Crawford in her now seminal 1992 article 'The world in a shopping mall', where she uses the case of the West Edmonton Mall in Canada to discuss the extent to which retail design has been refined to influence consumers. In her description of the mall she writes:

> Inside the mall presents a dizzying *spectacle* of attraction and diversion… Confusion proliferates at every level; past and future collapse meaninglessly into the present; barriers between real and fake, near and far, dissolve as history, nature, technology, are indifferently processed by the mall's fantasy machine. (Crawford, 1992, p. 126, my emphasis)

Her descriptions could apply to any mall in the world – particularly in Dubai where the shopping malls are a continuation of this vision but at a more much elaborate and exaggerated scale. This is not just for aesthetic purposes or to attract visitors. These effects are designed deliberately, based on what Crawford terms the 'science of malling'. She points out that this is based on models developed by specialized consultants using techniques of demographic and market research. One of the pioneers of mall design, architect Victor Gruen, proposed an ideal matrix for mall-building which 'combined the expertise of real estate brokers, financial and marketing analysts, economists, merchandising experts, architects, engineers, transportation planners, landscape architects and interior designers' (*Ibid.*, p. 127).

Based on these extensive models and research, a 'mix' is created which for each mall is its unique blend of tenants and department-store anchors. This is strictly governed by mall managers through leases, which determine among other things, décor and prices. Such controls target specific consumers through what is referred to as 'psychographics' which are marketing profiles based on customers' aspirations and needs. Crawford views this as something inherently negative by noting that 'the variations are endless, but whatever form the system adopts, the message conveyed is the same – a repeated imperative to consume' (*Ibid.*, p. 129).

This is critical because 'consumption increasingly constructs the way we see the world' (*Ibid.*, p. 129). She bases her analysis on a variety of retail experts such as William Weiss (1976) who argued that the best measure of social consciousness is the *Index of Consumer Sentiment*, which charts optimism about the state of the world in terms of willingness to spend. This is tied to the notion of identity construction:

> … for many the very construction of the self involves the acquisition of commodities. If the world is understood through commodities, then personal identity depends on one's ability to compose a coherent self-image through the selection of a distinct personal set of commodities. (Crawford, 1992, p. 129)

Mall design is increasingly focused on influencing consumer behaviour and encouraging consumption – but this is not based on real needs. Rather by 'barraging' consumers with messages (advertisements) even before they enter the mall, a set of 'false needs and wants' is created. Thus the shopper arrives at the mall with a confused set of wants – a kind of ambiguous, unstable state. This is further enhanced, according to such analysis, by extending the period, inside the mall, of 'just looking' – thus encouraging 'cognitive acquisition', the imaginative prelude to actual buying. Thus 'shoppers mentally acquire commodities by familiarizing themselves with a commodity's actual and imagined qualities' (*Ibid.*, p. 130). Specific design features influence, or determine, such behaviour:

> Dramatic atriums create huge floating spaces for contemplation, multiple levels provide infinite vistas from a variety of vantage points, and reflective surfaces bring near and far together. In the absence of sounds from outside, these artful visual effects are complemented by the 'white noise' of Muzak and fountains echoing across enormous open courts. The resulting 'weightless realm' receives substance only through the commodities it contains. (*Ibid.*)

Such a state of suspension resembles the mindset of drug users. Joan Didion (1979) writes that the mall is an addictive environmental drug, where 'one moves for a while in an aqueous suspension not only of light, but of judgment, not only of judgment but of personality'. Within retail jargon there is actually a term describing such actions – the Gruen Transfer, which designates the moment when a 'destination buyer' with a specific purchase in mind is transformed into an impulse shopper, a crucial point immediately visible in the shift from a determined stride to an erratic and meandering gait. Yet as Crawford points out, shoppers do not perceive these effects as negative. Studies have shown that there has been an increase in time spent at the mall (81 minutes for malls in the US in 2005).

Certain retail strategies, besides the actual physical design of the mall, further encourage consumption; for example, 'indirect commodification' which is the placing of non-saleable objects and images in the commodified world of the mall. Here the basic marketing principle is 'adjacent attraction', where 'the most dissimilar objects lend each other mutual support when they are placed next to each other' (Crawford, 1992, p. 131). Crawford lends credence to her argument by quoting urban sociologist Richard Sennett, whose writings – particularly in *The Fall of Public Man* (1977) – clearly favour a romantic, and perhaps idealized version of a city (New York). He explained this effect as a temporary suspension of the use value of the object, its decontextualized state making it unexpected and therefore stimulating. Thus placing an ordinary pot in a window display of a Moroccan harem transforms the pot into something exotic, mysterious and desirable, according to Crawford. Of particular interest is her analysis of how this process is related to the 'spectacle' based on what is termed indirect commodification, which 'can also incorporate fantasy, juxtaposing shopping with an intense spectacle of accumulated images and themes that entertain and stimulate and in turn encourage more shopping' (Crawford, 1992, p. 131). In shopping malls, the very fact that they are enclosed further enhances this, since space, time and weather are suspended. And because of the connection between unexpected settings and familiar products the shopping experience is 'reinvigorated'.

As noted, the 'science of malling' is based on extensive research carried out by various institutions and retail consultancies such as The International Council for Shopping Centers (ICSC), a US based retail consultancy with the motto 'Serving the global retail real estate industry'. Examining some of its studies shows that there is a deliberate attempt to influence consumer behaviour. One study is titled 'Converting browsers into spenders', [2] and here the author elaborates on the demographic profile of a typical mall user (a female, 39 years of age, living in a three person household, with a median income of US$51,000). Furthermore, 44 per cent of 'consumers went to the mall for shopping/browsing rather than to shop at a specific store or make a purchase', which is viewed with some alarm by the study. Some of the terminology is particularly interesting – showing the degree to which the movement/behaviour of people is classified and structured in a quantitative manner. For instance there is something called 'conversion rate' – the ratio of number of shops entered per trip and the number of shops where an actual purchase is made; a 'walk-out' rate – leaving the mall without purchasing anything. And to understand the 'predatory nature' of mall design, the author concludes: 'With customer already inside the store, half the battle is won. The other half of the battle is for retailers to meet the consumer's evolving needs and *close the sale*'.

In another article a consultant with ICSC discusses some of the trends affecting the retail industry. Here again the terminology used is interesting as it relates to the actual design of these malls which are described 'as living, breathing entities'. Traditional mall design is criticized because it turned inward, so that in terms of the mall's exterior design there is less 'curb appeal'. Furthermore, to enhance the appeal of shopping centres, attention should be paid to 'place making' by integrating them with the surrounding community, and also by creating a sense of place for consumers through the provision of children's play areas, ample restrooms, soft seating areas, and wider walkways in the food courts – which are mostly features pertaining to the interior spaces of malls rather than making any significant contextual links. But, this could be accomplished by a 'cross-pollination of retail concepts' such as open air shopping centres and enclosed malls – 'hybrid venues'. The overall objective is, and the bluntness with which this is put forward is striking, to increase 'focus on overall environment to appeal to consumers' senses and emotions'.[3]

Such blatantly deterministic, and perhaps predatory, jargon would seem to reinforce the perception of traditional urbanists – e.g. Crawford and Sennett – that shopping malls are inherently evil since they have led to a decline in public life, are undermining the 'life and culture of the traditional city', and have contributed to the 'death of city architecture'.[4] An active consumer has been turned into a passive spectator. For instance, the replacement of haggling with a fixed price system would be one example. But ultimately the imagery associated with the mall – the spectacle – has played a large role in this:

> In this overcrowded marketplace, imagery has become increasingly critical as a way of attracting particular shops and facilitating acts of consumption. Through a selective manipulation of images, malls express a broad variety of messages, about the world both outside and inside the mall. (Crawford, 1992, p. 136)

I would argue that underlying all these discourses are two assumptions: people are passive recipients of suggestive, subliminal messages turning them into mindless consumers; and that consumption – enjoying oneself in a shopping centre, for example – is something inherently negative. Clearly neither of these assumptions reflects reality, nor are they particularly helpful in illustrating the complexity of urban interactions. People navigate different settings and spaces, switching easily between 'temples of consumption' and more mundane urban settings. The everyday is a setting where such negotiations and contestations take place. A more apt depiction would be of a 'shrewd' consumer – based on his needs and wants – *navigating* appropriate spaces. In the following section, I briefly present the recent shift in the study of urbanism whereby the everyday is becoming a subject worthy of study and investigation.

The Everyday and the Informal

Malcolm Miles, Tim Hall and Iain Borden (2004), in *The City Cultures Reader*, devote a considerable part of their collection to the everyday aspects of urbanism. They argue that the everyday life of cities is often hidden away. It is also deliberately ignored by city officials, who like to emphasize what they perceive as the positive side of their respective cities, which is in turn reflected on those responsible for shaping and designing the built environment. But, this is not the real city – only some version of it – as they observe:

> If you want to find out about the everyday lives of cities, read detective novels, the local newspaper, the notices pasted to lampposts and corrugated iron fences telling that someone's pet cat has gone missing, and the graffiti that obscures these traces of everyday life. (Miles *et al.*, 2004, p. 258)

Much of the emphasis on the everyday is based on the writings of French theorist Henri Lefebvre (1974) in the *Production of Space*, where he attempted to provide a total theory of space. The relevance of Lefebvre's ideas to everyday life are that his schema encompasses both the production of space through professions such as architecture and planning and its experience and negotiation through the practices of everyday life. According to Lefebvre, everyday life is lived within the spaces shaped by the powerful, or left behind by their shaping, but it is not determined by them. In a similar vein Michel de Certeau (1984), in *The Practice of Everyday Life*, recognizes 'strategies' by which the powerful produce instrumental or functional space, but argues that through the 'tactics' employed in the experience and negotiation of these spaces everyday life is able to subvert or elude the imposition of dominant meanings of space. Such ideas had widespread implications. For instance Tim Edensor, in his application of de Certeau's ideas to the culture of the Indian street, writes:

> His evocation of the plethora of desires that are stimulated through the relationship between sensual bodily movement, fantasy and reverie convincingly refute deterministic notions of pedestrians being shaped mentally and physically by urban space and its control. (Edensor, 1998, p. 219)

As Miles *et al.* (2004) observe, critical social scientists have begun to unearth the performity of meaning and the complex hidden geographies of the everyday use of space. Even Margaret Crawford in her more recent writings, particularly her by now classical collection *Everyday Urbanism* published in 1999 with J. Chase and J. Kaliski, begins to tackle the issue of informality. She writes on the spatial expressions of informal economies, as in street vending and garage sales in US cities, seeing such manifestations of a spatiality of occupation as offering a counter-argument to those of the dominant spaces of malls, and as evidence of the survival of spaces of public association and exchange despite the encroachment of privatized spaces on a more conventionally defined public realm. She writes that 'Woven into the patterns of everyday life, it is difficult to even discern these places as public space', but that, located behind the private, commercial and domestic realms they '… contain multiple, and constantly shifting meaning rather than clarity of function' (Crawford, 1999, p. 28).

In the introduction to *Everyday Urbanism* she defines the everyday as follows:

> ... everyday describes the lived experience shared by urban residents, the banal and ordinary routines we know all too well – commuting, working, relaxing, moving through city streets and sidewalks, shopping, buying and eating food, running errands... The utterly ordinary reveals a fabric of space and time defined by a complex realm of social practices – a conjuncture of accident, desire, and habit. (Crawford, 1999, p. 8)

The everyday is viewed as a site of endless possibilities and having 'the potential for new social arrangements and forms of imagination'. Furthermore, she is also influenced by the writings of Lefebvre, Debord and de Certeau, who view daily life 'as a site of creative resistance and liberatory power' (*Ibid.*, p. 9). Lefebvre (1971) was of particular influence; in his writings he distinguished between two simultaneous realities that exist within everyday life: the *quotidian*, the timeless, humble, repetitive natural rhythms of life; and the *modern*, the always new and constantly changing habits that are shaped by technology and worldliness. Based on this, Crawford notes her approach as being full of possibilities in reclaiming elements of the 'quotidian':

> We have tried to focus on ... the possibility of reclaiming elements of the quotidian that have been hidden in the nooks and crannies of the urban environment. We have discovered these qualities in overlooked, marginal places, from streets and sidewalks to vacant lots and parks, form suburbia to the inner city. (Crawford, 1999, p. 10)

Her approach is grounded in a belief that 'lived experience' is more significant than the physical form of the city – putting her in strong opposition to the proponents of formal urbanism. In such an approach, difference – the recognition of an other – is 'negated' yet is 'the most salient fact of everyday life' (*Ibid.*). She argues for a methodology that is based on mapping the city's social geography – and thus locating these differences that constitute the daily experience of city residents. These sites, or intersections with the city – and here she is clearly influenced by de Certeau – constitute places of multiple social and economic interactions, where differences collide or interact and thus are 'the most potent sites for everyday urbanism' (*Ibid.*, p. 11). They are also sites of resistance; by recognizing the temporal and spatial characteristic of places, residents begin to formulate 'tactics' which challenge the strategies of those in power and in this way the sites of the everyday become also sites of resistance.[5]

Other scholars, such as urban geographer Michael Peter Smith (2005), have adopted a similar viewpoint, calling for an examination of the everyday as a counterpoint to the global city literature with its conventional emphasis on 'spaces of flow'. Dubai represents a rich arena for observing these propositions. A city that is seemingly defined by spectacle, it nevertheless contains less spectacular sites as well, as I indicated in the introduction to this chapter. In the following sections I will examine both aspects in relation to its retail landscape, suggesting that denying people choices, i.e. the ability to navigate freely between the exclusive and non-exclusive, may be one particular negative development that could prove to be problematic.

Spectacular Shopping in Dubai

Dubai, more than any other city in the Middle East is defined by, and is an expression of, commerce. The spectacular notion of the city's retail landscape is evident in two respects: the sheer size and scale of its mega-malls, designed to surpass and exceed other malls throughout the world; and the particular themes which are adopted by these malls. Here they do not just become functional devices for selling merchandise, but are designed in a way that entices consumers by offering them an 'experience'.

Size: 'Bigger is Better'

Dubai is dominated by malls and has based its development strategy to a large degree on becoming a global player in retail. In 2008 the city had some thirty-five shopping centres covering an aggregate space of 14 million square metres – planned to increase to 40 million in the coming years.[6] While these numbers are impressive, individual centres exceed global standards. For example, Dubai Mall, set to become the world's biggest mall, as well as Mall of Arabia and Dubai Festival City will have a combined 1.2 million square metres.[7] GLA (Gross Leasable Area) is an indicator of retail space and it shows that Dubai Festival City has an estimated GLA of 195,000 square metres and another 58,000 square metres is under construction. Dubai Mall, part of the Burj Dubai development, is offering around 450,000 square metres of GLA. The latter is particularly impressive if we consider that the Mall of America in Bloomington, Minneapolis and one of the largest in the US offers approximately 260,000 square metres of GLA.[8]

According to the UK-based consultancy Retail International, it is anticipated that by 2009 retail activities in shopping centres will contribute about 50 per cent of Dubai's GDP. In other cities within the region the figure is closer to 20 per cent. Also, the city will represent 34 per cent, or more than a third, of the GCC's total retail development from 2006 to 2009, according to all the projects announced to date. In 2009, the per capita GLA in Dubai will reach 27.26 ft^2 (2.53 m^2), much higher than its nearest rival, Doha, which is expected to reach 6.84 ft^2 (0.64 m^2) per capita.[9]

Globally, the UAE ranks second after Hong Kong in recreational shopping. According to the ACNielsen Online Consumer Confidence Survey conducted in forty-two markets, 30 per cent of consumers in the UAE go shopping 'at least once a week', while the figure for Hong Kong is 36 per cent. To emphasize further the UAE'S love of shopping for entertainment, the combined UAE percentage of respondents who shop for 'something to do' either 'twice a week or more', 'once a week', 'once a month', or 'less than once a month' was recorded among the top ten worldwide, at 84 per cent.[10] Clearly this would increase if only Dubai was taken into account.

Malls are developed by both public and private developers. Among the biggest is Emaar Properties. Emaar is planning about 200 new shopping malls with an investment of Dh15 to Dh20 billion (US$4.1 billion to US$5.4 billion). It is expanding its presence outside the region as well, in an area stretching from Morocco to India. Nakheel, another public company, whose real estate portfolio exceeds Dh110 billion (US$30 billion), launched its own retail division called Retail Corp. They are responsible for the Ibn Batuta Mall named after the famous Arab explorer. Private developers are involved as well, for example Al Futaim Group (Mall of the Emirates), and the Galadari Group (Mall of Arabia). When completed, Dubai's Mall of Arabia, Dubai Mall, Mall of the Emirates and Ibn Batuta Mall will be among the world's top five shopping malls in terms of size.

The Mall of Arabia, being developed as part of the City of Arabia area in the Dubailand theme park with 600,000 square metres will be the largest. Among its attractions is the world's largest Starbucks, which will be built in the centre court of the mall. More malls are on their way. The Walk at Jumeirah Beach Residences, has a GLA of 71,500 square metres and has recently been opened. Mirdif City Centre with a retail area of 183,000 square metres and Dubai Marina Mall with 77,000 square metres opened in 2009.

Such rapid expansion and proliferation of shopping centres raises the question of saturation. The previously mentioned ICSC has in fact devoted a number of studies examining the retail market in the region. The GCC, led by Dubai, is, according to these studies, a perfect market for such expansion, mostly because it is the world's seventeenth largest economy and includes about 500,000 'high-income' professionals.[11] These optimistic numbers were, of course, based on the economic situation prior to the 2009 financial downturn. In fact some analysts have cautioned that Dubai's 'passion for mall building' could lead to an oversaturated retail market, particularly with regard to consumer confidence in the UAE, which has been declining slightly according to various retail consultancies. Such figures may be offset by the fact that until 2008 it was expected that 55 per cent of the money spent in Dubai's malls would come from tourism.[12] Given the decline in consumer spending, as well as the reluctance of people to travel, the financial viability of these malls may be in question – at least in the short term.

Theming: The Culture of Consumption

The city has both large mega-malls and smaller-scale malls serving specific communities. One of the oldest shopping malls in Dubai is the Al Ghurair Mall in Deira. A sprawling complex, it resembles a traditional *souq*. The 1980s and 1990s, however, witnessed the construction of a series of 'modern' shopping centres which adopted Western typologies: the use of anchor stores; a proper store mix; presence of food courts; exclusively inward orientation and blank anonymous exteriors. Deira City Center was for many years considered representative of this trend. However, as these centres proliferated developers turned to the notion of 'theming', common in other parts of the world as well. The idea here is to offer the consumer some sort of experience based on a certain theme: an Italian/Renaissance streetscape (Mercato Mall); an Oriental *souq* (Madinat Jumeirah); or an Egyptian Temple (Wafi Center) (figure 7.1). Another mode of theming is to link these centres with a specific event. This could be in the form of a winter landscape and ski slope (Mall of the Emirates); association with an iconic structure (Souq Bahar and Burj Dubai); or the presence of 'the world's largest aquarium' (Dubai Mall) (figure 7.2).[13] There is actually a term for this in the retail industry: 'entertainment

7.1. Mercato Mall, designed to resemble an Italian Renaissance Palace.

7.2. The giant aquarium inside the Dubai Mall.

anchor'! History as theme is also present in other malls in the city: Khan Murjan, which is an underground extension of the Egyptian themed Wafi Mall, named after the famous Baghdad *caravenserai*; Mercato based on an Italian cityscape; Souq Bahar which is built to resemble a Mameluk castle (figure 7.3).

7.3. Khan Murjan, an underground shopping centre evoking its namesake from Baghdad.

Taking this whole notion of theming to extremes is the Ibn Batuta Mall. While conventional in its layout – essentially an oversized, one storey, half mile long, strip mall – it is broken down into zones, each of which was visited by the explorer on his travels. Thus, there is a Chinese Court, an Egyptian zone and so on. These zones contain an exhibition of items relaying to the curious visitor aspects of the traveller and Arab culture in general. Interactive exhibitions and 'replicas' of famous artefacts displayed in museums elsewhere complete the image of a cultural centre in the midst of a shopping mall (figure 7.4.).

7.4. The North African court inside the Ibn Batuta Mall.

These developments are characterized by their scale as well as an exaggerated and heightened use of themes; the meaning behind this becomes clearer if we examine the marketing campaigns run for some of these projects. For instance Emaar, developer responsible for the Dubai Mall, uses the following advertisement:

> We will re-define how 2 billion drink coffee. How people from 2 continents travel. How 21 different countries dress up. How 1500 different dialects communicate. How 400 million homes get furnished. How over 150 cultural beliefs are celebrated. How 100,000 brands get recognized. How 750 billion US Dollars will be spent on shopping.
>
> We will re-define shopping.

This is followed by a full page image of three ultra-chic female models, dressed in black, closely huddled together in one anonymous mass (figure 7.5), upon which is superimposed the following sentence: *Emaar Malls. Re-defining the world of shopping.* Another page then displays the following:

2 continents
2 billion people
100 malls
1 company

While the objective is clearly profit and increasing sales, the strategy adopted is one that seeks to influence potential buyers. A lifestyle is proposed which, through

7.5. A version of the Emaar advertisement displayed at Dubai airport.

the sheer power of imagery, is supposed to turn people into willing consumers of luxury goods. In that process malls do not just become outlets for goods but also settings that celebrate multi-culturalism, all unified under one singular purpose. Such strategies are not unique to Dubai of course – the whole industry of advertising is dominated by these seductive images and slogans. It is primarily based on motivational research, popular in the 1950s and 1960s, which argued that people's behaviour could be influenced through subliminal messages addressing their emotions (e.g. Packard, 1957). Taking this a step further, entire environments are now designed in a way that would affect consumers' perception and behaviour – also known as 'life-style marketing'. Here marketing is geared beyond needs to explore the consumers' 'deepest longings'. Thus the 'shoppers' fantasy of living better has become more important than the actual product' (Kelley, 2005). Another tactic involves creating a never ending stream of desires, beyond one's immediate needs, by combining things in a novel way: 'edu-tainment, info-tainment' and so on (Poynor, 2005).

This focus on consumption has not been without its critics. For instance, the UAE's Department of Planning and Economy (DPE) warned in a 2008 report that this culture of consumerism could seriously dent the country's future economic growth if the current trend continued. The DPE noted that consumer spending had surged 122 per cent during the last five years, jumping 17.7 per cent to Dh320 billion ($87.1 billion) – almost half the UAE's gross domestic product (GDP). The department said daily per capita consumer spending in the UAE stood at $27, more than seven times higher than the average daily spending in the rest of the Arab world.[14]

Malls as Meeting Spaces or Circumventing the Spectacle

Based on these economic data such strategies may actually work in terms of generating profit, but a more interesting question pertains to the extent to which mall users engage in activities that do not necessarily have to be described as consumerist. In other words, do these exhibits actually attract people, and in what other activities do they engage? The notion of the mall as a meeting place – a third space as defined by sociologist Ray Oldenburg (2000) – has, of course, been researched *ad nauseam* in a way that contradicts Margaret Crawford's early assertion that malls are more or less machines for shopping, determining consumer behaviour – which does not seem to be the case according to my observations.

In Ibn Batuta Mall, the position of the mall as a 'third space' is indeed confirmed; it is not merely a space of consumption, but offers users a place where they can display their ethnicity, engage in various work related activities, or simply socialize with others. Here the spectacle does not become a numbing device goading consumers into buying, but instead consumers actively adapt the spectacle to shape their own perceptions and expectations.

One of the interesting features of this mall is that the entrances are, in some instances, used to create a sort of public space rarely seen in the city. For instance, the entrance from the Chinese court side leads to a large space on to which open a series of restaurants. In addition there is also a convenience store, which is used by mall goers but also many outside visitors. Indeed, I observed a group of teenagers, who had just finished school, entering the store and purchasing soft drinks as well as a packet of cigarettes. They then proceeded to sit outside the store, using the café chairs. This particular section of the mall has become a hideaway, a place where one escapes the gaze of adults. Typically, one would encounter such behaviour in traditional streets and alleys – yet here the mall, a place that is supposedly only meant for consumption, is transformed into this 'liberating' space, where teenagers engage in rites of passage into adulthood. In general the whole setting has the feel of a pleasant courtyard, a feeling that is enhanced by the use of wooden walkways. My observations have shown that a significant number of visitors – particularly to the café – do not go to the mall to shop, but use the setting for reading, meeting friends and so on. The whole notion of the mall as a community centre acquires a fascinating dimension once one steps into the mall itself. Immediately noticeable are people sitting on benches in the mall's public spaces or in its different cafés, surfing the internet on their laptops, facilitated by a free wireless internet service.

Another interesting feature pertains to the previously mentioned exhibition stands, which are spread throughout the mall. One particular question that I was interested in is to what extent they are used by mall shoppers. My observations show that there is indeed an active engagement with these displays. One particular area in the Egypt section of the mall – which is the largest – contains a variety of maps and objects related to the various regions visited by Ibn Batuta. For many shoppers who stop to look at them, they are used as devices to reinforce a sense of identity: two elderly Pakistani men standing in front of a map and pointing to Pakistan; or a couple of Indian labourers looking at a map of India and trying to identify their city; others would take photographs alongside exhibits related to their home country. Taking photographs and videoing the setting also illustrate that the mall has moved beyond its function as a place of selling goods and is becoming a space of memory as well. Furthermore, the location within a mall encourages people to talk and be more interactively involved with the exhibit than if they were in a museum, for instance (figure 7.6).

Less Spectacular Malls

Dubai, surprisingly, has its share of less spectacular malls as well. In an effort to cater for low-income users some developers began targeting areas which are home to thousands of labourers, such as Al Quoz Industrial Area, which stretches from Mall of the Emirates – parallel to Sheikh Zayed road – until it almost reaches the limits of the Burj Dubai complex. As the name indicates it is an industrial area with warehouses and light industries. While acquiring notoriety recently for various fires that broke out in some of its old and dilapidated structures, it also contains

7.6. An exhibition depicting the travels of Ibn Batuta surrounded by clothing boutiques.

residences – better known as labour camps – for thousands of workers. Unlike the infamous Sonapur camp – referred to by the Human Rights Watch group and in turn by countless media articles, as an example of exploitation and abuse – which is located in the desert near the border with Sharjah, Al Quoz is to a large extent an integral part of the city fabric. While it was initially located on the city's outskirts it is now surrounded by various high-end projects which will, given developments taking place, lead to the area's eventual demise (figure 7.7).

Al Quoz has no public space, no clearly defined public realm allowing for gatherings, nor even a park, but is rather composed of roads arranged in a grid pattern. Until recently it had no major shopping centres, healthcare facilities and

7.7. The distant skyline of Dubai as it appears from Al Quoz Industrial area.

7.8. The Grand City Mall of Al Quoz.

so on. In 2006 a mall operator, Regency Group, opened a 'low-cost' shopping mall 'built by labourers for labourers' and named Grand City Mall. The mall contains the typical stores – a hypermarket, various food venues as well as thirty-five different retail outlets. In addition, there is a pharmacy, travel agent and a driving school – key facilities for this particular segment of the population (figure 7.8).[15]

The mall itself is located at a traffic intersection and is not surrounded by any buildings. Close by are a variety of housing structures and labour camps, but its location at the edge of the industrial area, rather than in the centre, makes it somewhat difficult to access. Yet in spite of its relative remoteness, I observed a sizeable number of users. In fact, the area around the entrance which is wider than a typical sidewalk, was used by many people, standing around, talking and so on. Also, a large South Asian restaurant, named 'Pataan', faced directly onto the open space in front of the mall. Various notices and flyers were mounted on the centre's wall, put there, for instance, by people seeking accommodation, as can be found in many other places in the city which cater for low-income users. Inside, the mall is clean and well organized. A security guard is visibly placed at the entrance. Users are mostly male, although I did see a few female customers (figure 7.9). Overall, by adopting the strategies of larger malls, the centre attracted users not just for shopping, but also as a gathering place, a setting for reinforcing one's sense of identity (the ethnic restaurant) – even in an area as desolate and grim as Al Quoz.

While the mall no doubt serves an important need for residents in the area, I was struck by the extent to which the city of Dubai – its skyscrapers and luxurious developments – appeared so remote. Burj Dubai is visible from all over Al Quoz, particularly around the Grand City Mall, its distance, but also its sheer extravagance

7.9. Users congregating around the mall's entrance.

is evident. For those using the mall, the city appears inaccessible. For them, Grand City Mall is perhaps their only glimpse of what 'the other' Dubai can offer. Such directions will be further reinforced since newly constructed labour camps – which are near Jebel Ali, the border with Abu Dhabi – are gated and will contain their own shopping centres and means of entertainment. In this way labourers and workers are further isolated from the city – reinforcing their sense of transience.

The discussion so far has centred on a critical assumption that consumers will blindly follow what is on offer in these spectacularly themed developments. Thus the power of capital, somehow made more appealing by the spectacular, will act as a determining factor – causing people to spend their money on unnecessary items. These views have been criticized, as I noted earlier – people are not 'cultural dupes'; in fact they adopt strategies which circumvent these spectacular developments, seeking instead an experience that is not tied to imagery or the appeal of the spectacle. They are not passive, nor does the proliferation of the spectacle cause them to be unwitting participants in capitalist exploitation. I have illustrated this by examining the behaviour of mall visitors in one particular case, the Ibn Batuta Mall, the ultimate example of a spectacular development. I illustrate this further by looking at the 'everyday retail experience' in the city in the following section.

Informal Dubai

The informal economy, also described as the shadow, underground, parallel, or grey economy, is defined by economists as business activities whose participants have failed to pay tax or comply with regulations. In many instances, however, it also means illegal activities such as prostitution and drug dealing. It is usually associated with things happening at the margins of developing countries – a hawker's stand in Thailand, a roadside vendor in Ghana, a vegetable market in Cairo. Yet increasingly such activities exist in rich countries as well. According to economic data, the share of the informal economy in developing countries is about 41 per cent while in industrial nations it reaches 18 per cent.[16]

The UAE, and particularly Dubai, is viewed as a centre point in this illegal trade. For instance, counterfeit drugs, a $60 billion a year industry, is one particularly interesting example. In places such as Dubai and Hong Kong, because of their open trade policies, free ports and absence of import and export duties, the trade in counterfeit drugs has flourished. A recent report noted that Dubai attracts counterfeiters for the same reason that it attracts honest traders: its strategic location on the Gulf makes it ideal for the movement of goods between Asia, Europe and Africa.

The report cites as evidence that one-third of all counterfeit drugs confiscated in Europe in 2007 came through the United Arab Emirates. The UAE is part of a supply chain which runs from counterfeit drug manufacturers in China through Hong Kong, onward to the United Arab Emirates, Britain and the Bahamas, ultimately leading to internet pharmacies whose American customers believe they are buying medicines from Canada.[17]

Yet, in spite of the UAE playing such a significant role in large-scale informal trade, and acting as a gateway of sorts for the rest of the world, the situation differs at the city scale. In Dubai certain conditions preclude the presence of a visible and active informal economy. For example, there is no poor rural population migrating to the city in search of jobs, nor a highly dense city teeming with people in which an informal economic activity can take hold. Moreover, illegal migrants (defined as those entering the country without a valid visa or who have overstayed the permissible time without renewing their residency) are actively pursued by authorities, jailed and subsequently deported.[18] And, closely related to that, there is a strong security presence on the street ensuring that law and order are followed – any deviation from behavioural norms is immediately noticed. Thus, unlike other cities in the region – particularly ones with a poor population such as Cairo – the first impression is that Dubai is more or less regulated and orderly. But forms of informality do exist. In fact, according to some observers, Dubai owes its very existence to informality – from the early days of smuggling gold and other goods to becoming a major 'transition point' in transferring illegal amounts of money, as well as being a centre for money laundering. According to Tom Porteous, places like Dubai have become 'key service stations on the highway which links the formal, legal world of democratic peace, to the informal, extra-legal world of war, poverty and dictatorship [and] instability'.[19] Of course, given the nature of these activities they are not visible; their very existence relies to a large extent on rumour, and they do not have a direct impact on urban space. Of more significance are the everyday markets which are frequented by the city's poor migrant population and whose services cater for them. They represent a stark counterpoint to the spectacular retail landscape and in them one can observe displays of ethnicity and gatherings of compatriots; they are accessible to all.

These settings can be viewed as an attempt to circumvent 'spectacular Dubai'. A series of mechanisms are employed such as writing graffiti, taking over of left-over spaces, personalization of semi-public spaces such as balconies in residences, overt displays of ethnicity, restaurants as well as supermarkets catering for different ethnic groups. At the level of retail, selling counterfeit goods could be construed as one form of 'contesting' the city's 'official' retail landscape. Such visible manifestations of circumvention do in fact suggest that people in globalizing cities are not merely pawns within a capitalist scheme – as theories of a Debordian spectacle may suggest – but are actively engaged in a process of forming and shaping their identity in a city which denies them such possibilities. In the following sections, I explore the extent to which an examination of these everyday settings may offer insights into the degree to which the spectacular is both navigated and, in some instances, circumvented. These assessments are based on observations and field notes within the following areas of Dubai: Souk Naif; Hudeiba Street; Karama district; Hamriya neighbourhood and Rashid Colony. All are settings associated with middle- to low-income users, catering for the city's various sub-cultures – while the spectacular city appears in the distance.

Territorial Identity/Assertion of Sub-Cultures

Within the city of Dubai are a variety of areas, neighbourhoods and strips of streets which are linked to different ethnic groups. While the city has a plethora of ethnic groups, it is dominated by the South Asian community (India, Pakistan and Bangladesh) who represent 76 per cent of the total population; the remainder is divided among various nationalities with percentages ranging from 1 to 3 per cent. Among this group, the Filipino community is particularly well represented. While overt displays of ethnicity are discouraged, certain settings within the city are closely linked to some of these groups. Specifically the South Asian community is associated with places such as Meena Bazaar, and the Souk Naif/Sabkha area.

The Filipino community gravitates towards a stretch of street in the Satwa district known as Hudeiba. Many have taken up residence in the district as it is still relatively affordable even though they are employed in places which are at a considerable distance away, such as Al Quoz Industrial Area, Jebel Ali or many of the free zones such as Internet City and Media City. Various message boards advertising rooms 'For Filipinos' further accentuate the ethnic character of the district (figure 7.10).

The Karama district in Bur Dubai contains a mix of Filipinos and South Asians, although the sheer number of the latter clearly dominates. The ethnicity of these places is marked by a series of indicators, which sets them apart from the rest of the city. One particularly poignant marking are flyers and advertisement, as well

7.10(*a*). Hudeiba Street, a centre for the Filipino community.

7.10(*b*). Advertisements placed on an electric box, geared to the Filipino community.

as graffiti – migratory traces – illustrating the degree to which these territories are carved out from the surrounding cityscape.

Walking through any of these districts a clearly noticeable feature are the flyers, handwritten or typed on a computer and posted on walls, lamp posts and phone booths. While some offer services of various kinds, they are dominated by advertisements for apartments, rooms, and for the most part bed spaces. What is of interest is that the sought-after clientele is clearly marked by ethnic background, social status as well as lifestyle. For example, one flyer in the district of Satwa reads (cited here with its spelling mistakes) (figure 7.11):

Three bed space available

for only executive indian muslim bachellors

(non smoking and non drinking)

to share with same

7.11. Handwritten and typed advertisements and flyers; one reads 'for decent bachelor muslims only'.

In Hudeiba Street, also known as little Manilla, the following flyer was typical:

FOR FILIPNO ONLY

Room/Partitioned Bed Space

available for families and ladies, behind Lal's supermarket near al bada park

These advertisements circumvent official channels for renting living spaces; they could also be considered a form of informal residency since the act of subletting bed spaces, for example, is not explicitly endorsed or sanctioned by law. The advertisements add a sense of randomness to the carefully maintained order of the city – through their arrangement on the wall, the mixing of computer typed and handwritten flyers, and the overlapping of various papers – and they offer a glimpse into the everyday lives of the city's low-income residents and their struggle to find a place to live. Other means of expression are graffiti messages which are typically written in Arabic and relate to expressions of identity, soccer proclamations and so on; in some instances they express political views such as the supremacy of Yemen, for instance. Both flyers and graffiti messages seem to aid the formation of ethnic sub-groups; given the degree to which the authorities discourage any political expression and in the absence of effective community centres within neighbourhoods, they become the only means through which an identity is carved out and established within the larger city.

Selling Counterfeit Goods

Selling fake brands, while prevalent in the past, is pursued quite aggressively by the authorities and offenders are jailed and deported – or at least this is the official portrayal in the media. Yet within the city there are a number of places notorious for such activities. For instance, the district of Karama is known as a market for cheap and counterfeit goods.[20] According to one observer:

> These goods usually end up in places like Dubai's thriving Karama shopping centre where scores of shops compete to sell the cheapest brand name to the not so unsuspecting tourists who come in their droves to hunt for that supposedly branded bargain.[21]

The market is located in a large interconnected residential complex which contains a variety of stores on the ground level (figure 7.12). Passing through one

7.12. The sprawling complex of Karama Souq, which is located at ground level, while upper storeys are residences.

encounters these fake brands in display windows in addition to constant calls from merchants enticing potential buyers by claiming that they sell 'Rolex' watches. If interest is shown, potential purchasers are taken inside the store where a shoebox is produced containing watches of any brand imaginable. Of impeccable quality, they are sold at bargain prices – a fraction of the cost of the genuine article. These activities take place without fear of being caught by the authorities. They are seemingly tolerated. What is of particular interest is that I observed *Tour Dubai* buses taking tourists through the district – without actually stopping. The informal and less spectacular is used and portrayed as a spectacle. In common with similar settings, it has a variety of ethnic restaurants; it is also a popular hangout for the city's poor and middle-income population. A centrally located park is a major gathering point and various street corners act as 'incidental' gathering spaces.

The market has attracted the attention of Western journalists searching for a more authentic Dubai, going beyond the official, luxurious image. A report by Joy Lo Dico in *The Independent* described the district of Karama as 'a little series of boxy concrete residential blocks containing shops selling old furniture' but it also 'boasts a thriving counterfeits market'. She then describes her experience as follows:

> It was the first place I heard the mantra that then followed me through the old town: 'Rolex! Tag Heuer! Cartier! Omega!' An Iranian spotted me as a potential buyer and led me up some back stairs to a room stacked high with handbags, shoes and trays of watches. He gave me a Coca-Cola while he displayed his wares. 'You like Gucci?' he asked. 'Juicy Couture? Everything's very good quality'. I declined his offers and moved onto a store where the Keralan shopkeeper let me try on a burka and a belly-dancing outfit. I left with a camel puppet as a souvenir.

Her description of the context in which these interactions occurred is also interesting since it reveals the multicultural nature of these districts; streets filled with African women in flowery headdresses, Chinese labourers, Indian stall-holders and mechanics who are 'all following the pulse of money'.[22]

Another setting known for selling counterfeit goods is Meena Bazaar, an area linked to the city's South Asian community. While not as prevalent as in Karama, my observations resulted in numerous encounters where I was offered various items of dubious origin. Also, there were sellers of pirated movies on DVD (mostly of Indian origin) which were displayed in dark alleyways on a piece of cloth (figure 7.13). In some instances, Chinese sellers with bags containing such items enter fast food restaurants and offer their merchandise to interested customers – although this has been actively pursued by the authorities and is not as prevalent as it once was. Yet it is quite remarkable that even within a highly controlled society such as Dubai, which is projecting itself as a modern and orderly city, and where the city's urban form does not encourage the proliferation of these centres (wide open streets where any form of deviation from the norm can be easily spotted), such activities do take place.[23]

7.13. Informal selling of bootlegged DVDs in an alley connecting Meena Bazaar to a main thoroughfare.

Ethnic Restaurants

Ethnic restaurants play a significant role in that they allow the city's residents to maintain links with their home countries; they are an affordable alternative to the more expensive fast food outlets in shopping malls and in the city's streets. Supermarkets also cater for specific ethnic communities, selling merchandise and groceries that are geared only to them. In Hudeiba Street for instance, the centre of Dubai's Filipino community, are a variety of ethnic supermarkets, eateries and shops selling different wares catering both for expatriates and locals. This strip of street, extending from the Iranian Hospital to the Satwa bus stop, is referred to by Filipinos as Dubai's 'Little Quiapo' after Manila's busiest commercial district (figure 7.14). According to one account:

> This area offers a slice of home for thousands of Filipinos in Dubai where they socialise with
> their kababayans [compatriots] in restaurants offering Filipino food or while killing time on
> the steps of Al Maya Lal's. A Filipino-style ukay-ukay [secondhand] shop sits next to a row
> of Filipino restaurants, where bargain-hunters rummage for pasalubong [homecoming gifts]

7.14. A supermarket in Hudeiba Street is a major gathering point for the Filipino community.

like shirts, electronics, toys and perfume to fill up their balikbayan [returners'] boxes. Filipino delicacies and foodstuff – from balut [boiled fertilised duck egg), daing na bangus (dried milk fish), chicharon [chicken skin or cracklings] and longanisa [Philippine-style sausage that evolved from the Spanish chorizo] – are in steady supply at Al Maya Lal's as well as a number of supermarkets and grocers in Satwa.[24]

The numerous restaurants catering for the South Asian community, and associated with similar settings back home, include places known throughout their respective communities, such as Karachi Darbar or Bombay Fast Food Restaurant. My observations in Rashid Colony, a nondescript public housing scheme on the city's outskirts, shows that the presence of these two eateries, in addition to several others, enhances the ethnic character of the district to the extent that a place such as Bombay Fast Food becomes a destination visited by people from different parts of the city – and even from different Emirates. This latter establishment has been in operation for more than 30 years, thus creating a sense of identity for the city's migrants. Some such as Karachi Darbar, due to the familiarity of the food and their cheapness, become a hangout, or place for a break for the city's low-income population. For example, I observed that they are frequented by a large number of taxi drivers (figure 7.15).

Other ethnic groups are represented as well such as the Iranian community who have a series of restaurants that cater for them. Among them, Special Ustadi Restaurant, described in Chapter 3, is of particular significance. These settings add a sense of history and identity to a city that is increasingly focused on generic food chains. These eateries also become places that attract large gatherings of people. Thus they act as anchor points within some of these districts. In one interesting

7.15(*a*). Bombay Fast Food Restaurant in Rashid Colony, attracting a large number of visitors on a typical evening.

7.15(*b*). Karachi Darbar Restaurant in Rashid colony, a well known chain in the city serving predominantly low-income users.

instance, in Meena Bazaar, I saw a large number of Indian low-income workers watching cricket on a TV inside a restaurant. The food, the activity being watched, as well as the presence of compatriots. all contribute to strengthening community bonds among this ethnic group – thus reinforcing their sense of identity. All these

7.16. In Meena Bazaar a game of cricket shown on TV inside one of the many eateries attracts the attention of passers by.

instances reveal that a parallel, alternative order is being constructed, catering for a particular ethnic group, slipping between the cracks of the orderly, spectacular city (figure 7.16).

Ethnic Markets

Dubai has, of course, its share of renovated, 'historic' markets which cater for the tourism industry. But there is also a set of markets which while not informal nevertheless offer an interesting counterpoint to the spectacular malls. One of these is Naif Souq located in an area of Dubai known as Sabkha, one of the older parts of the city. It houses a large low-income expatriate population and has one of the highest densities in the city. It is known for its various commercial outlets and also has a major bus stop (figures 7.17 and 7.18). One observer describes it as follows:

> If you are a bargain hunter, a fun place to search for those special purchases in Dubai is the Naif Souq, nestled in a warren of alleyways near the police station. Here, you can find anything from bolts of cloth and glass bangles to crockery and ready-made garments.[25]

The district contains a market which was popularly known among expatriates from the sub-continent as Chapra Bazaar, or the 'Shed Market', as all the shops were made of metal and aluminum with asbestos sheeting for roofs. Recent renovation efforts replaced this run-down market with a traditional looking version,

7.17. An outdoor cafeteria in the Naif Souq area.

7.18. The original Naif Souq prior to its destruction in a fire in summer 2008.

specializing in selling fabrics and clothes. The informal collection of stores has thus been formalized in a way – turned into a 'spectacular' version of a traditional market. What is of greater interest, however, is the surrounding area. Here one can find a series of shops, vendors and hawkers selling a variety of merchandise and catering for a wider segment of the population. In a maze of narrow alleyways one encounters porters, gatherings at street corners, tea shops and ethnic eateries. A small microcosm of similar settings in India and Africa are thus created in this part of the city. These places serve an important communication function. Interviews revealed that people come to them on a regular basis to interact with others and meet friends. People from certain areas in their home countries know where to find their compatriots in Sabkha; through them they may receive news from home. Witness the following account:

> Strike out on Al Sabkha road and it is the twists and turns of Tamil, a few steps down Al Borj street and it is the thick flavor of the Hindi dialect spoken in the western Indian state of Rajashan complete with the cuss words, about turn and head down the street leading to Sabkha bus stand and it is the lyrical Bhojpuri of Bihar and parts of Uttar Pradesh that greets your ears, stand firm in the middle and it is either the Hyderabadi Hindi … or the utterly unintelligible to your ears Telegu.[26]

In the summer of 2008 a fire broke out in the traditional Naif Market leading to its complete destruction. Many low-income workers lost their livelihood over night. Coming to their aid were Indian community organizations such as the Dubai Kerala Muslim Cultural Centre in addition to various individuals offering them stipends and food.[27] Such an overt display of community action is rare, but it shows the extent to which these ethnic districts are entrenched in the city's fabric and everyday life. The almost complete absence of the state, whose role is relegated to relocating and rebuilding the original, is compensated by these charity and community centres.

Meena Bazaar, referred to earlier, is another interesting area catering for a mix of users, including locals but dominated by South Asians. The mix of shops indicates that it serves both a low-income and middle-class clientele (figure 7.19). The area figures prominently in the consciousness of UAE citizens. One notes that: 'The bazaar lives up to its name and it reminds me of a typical bazaar in Mumbai. I just love it here'.[28] Modelled after a similar bazaar in India, it is also known as Cosmos Lane, named after a building with a huge 'Cosmos' sign (the name of a store) built in 1974. While the area has a definite commercial character, it also serves as a meeting place, drawing people from various parts of the city – single men, families and single women. Adding to the ethnic character of the setting there is a Sindhi temple and ceremonial centre which is heavily frequented, although it is located in a side alley and has no externally visible architectural signs. Eateries serving South Asian fare are to be found throughout the various lanes which for the most part follow a traditional morphology of irregularity (figure 7.20). Thus, given all these indicators, the area acquires a distinct character setting it apart from the remainder of the city. It is relatively hidden and is only known to 'insiders' or long-time residents. Yet its very presence and popularity shows that people do indeed find ways to circumvent and navigate the spectacle promoted in shopping malls. And this is not just restricted to the poor. In fact one resident notes that the mixing of rich and poor is what makes this area interesting: 'I can afford to live in a less congested residential area in Deira or Bur Dubai but I will never get the same energy and synergy that exists in this place called Meena Bazaar'.[29]

Various media reports portray these settings as exotic locales – places where one can find some sort of authentic experience in contrast to the 'high style' living on Sheikh Zayed Road. They thus resonate with a desire to move away from the

7.19. The main shopping road in Meena Bazaar. Street corners become main points for gatherings.

7.20. The Meena Bazaar area is also a place of residence for many low-income expatriates.

perceived 'artificiality' of themed shopping malls. Interestingly, the anonymous, unremarkable architecture of these settings seems to be a perfect environment for the unfolding and display of one's ethnicity. They act as a neutral backdrop, allowing for a certain degree of personalization, for example the hanging of lights to celebrate the Diwali festival, or writing of graffiti. One could perhaps describe them as the 'anti-spectacle'. Yet they also point to larger issues hinted at the beginning to this chapter, which I discuss in the concluding section.

Dangerous Spectacles

A recent media report indicated that a Dubai-based businessman has decided to build a replica of the French city of Lyon in a yet to be decided location in the city.[30] So clearly the trend for the spectacular, the superlative, the constant questioning of authenticity and the ultimate meaning of fakery and artificiality continues unabated. But one characteristic of the spectacle, as Debord informs us, is its capacity to move beyond borders – a diffusion, or what he calls 'the integrated spectacle'. He writes:

> … a third form has been established, through the rational combination of these two [the concentrated and the diffuse spectacle], and on the basis of a general victory of the form which has showed itself stronger: the diffuse. This is the *integrated spectacle*, which has since tended to impose itself globally. (Debord, 1988, p. 8)

Such prophetic proclamations can be observed in the Middle East where the *Dubai Spectacle* is being portrayed as a model enviously eyed by its neighbours. Nowhere is this more evident than in Cairo. As I have shown, there are Egyptian references in Dubai's architecture – yet increasingly there have been adaptations of Dubai-based ideas in an Egyptian context. These include the Maadi City Center, a massive shopping mall built by a Dubai based investment company; Uptown Cairo, a gated community project near Salah ud-din's citadel, where Emaar is adopting a marketing strategy relying on Arabian themes; or the City Stars Mall, which in its architecture replicates Pharaonic elements. Even cities with substantive history are not immune to notions of theming and commodification. Similar developments are taking place elsewhere in the region. Such approaches, while not particularly harmful in a desert context where there are no contextual constraints, become problematic in a city such as Cairo which contains large pockets of poverty. The upscale Uptown project, for example, overlooks the notorious Manshiet Nasser slum, one of the largest informal settlements in the city. This juxtaposition of extreme wealth and abject poverty will inevitably result in social problems and unrest.[31] I return to this issue in more detail in Chapter 9 where I discuss the influence of Dubai in the wider region – *Dubaization.*

Here the spectacle is not just a way to induce passivity in the population or a tool of domination, but is used to mark, to segregate and to separate people along socio-economic lines. And it is precisely this last point which underlies my main argument. The spectacle in itself – themed developments etc – is not harmful to anybody. It becomes a problem when there is a lack of choice; when developments are increasingly geared to a specific segment of society, thereby excluding a large poor population. Also, relegating the use of informal markets to the poor marks them and creates ghettos within the city, discouraging their use by the remainder of the population. Great cities are by their very nature integrative – the spectacular co-exists with the informal, and city residents have the choice to move between these two worlds.

In my discussion earlier I tied these issues to Debordian theories of spectacle and the extent to which spectacle can induce passivity in the population. Taking this a step further, David Harvey (2006), for instance, in his discussion of 'geographies of exclusion', argues that neoliberal urban development, i.e. capitalism, favours or leads to a geography that caters for the rich. What I have tried to illustrate in this chapter, however, is that while this may be true at some level, a closer examination of the spaces of the everyday – and here I am following theories of transnational urbanism as developed by Michael Peter Smith, for instance – reveals that strategies are adopted by migrant and local populations that mitigate these exclusionary directions by creating and adapting spaces to their needs – in a way providing an alternative landscape (Peter Smith, 2001).

In Dubai such areas of informality do exist and are thriving. But recent indicators suggest that the city is moving towards exclusivity. A real estate company – Meraas – had been given the task of redeveloping these older areas, which means turning them into upscale mixed-use developments; the poor, informal markets

7.21. Graffiti in Rashid Colony – 'We won't leave'.

will be – and some have been already – relocated to the city's edge.[32] Rashid Colony, site of the Bombay Fast Food Resturant and Karachi Darbar, is slated for demolition in spite of strong resistance from residents (figure 7.21).[33] The urban diversity and healthy mix of socio-economic groups will be a thing of the past. And if this dystopia comes true, Debord's society of the spectacle will have finally come to full fruition in the deserts of the Middle East.

Notes

1. For an interesting example see the following article: Zacks, Stephen (2007) 'Beyond the spectacle', *Metropolis*, November. http://www.metropolismag.com/cda/story.php?artid=3047. Accessed 16 November 2008.

2. Soriano, Veronica (2006) 'Converting browsers into spenders', *Research Review*, **13**(2), pp. 9–13.

3. Contis, David (2006) 'Understanding Macro Trends Affecting the Industry', *Research Review*, **13**(1), pp. 6–9.

4. This quote is from *The Guardian*'s architectural critic discussing the recently opened Westfield mall in London. He observes that it 'looks like a cross between a giant 1980s airport terminal and, well, a big, brash and shiny shopping mall of the sort you might expect anywhere today from Des Moines to Dubai via Shanghai and Sydney'. And in a typical architectural response: 'in the short to medium term, Westfield is just a tiny step towards our collective desire to undermine the life and culture of the traditional city, along with its architecture, and to shop and shop some more'. Glancey, Jonathan (2008) 'Westfield mega mall: the death of city architecture','' *The Guardian*, 3 November. http://www.guardian.co.uk/artanddesign/2008/nov/03/westfield-shopping-centre. Accessed 12 November 2008.

5. Crawford (1999) notes that 'Both Michel de Certeau and Henri Lefebvre argued that the temporal is as significant as the spatial in everyday life. De Certeau drew a distinction between two modes of operation: strategies, based on place, and tactics, based on time. Strategies represent the practices of those in power … [they] establish a "proper" place, either spatial or institutional, such that place triumphs over time… In contrast, a tactic is a way of operating without a proper place, and so depends on time. As a result tactics lack the borders, necessary for designation as visible totalities: "The place of a tactic belongs to the other." Tactics are the "art of the weak", incursions into the field of the powerful. Without a proper place, tactics rely on seized opportunities, on cleverly chosen moments, and on the rapidity of movements that can change the organization of a space. Tactics are a form of everyday creativity … By challenging the "proper" places of the city, this range of transitory, temporary, and ephemeral urban activities constitutes counterpractices to officially sanctioned urbanisms'. (p. 12)

6. Maceda, Cleofe (2008) 'Number of malls in Dubai to double', *Gulf News*, 19 February, p. 50.

7. Ditcham, Robert (2007) 'Neighbors vie with Dubai for retail glory', *Gulf News*, 24 February, p. 29.

8. http://www.easternct.edu/depts/amerst/MallsLarge.htm. Accessed 17 February 2008.

9. MECS, *Middle East Council of Shopping Centres: Newsletter*, 2006. http://www.mecsc.org/newsletter/nledt_view.php?id=110. Accessed 17 February 2008.

10. AME Report (2006) *UAE Shoppers ranked Second in Global ACNielsen Survey on Recreational Shopping.* http://www.jump.co.za/blog/2006/08/uae-shoppers-ranked-second-in-global.html. Accessed 10 February 2008.

11. See Thomson, Simon (2006) 'The Middle East retail real estate dynamic', *Research Review*, **13**(1), pp. 36–40; see also McArthur, Phil (2006) 'A retail oasis: the Middle East industry', *Research Review*, **13**(1), pp. 41–43.

12.   Salama, Vivian (2008) 'Dubai Mall to be global landmark', *The National*, 7 September, p. 4; also see Maceda, Cleofe (2008) 'Dubai retail market could see saturation', *Gulf News*, 2 June, p. 36. Recent economic development at the time of writing may lead to a decline in visitors from Europe which would in turn negatively impact the profitability of malls and perhaps lead to a revision of the city's retail policy.

13.   A *Gulf News* survey which asked readers about their favourite mall had the following results: Alghurair 3 per cent; Burjuman 7 per cent; Deira City Centre 27 per cent; Dubai Outlet Mall 1 per cent; Festival City 11 per cent; Ibn Batuta Mall 10 per cent; Mall of the Emirates 32 per cent; Mercato Mall 2 per cent; Wafi City 1 per cent; Other Malls 6 per cent (31 October 2008, p. 13).

14.   Bowman, Dylan (2008) 'Retailers, banks under fire over consumer spending', *Arabian Business*, 28 June. http://www.arabianbusiness.com/523179-retailers-banks-under-fire-over-consumer-spend ing?ln=en. Accessed 3 November 2008.

15.   Ditcham, Robert (2006) 'Low-cost mall to open in Al Quoz Industrial area', *Gulf News*. 7 August. http://archive.gulfnews.com/articles/06/07/07/10052207.html. Accessed 16 November 2008.

16.   *The Economist* (2004) 'In the shadows', 17 June. http://www.economist.com/finance/display Story.cfm?story_id=2766310. Accessed 20 February 2008.

17.   Tharoor, Shashi (2008) 'A spreading danger', *International Herald Tribune*, 9 July.

18.   The number of these 'illegals' varies and they are frequently subjected to deportation once caught; usually they enter on a visit visa, overstay, and thus their status turns to illegal; in 2007 an amnesty was granted for these workers; by turning themselves in they would be spared a penalty and are allowed to return home; see for example Malik, Talal (2008) '83,000 illegal residents in Dubai', *Arabian Business*, 18 February. http://www.arabianbusiness.com/511539-83000-illegAl resi dents-in-dubai?ln=en. Accessed 1 March 2008.

19.   Porteous, Tom (2006) 'Dubai Inc. and the war on terror', *Agence Global*. http://www.agence global.com/article.asp?id=833. Accessed 23 February 2008.

20.   A residential district initially planned as a low-cost housing suburb for locals in the 1960s. In the early 1980s a large Omani contingent, about 8000 originally displaced from Zanzibar in the 1960s, were offered housing in what is known as Hamdan Colony, which dominates the district today. In the late 1970s and early 1980s as locals moved out, the area was being developed into a residential district with low-income public housing schemes (also see Wilson; 1999).

21.   Phillips, Alex (1998) 'Counterfeit Clobber', *Al Shindagah*, September. http://www.alshindagah. com/september98/counterfeitclobber.htm. Accessed 12 February 2008.

22.   Lo Dico, Joy (2008) 'Head for heights in Dubai', *The Independent*, 19 April. http:// www.independent.co.uk/travel/middle-east/head-for-heights-in-dubai-811621.html. Accessed 3 November 2008.

23.   A recent media report in the local English newspaper describes the nuisance which these illegal vendors pose, also noting that there is a fine of up to 5,000 DH for participating in any transaction involving fake merchandise: 'Vendors hide in the numerous alleys that connect to the Gold souq from the central district's business areas... The vendor said that his target is to sell half a dozen counterfeit watches every day. "There is a lot of competition in this field. I work on a commission basis and so my earning depends on how much I am able to sell. You will be surprised at the number of residents coming to buy counterfeit goods from us. It is easy to sell counterfeit goods to young tourists who are unaccompanied by grown ups' (Menon, Sunita (2008) 'Clamour of hawkers with fake goods drive shoppers away', *Gulf News*. 22 August, p. 5).

24.   Hilotin, Jay B. (2007) 'Dubai's own little Manila', *Xpress*, 19 October. http://www.xpress4me. com/news/uae/dubai/20003763.html. Accessed 14 January 2007.

25.   Saberi, Mahmood (2007) 'Shedding a look, but not the bargains', *Gulf News*, 21 December, p. 9.

26.   Kutty, S. (2002) 'Meeting point, message circle', *Khaleej Times*, 29 May, p. 7.

27.   Gulf Today (2008) 'Indian groups collect DH 600,000 for victims', *Gulf Today*, 7 April.

28.   Al Serkal, Mariam (2008) 'Bur Dubai Meena Bazaar remains a good deal', *Gulf News*, 18 April. http://www.gulfnews.com/nation/Heritage_and_Culture/10206478.html. Accessed 18 April 2008.

29.   *Ibid*.

30.   Sciolino, Elaine (2008) 'Smitten by Lyon, a visitor tries to recreate the magic', *The New York Times*, 28 January. http://www.nytimes.com/2008/01/28/world/europe/28lyon.html?_r=1&oref=slogin. Accessed 1 March 2008.

31.   For further information on this see Elsheshtawy, Yasser (2008) The global and the everyday: situating the Dubai spectacle', in Kanna, Ahmed (ed.)*The Superlative City Dubai and the Urban Condition in the Early Twenty-First Century*. Cambridge, MA: Harvard University Press; also Elsheshtawy, Yasser (2008) 'The Impact of Globalization on the Sustainability of the Arab City'. *Report on the Status of the Arab City*. Beirut: UN-ESCWA.

32.   Reuters (2007) 'Gov't plans to overhaul old Dubai', *Arabian Business*, 25 November. http://www.arabianbusiness.com/504726-govt-plans-to-overhaul-old-dubai. Accessed March 1, 2008. According to the report: 'The developer … plans to transform some of the city's older districts, including Satwa, Al Wasl and Al Safa, areas housing thousands of people living in villas and low-rise apartment buildings'. There are also frequent reports about relocations of old markets to outlying areas; in addition labourers are housed in labour camps far removed from the city.

33.   Menon, Sunita (2006) 'Move out board tells Rashid colony tenants', *Gulf News*, 1 November. http://archive.gulfnews.com/articles/06/11/01/10079087.html.

Chapter 8

Transient City:
Dubai's Forgotten Urban Spaces

'The panorama-city is a 'theoretical' (that is, visual) **simulacrum**, *in short a picture, whose condition of possibility is an oblivion and a misunderstanding of practices. The voyeur-god created by this fiction, who, like Schreber's God, knows only cadavers, must disentangle himself from the murky intertwining daily behaviors and make himself alien to them. The ordinary practitioners of the city live 'down below', below the threshold at which visibility begins. They walk – an elementary form of this experience of the city; they are walkers,* **Wandermaenner**, *whose bodies follow the thicks and thins of an* **urban 'text'** *they write without being able to read it.'*

'The networks of these moving, intersecting writings compose a manifold story that has neither author nor spectator, shaped out of **fragments of trajectories** *and alterations of spaces: in relation to representation, it remains* **daily** *and indefinitely other.'*

'A **migrational**, *or metaphorical, city thus* **slips** *into the clear text of the planned and readable city.'*

Michel de Certeau (1984) *The Practice of Everyday Life* (my emphasis)

Chapters 4 to 6 looked at Dubai's historical origins and developments and discussed the various planning and architectural strategies employed to establish its credentials as a global city. Beginning in Chapter 7 and continuing in this chapter I am setting up a counter narrative by looking at the city's less spectacular aspects. In Chapter 7 my focus was on the retail environment and in this chapter I look at the city's urban public spaces – the gathering spaces of the low-income inhabitants, migrants, workers and others. These spaces are hardly discussed in the literature on Dubai which is dominated by writers who have merely experienced the city in passing, leading to all sorts of misrepresentations focusing on extremes: luxurious megaprojects or the abject squalor of desert-based labour camps. Both clearly exist, but within this spectrum is a wide range of settings that defies easy categorization and seems to escape the gaze of observers – the spaces of everyday life.

Even a brief visit would confirm that Dubai is not a city in the conventional sense, but rather a set of 'cities' connected by a network of highways, where there hardly any pedestrian circulation and everything is geared towards consumption (Figure 8.1). This is, of course, the planner's view – a view from above, where

8.1. Observing the spectacle – a visitor at the 2007 Dubai Cityscape exhibition.

successful cities are conceived as nodes on a network, command points in a global economy. Here, there are no real people – merely passive consumers, following the dictates of global capitalism as espoused by theories of spectacle which I have discussed in previous chapters.

But, if one is to truly understand the city of Dubai, one needs to move in closer, to places where everyday life takes place. There one will find a series of vibrant spaces which offer a sense of comfort and inclusiveness for the city's migrants – thus creating a 'migrational city' which 'slips into the planned city' according to Michel de Certeau (1984). The significance of these spaces stems from the fact that they are a 'haven' for the city's multi-ethnic community, a setting where users from lower socio-economic backgrounds can interact, without having to enter into the more exclusive zones reserved for higher-income segments of society.

By focusing on the spaces of the everyday, rather than the abstract spaces of economic flows, I am responding to a shift in global city research whereby the emphasis has moved towards establishing uniqueness and differences between cities, rather than similarities. To that end, I have conducted an extensive survey of Dubai's urban public spaces, in areas such as Deira, Satwa and Karama, used by the low-income population. Through this narrative I attempt, using de Certeau's constructs, to read the 'urban text' written by the city's migrants.

My examination of the spaces of the everyday is preceded by a description of Dubai's unique urban geography, as well as its position as a primary migrant city and all the problems which that entails. This part also includes information on the city's migrants. The purpose here is to set the stage for the survey which follows.

Here, I offer an analysis of these 'forgotten' urban spaces, situating them within the city and showing how they are a prime example of what I have called 'transitory spaces'. I follow this by discussing the strategies which are employed by the city to turn it into an exclusive space reserved for the rich – specifically through its housing policy. I conclude the chapter with an attempt to identify some of the unique qualities of these transient settings and how they have become a way of identifying transnational cities – a category which seems to describe Dubai more accurately than 'global city'.

But I begin, as in the previous chapters, with a theoretical framework. Dubai, in its efforts to become a global city, has in fact been following the dictates of global city theory, particularly in matters related to social exclusion and the role of migrants etc. It would therefore be helpful to establish what the literature tells us about global cities and how that construct itself underwent numerous transformations, leading to a more specific approach tied to local contexts, hence the emergence of 'transnational cities' (I discuss this in more detail and as it relates to Arab cities in general in Chapter 2).

Globalization and Cities

The global city construct, initially articulated by Friedmann and Wolff (1982) and further developed by Saskia Sassen (2001) and many others, underwent numerous transformations. Moving away from its earlier focus on certain cities (London, New York, Tokyo) or on certain regions (the Western hemisphere), together with a growing realization of its historicity, prompted many writers to call for a re-examination (e.g. Robinson, 2002; King 1990a, 1990b; Abu Lughod, 1995). Due to these criticisms a shift has occurred in global city theory, focusing on 'other' cities as well as re-examining notions pertaining to some of its main constructs. Namely, social exclusion (or polarization) and the extent to which local agents interact with globalizing influences. Underlying these reconstitutions is a realization that people are not passive recipients of globalizing influences, but are actively engaged in shaping and modifying them. This has also been called an 'agent-centred' critique of globalization and that a more accurate depiction would be 'globalizing cities' (Marcuse and van Kempen, 2000; Brenner and Kiel, 2006). The following sections establish some of the criticism that has been directed at the global city rhetoric and illustrate the shift that has occurred in more recent scholarship.

Social Exclusion

Social exclusion or polarization was considered one of the main identifying characteristics of global cities (e.g. Friedmann, 1986). Yet the notion of exclusion needs to be more clearly defined. It does exist in a variety of forms and degrees and in some instances is critical to maintaining a balanced urban order. Urban sociologist Ali Madanipour (1998, p. 183) notes that the 'overall constitution of the social world is such that different forms of exclusion are fundamental to any social relationship' and that 'we are all engaged in exclusionary processes that are essential for our social life'. He argues that these processes of integration are placed on a continuum where we have two extremes with a wide variety between them. Looking at globalizing cities we can see that there is indeed great variation in the extent to which exclusionary practices are expressed spatially. These may range from the explicit (walled compounds; security cameras; armed guards etc.) to more subtle means whereby exclusion is communicated via environmental cues and the marking of boundaries (location; luxurious entranceways; distance from public transport; etc.). Recent scholarship has begun to address these subtle distinctions whereby the boundaries between rich/poor are, in some instances, not clearly defined (e.g. Nagy, 2006; Leonard, 2007). Cities in the Arabian peninsula, for example, do not have ethnic spaces that are marked by 'rigid and threatening' boundaries, as Sharon Nagy (2006) has pointed out in her examination of Doha, Qatar; similarly, Katie Walsh (2006) explores the life of a British expatriate hairdresser living in the low-income district of Satwa, Dubai, describing her interactions with a variety of ethnic groups. Contrast this with São Paulo's characterization as a 'city of walls' by Theresa Caldeira (2000).

The Local/Global Dichotomy

Another construct which is beginning to receive critical attention is the local/global dichotomy. Typically, the global is viewed as a space of sameness and economic flows while the local becomes the site of difference, struggle and resistance. Such categorizations have resulted in epistemological problems critiqued by a number of authors such as Janet Abu-Lughod (1995) and David Ley (2004). This view is also echoed by Michael Peter Smith (2005), who argues that they are an outcome of 'urban structuralism' where we have a global-local dialectic in which there is a 'systemic disjunction between local and global processes'. Given the limitations of the global-local dichotomy, there is a need for what Ley calls 'theoretical adjustments', incorporating other scales which would include the regional, national and supra-national (but not yet global). Lisa Benton-Short (2005, p. 957), for example, notes that: 'global immigrant destinations are the nodes from which complex linkages are formed with the economic periphery', citing as evidence the immigrant population in Amsterdam who form 'transnational' networks with their countries of origin.

Fixed Categories

Another criticism directed at world city research is that it propagates the categorization of cities, thereby 'privileging' the West as the source of 'economic dynamism' (Robinson, 2002). Cities are classified, ranked and so on, based on purely economic criteria – for example, the number of headquarters of transnational corporations, banks and law firms. Influenced by Sassen, the work of the Globalisation and World Cities (GAWC) Research Network in the UK is representative of this approach (Beaverstock *et al.*, 2000). Much criticism has been directed at this kind of ranking and categorization. In this view, a city's success is measured by the extent to which it has become global – which may have serious consequences for the poor or those without access to 'global resources' (Berner and Korff, 1995).

Jennifer Robinson (2002, p. 540) highlights the need for a 'view from off the map', noting that through such categorizations '… other aspects of city life in these places are obscured, especially dynamic economic activities, popular culture, innovations in urban governance and the creative production of diverse forms of urbanism'. She calls for more '… creative ways of thinking about connections across the diversity and complexity of city economies and city life' and for 'cities without categories' (*Ibid.*, p. 542). This new approach – looking at ordinary cities – places great emphasis on transnational connections; a spatialized account of 'the multiple webs of social relations' – thus these 'ordinary cities' have the possibility to imagine 'their own futures and distinctive forms of city ness' (*Ibid.*, pp. 545–546). In a similar vein Michael Peter Smith (2001, p. 246) argues for what he calls 'transnational cities' – sites which are characterized by diverse urban experiences and criss-crossing networks which 'defy easy boundary setting'.

Hybridity

The classic view of hybridity, a concept articulated by Homi Bhabha (1994) and others, suggests that the 'global citizen' engages in a fusion process where old and new cultures intermingle, creating new forms, and through this a detachment from participating cultures can occur. According to Salman Rushdie (1991, p. 394), the migrant (the ultimate hybrid subject) 'celebrates … impurity, intermingling, the transformation that comes of new and unexpected combinations'. This concept received considerable scrutiny within the cultural studies literature, for example, Nezar AlSayyad (2001) in *Hybrid Urbanism*, or Jane Jacobs (2001) in *Edge of Empire*. AlSayyad (2001, p. 8), making the case for hybridity, argues that in cities throughout the world globalization led to creation of 'third places', in-between spaces of 'spatial reconciliation of incommensurable constructions of subcultures'.

For some, hybridity and cosmopolitanism have become closely intertwined and, based on this, it has been argued that they are a 'predisposition of intellectuals' and 'bear an awkward elitism' (e.g. Hannerz, 1991; Anderson, 1998). Calhoun (2002) describes it as 'the class consciousness of the frequent traveler'. Mitchell (1997, p. 535) argues that 'the hype of hybridity' is 'increasingly disarticulated from history and political economy'. Cheah and Robbins (1998, p. 301, emphasis added) notes that '… *the hybrid viewpoint belongs to the west*, where its subject, rather than universal humanity's view from nowhere, is no less and no more than "the migrant literary critic in the metropolis"'. Ley (2004, p. 161) describes it as a form of 'elitist universalism'.[1] Hybridity then is another form of imperialism (colonialism), but cloaked in a language that is more palatable.

It seems to me that when we look at social practices (i.e. culture) in relation to urbanism, the notion of hybridity is indeed problematic. Its implied notion of 'fusion', 'happy coexistence', etc does not bear much relation to reality (or only to some aspects). Close examination of migrant communities in *transnational* cities, for example, may reveal the persistence of social practices – which are ultimately reflected in the built environment. I would argue that using hybridity is a 'view from above', disassociated from daily practices. A 'view from below' is needed that would closely link observation and understanding of daily practices to urbanism and in turn feed into our understanding of how global processes affect our cities.[2] There are countless examples for such an approach such as Tim Bunnell's (1999) assessment of skyscraper development in Malaysia.[3] Another excellent study is by Lisa Benton-Short *et al.* (2005) ranking immigrant cities, and calling for an emphasis on 'cultural globalization'.

Towards a Grounded Transnational Paradigm

An emerging body of research is beginning to respond to this growing criticism, dubbed by Peter Smith (2005) 'second wave globalism'. A new, more accurate heuristic approach is being used – transnationalism – which is defined as multiple ties linking people across the borders of countries, establishing various networks prompted by advances in telecommunications. According to Vertovec (2005) '... transnational practices and their consequent configurations of power are shaping the world of the twenty-first century'. Transnationalism has become associated with resistance, a subversion of global processes (Al-Rasheed, 2005), while in transnational sites we encounter places which, according to Peter Smith (2005), are 'pregnant' with power relations, where one observes relations of dominance/ accommodation/resistance, all occurring simultaneously. Within such sites both global (interacting with home countries; sending back remittances) and local processes (daily life interactions; meeting others; visiting a mall; social resistance to perceived injustices) occur almost simultaneously with one flowing into the other effortlessly.

One significant methodological concern is for research on transnationalism and diaspora to be 'grounded' in the everyday practices and lives of individuals (e.g. Ley, 2004). Transnationalism and migration are now understood as processes 'constituted through the dialectical relations of the grounded and flighty, the settled and the flowing, the sticky and the smooth' (Jackson *et al.*, 2004, p. 8). Thus, grounding research on transnationalism is about recognizing that it is locally lived and produced with particular people 'making their daily lives across worlds' (Lamb, 2002). Looked at in this way, the notions of social exclusion and the local/global dichotomy, discussed earlier, acquire more nuanced dimensions, recognizing that they are defined/practiced by local agents, who in turn modify their meanings and manifestations. Within the context of cities in the Arabian Peninsula – specifically Dubai, home to more than 200 nationalities[4] – such processes are intensified and observing them would make a substantive contribution to this debate.

Dubai, a Migrant City?

A recent study by Lisa Benton-Short *et al.* (2005) ranking cities in terms of immigration revealed that Dubai is at the top of the list based on the number of foreign born (82 per cent) followed by Miami (51 per cent) and Amsterdam (47 per cent). As the authors point out the data deceptively suggest diversity and multi-culturalism; a closer look reveals that a majority of the foreign-born are from one region – 67 per cent are from India and Pakistan (figure 8.2), in addition to not being a city (country) that allows immigrants to become citizens (obtaining citizenship for expatriates is next to impossible and can only be attained via a special government decree). The city has, in fact, a population structure that is

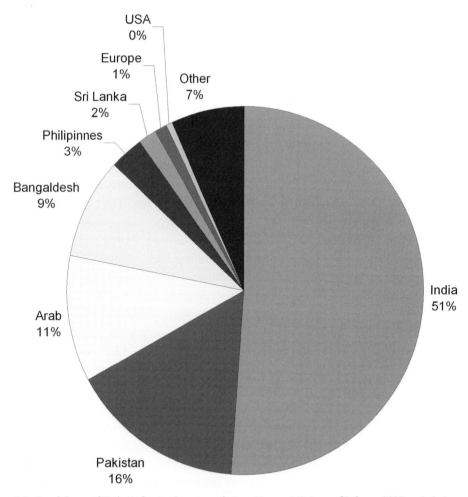

8.2. Breakdown of Dubai's foreign born population. (*Source*: Ministry of Labour, 2005 statistics)

unique in the world. In the absence of any official statistics, estimates put the local population at around 10 per cent. Yet two informants have suggested to me that the real proportion is only about 4 or 5 per cent.[5]

Furthermore, the demographic imbalance is evident in the male/female ratio. According to statistics for 2006, released by the Dubai Statistics Department, out of a total population of 1.422 million around 75.5 per cent were male while 24.5 per cent were female.[6]

Being a minority in one's own country has, understandably, caused some anxiety. A government official notes that 'We are facing a grave issue that demands a swift solution. We are shackled and I want a solution now before I become a mere one per cent', and 'the flood of the foreign labour was wiping out the character of the country where some areas now resembled parts of India or Pakistan' (quoted in Davidson, 2005). In an effort to control this, a recent government decision has labelled the large expatriate population as 'temporary workers', as opposed to immigrant workers. More recently, efforts are underway to introduce a law which would set a maximum stay of 6 years for unskilled labourers. On the other hand, it is not possible for expatriates of any kind to obtain citizenship irrespective of the number of years spent in the country.[7] Examining data pertaining to length of stay in the city shows that for the majority it varies between 4 and 15 years, and for a sizeable number exceeds 20 years. Furthermore a breakdown by level of education shows that on average those with a higher degree (i.e. skilled) stay longer (table 2a and 2b).

Table 2a. Length of stay for Dubai's immigrant community.

Period of Residence (years)	<1	1–4	5–9	10–14	15–19	>20
	2.6%	8.3%	8.3%	9.5%	5.1%	6.7%

Source: Dubai Municipality; 2000 data.[8]

Table 2b. Length of stay for Dubai's immigrant community based on level of education.

Period of Residence (years)	<1	1–4	5–9	10–14	15–19	>20
Basic Education	0.5%	8.2%	5.8%	2.5%	1.2%	1.8%
Higher Education	1.4%	13%	8.1%	4.2%	2.6%	3.5%

Source: Dubai Municiaplity; 2000 data.[9]

Those who have lived in the city since birth number 24 per cent. Yet unlike other places where residents are given the option of permanent residency or citizenship, as I noted earlier no such possibility exists in Dubai. Thus the general sense of living in Dubai for its long-term population is that of a visitor – somebody who eventually leaves regardless of how long they stayed.[10] For those who were born in Dubai the problem is even greater, with one resident noting: '… if people like us who may spend another 30 years of their lives here – our future is as uncertain as someone entering the UAE for the first time'.[11] Further adding to the tenuous status of migrants is the sponsorship system (*kafala*, the Arabic term connotes that someone is 'being taken care of'), whereby each foreign labourer must be sponsored by a local (named *kafil*) who in some instances withholds passports, or prevents workers from switching jobs etc. The system has been criticized for giving employers too much power over their employees (e.g. Gardner, 2008).

Housing such a large expatriate population has its own problems. A study by Zachariah *et al.* (2004) on Indian workers points out that 26 per cent of immigrants lived in apartments and another 27 per cent in portions of apartments in the cities of Abu Dhabi, Dubai and Sharjah. Another 15 per cent lived in rented rooms in cities. The rest (about one-third) lived in worker camps. The majority of immigrants in these cities lived in apartments, in portions of flats or rented rooms and paid rent from their earnings. The authors note that two-thirds belonged to this category. Furthermore, in Dubai, labour camps are located 15 km away from the city (in Sonapur) where 88 per cent live in rooms with average occupancy ranging between four and eight. Even within the city recent rent increases have led many low-income workers to rent bed-space, share accommodation in squalid high-density conditions, or even to sleep in the city's public spaces and parks – heralding the emergence of a homeless population. These remain the only alternatives in the absence of any effective low-cost housing programme.[12]

The lives of Dubai's migrant community have been widely documented in the popular press as well as in various human rights reports. The focus here is mostly on the city's construction workers, who number roughly 300,000 according to Human Rights Watch (2006). They are employed by various contractors and development firms who house them in labour camps. The abject conditions under which these workers live has been pointed out in a Human Rights Watch Report, following visits to several of these sites. For most of these workers the city represents a distant image which can only be seen from buses taking them from their accommodation to the construction sites. At weekends travel to the city is either too expensive or they simply prefer to stay with their compatriots at the camps. Until 2007 public transport was dilapidated, with old buses and no airconditioning, unlike the well maintained buses in the city itself.[13]

Another aspect of this problem pertains to the 'bachelors' who live in the city itself and are employed in its service sector. According to some estimates there are about 500,000 bachelors living in Dubai. Many are married but cannot afford, or are not allowed, to bring their families. They usually rent rooms in villas located in various neighbourhoods in the city. The authorities are increasingly seeing them as a blight on the city's carefully maintained image and are issuing eviction notices. Another sign that the city is increasingly 'turning its back' on these people is that the ultra luxurious shopping malls, 5-star hotels, and waterfront developments are geared to a very specific segment of society. While low-income people are not explicitly excluded, there are numerous signs and measures which indicate that they are not welcome. For instance, luxurious developments such as the Mall of the Emirates, or Madinat Jumeirah are located far away from the traditional city core and are designed to be primarily accessible by car; Deira City Center, a mall in the centre of the city, is surrounded by multilane highways and is almost impossible to access except by car, which according to Graham and Marvin (2001, p. 269) is a form of 'geographical distancing and biased infrastructure development'. The Burj Al Arab, the ultimate Dubai icon, actually has a gate physically preventing people from entering (unless a substantial fee is paid to be used at one of the hotel's facilities or, more recently, with a reservation at one of the luxurious restaurants and bars); in some instances the sheer extravagance of these projects acts as a psychological barrier to entry (as is the case with luxurious developments in many other cities). Public parks, while meticulously maintained and containing a variety of facilities, charge entrance fees. And more alarmingly, the authorities are beginning to contemplate building 'luxurious labour camps' with shopping and entertainment facilities far removed from the city – in a way discouraging those lower-income groups from entering the city in the first place.[14] My focus is on this group and one particular question relates to the degree to which this fractured demographic interacts with, and is reflected in, the city's urban form.

Social Geography

To understand fully the social structure of the city, I mapped its social geography using a methodology applied in London by Charles Booth at the end of the nineteenth century and applied to contemporary London by *The Economist* using 2001 census data (Cross, 2006; also Buck *et al.*, 2002). While Dubai lacks reliable statistical data, I used similar categories, assigning the following labels to its districts: wealthy; well-off; middle; poor. This categorization was based on a number of factors: density (from Dubai Municipality maps as well as site visits); housing conditions; use of public space; land use; character of population. The results are unavoidably impressionistic yet they nevertheless convey a preliminary social make-up of the city's spaces (figure 8.3).

The social geography analysis shows that the low-income population is concentrated in the central areas of Deira and Bur Dubai as well as parts of Jafiliya and Satwa. This excludes, of course, worker camps which are outside the metropolitan area within the desert (the most notorious, Sonapur, is located along Emirates Road and, as mentioned above, 15 km from the city; others are in Jebel Ali which is remote from any significant built up area). It is also of interest to note that areas of extreme poverty are located in close proximity to wealthy areas; for example, the run-down houses of Satwa contrast sharply with the 5-star hotels of Sheikh Zayed Road; or the ultra-luxurious Burjuman Mall juxtaposed with the middle-income area of Karama, and so on. What is also striking is that settings of extreme poverty tend to be somewhat hidden behind a 'veneer' of landscaping and well-off high rises. Venturing behind buildings along Baniyas Road in Deira, for example, will reveal a poor area, housing mostly Asian labourers. It should be noted that these are soft boundaries – in other words it is easy to penetrate these edges, and in some instances they are visible from the main street.

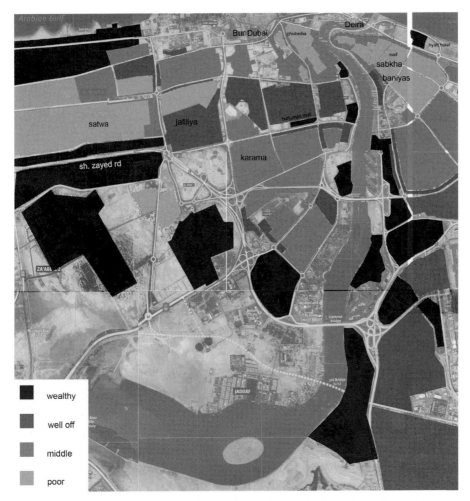

8.3. A social-geography analysis of Dubai indicating the distribution of areas by social status. (*Source*: Author)

Surveying the City's Urban Public Spaces: Transitory Settings

In surveying the city's urban public spaces my main criterion for identification was that they should be central gathering points for the migrant population, easily accessible, and contain a variety of activities as well as users. The following four sites and the areas surrounding them fulfilled these criteria: Baniyas Square, which also includes the Sabkha bus stop; the Ghubeiba bus stop in Bur Dubai; the Satwa bus stop; and, to a lesser extent, the Karama district (figure 8.4). These settings are located within poor to middle areas, surrounded by well-off and wealthy districts. They are not directly visible from the city's main highways and roads, but well-off/wealthy areas have to be 'penetrated' in order to access them, although the notion of soft boundaries, the ease of access, still applies. Thus, they are indirectly removed from the awareness of city residents, or are conceived as poor and dangerous places, filled with 'Indians' – according to popular perception.

8.4(*a*). An overall view of Dubai's central area indicating areas identified for mapping. (*Source*: Collage based on aerial imagery by courtesy of Dubai Municipality)

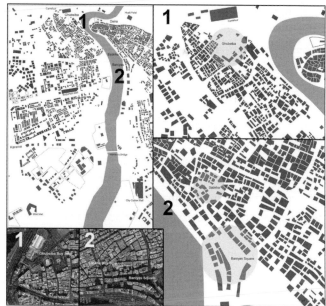

8.4(*b*). Figure-ground diagrams of selected areas identified for mapping. (*Source*: Drawings based on maps by courtesy of Dubai Municipality and Google Earth)

The methodology adopted for studying these spaces is qualitative and included a period of observation which involved note-taking and extensive photography. Many activities during the summer months take place at night. As such, some photographs were taken using long exposure times (10 seconds to 3 minutes). The resulting images convey some of the dynamism present. In addition, reaction to my presence provided me with some interesting data and gave me the opportunity to be immersed in the setting. Interviews, whenever possible, were conducted with people using the spaces. I have also used data from three informants, residents of Dubai, who supplied me with some inside information, critical due to the inherent difficulty in conducting fieldwork in the city.[15]

1 by the previously developed framework, I began with the following
Who are the main users of these settings? What activities do they
engage in? In addition, I was interested in the main nodes of gathering: Where
are they located? Also, I wanted to know the nature of land use in these spaces,
the type of stores, etc. In terms of cultural issues, how do residents display
their cultural background: Are there specific signs or markings, or do they hide
them? It should be noted that I am approaching this not as a social scientist, a
geographer, anthropologist or economist. Instead, coming from an architectural
background, and grounded in the methodologies of environment-behaviour
research, my main interest is in the interaction between the built environment
and human behaviour. This follows in the tradition of environment-behaviour
studies (EBS) using the work of pioneers in this area such as William Whyte and
Jan Gehl, who looked at the behaviour and interaction of users in public spaces in
New York and Scandinavian cities (Whyte, 1980; Gehl, 1987). I should also add
that there are considerable problems in conducting field research in the Middle
East, and in the Gulf specifically – plain clothes security are everywhere and I had
several encounters simply for photographing people. Thus information obtained
through observations and interviews is supplemented by secondary sources such
as newspapers and content analysis of media reports.

Description of the Spaces, Activities and Users

The four settings which I identified: Baniyas, Sabkha, Ghubeiba and Satwa have
several characteristics in common: location next to public transport (bus stops);
intense levels of commercial activity; location within, or in close proximity to,
poor areas. Furthermore, they have the highest residential density in the city,
ranging from 22,000 to 75,000 people per square kilometre (Dubai GIS Center,
2006). They are characterized by a very active and vibrant street life, to the extent
that they are main gathering points for low-income residents. This is particularly
the case for the latter three. I discuss the character and inner life of each of these in
the following sections.

Baniyas Square (whose historical origins and significance were discussed in
Chapter 4) is located in Deira. As can be seen from the social-geography analysis,
it is surrounded by well-off and middle areas. The well-off southern edge is close
to the Creek; the northern edge overlooks the district of Naif, one of the poorest
sections with the highest density. The square represents the heart of the central
business district and was known as a meeting place for Dubai's low-income
expatriate community (prior to its closure in 2006 due to the construction of a
metro station). Mostly low-income labourers from India, Pakistan, the Philippines
and elsewhere dominated the space. I also observed some Europeans from Eastern
Europe and the former Republics of the Soviet Union. With a few exceptions,
there were no locals. In spite of this absence, the area is well known among locals

due to the variety of shops that offer bargains; also its history as the centre of the city – in many ways signifying its entry into modernity – makes it memorable. One informant told me that the square was known for the presence of a cinema, as well as shops offering luxurious fashion items. However, as locals have moved out from the city centre to suburbs it has become a setting mostly associated with expatriates. Nevertheless, one could argue that by staying in the square it was possible to capture a limited microcosm of the city's population. The setting provided a retreat from work and shopping and allowed its users simply to sit and watch passersby. It also gave an opportunity for low-income workers to meet friends and family (figure 8.5).

The square and its surroundings are a setting for the exchange of messages and receiving news from home. Some low-income workers have no access to e-mail and cannot afford a cell phone. In being able to come to a space like this, they can obtain news from home, or ask someone leaving to send a message back. This has become so prevalent that surrounding areas are divided by nationality and ethnic background. Each member of a group would therefore know where to find his compatriots.[16] The following account is typical of the reason why many hang out in this space and why it is so important:

> Shamsuddin Kevi, from Kerala, who has been working for eight years as a driver in a trading
> company, said he meets his elder brother, Mohammed, an electrician, on most Fridays at the

8.5. Baniyas Square: traffic intersections are conducive to informal gatherings.

Square. 'My vacation is every two years', said Kevi. 'I came back a few months ago. It's hard to stay away from my wife, who's now six months pregnant with our first baby. On weekends, when I'm not busy, I can't help but think about her. I try to pass the time here and see my friends'.[17]

Others like the variety of people and the ability to meet and watch others:

Says Paluku Ndiwa, a buy-and-sell trader from Congo, 'It's like seeing the world pass right before your eyes because of the variety of people you can see in such a small area. It's one of my favourite hangouts with friends on weekends'.[18]

The square also has its share of European tourists, who argue that the space is similar to the squares in medieval Europe;

Kristopher Sretoslevov, an engineer from Bulgaria, likens Baniyas Square to the public square in Sofia. Says Sretslevov: 'This place reminds me of home somehow. Except that there's more variety of people here'. He was having a smoke on one of the benches with his colleague, Radostiu Dimov.[19]

The space is relatively empty during the day because of the heat, but in the evening it is crowded with people. This reaches a climax on Friday (the end of the weekend) when there are large numbers of people throughout the square. Particularly attractive are the green lawns, in the middle of the space, which are a place for people to sleep, eat or simply chat with others. Also, street corners, especially an area near the HSBC Bank, are gathering points for people, who simply stand there and talk while observing passersby. The overall atmosphere is one of relaxation and enjoyment.

The shops bordering the square are a mixture of Western fast food chains (McDonalds, KFC and so on) and regional restaurants catering for the various ethnic groups. The remaining commercial activities are dominated by electronics, clothing, bargain stores etc. In addition, the surrounding narrow lanes are well known for their hardware and building materials outlets. One area in particular is dominated by merchandise from China. The space at night is illuminated by neon signs which convey a vibrant, dynamic character, while two major streets, which define the square, add to the sense of movement present due to constant circulation of traffic. The architecture of the buildings around the square is an eclectic mix of post-modern structures on the more progressive, southern side and 1960s style, concrete structures on the northern side leading towards the traditional town with its maze of alleyways. Overall, the high-rise structures give a sense of containment and protection making it attractive for users.

Sabkha, Ghubeiba and Satwa are closely associated with low-income users, mostly from the Indian sub-continent (Afghanistan, India, Pakistan and Bangladesh;

but also Philippines and China). The Sabkha area is close to Baniyas Square, in the middle of the poor district of Naif. Ghubeiba is located on the other side of the Creek in Bur Dubai, near the historic Shindagha district. Satwa, on the other hand, is further away, bordered by the two wealthy areas of Sheikh Zayed Road and Jumeirah/Um Suqeim, both containing high-end residential villas for the city's well-off expatriate community. These three settings have major bus stops which draw in people from all over the city, contributing to the crowded feeling, particularly at the weekend. These bus stops are surrounded by commercial establishments which cater for the constantly moving, transient users. They include cafés and newspaper stands displaying mostly Hindi magazines and newspapers (figure 8.6). There are also seating areas. The food and drink served in these places are a reminder for the workers of places back home – the drink is similar, tea with milk served in plastic cups; in some instances they are even places for illegal consumption of alcohol.[20]

Because of their close proximity to bus stops, Sabkha and Ghubeiba are major hangouts for passersby. A fascinating sight, they include hundreds of people, simply standing, talking to each other or watching others. These places serve an important communication function. Interviews revealed that people use the space on a regular basis to interact with others and meet friends. People from certain areas in their home countries know where to find their compatriots in Sabkha or Ghubeiba; through them they receive news from home. In addition to these informal modes of communication, I observed a heavy use of mobile phones which many of these workers have; there are also a number of Internet Cafés close by and much used. Thus, ties to home countries are preserved, and these spaces become settings where such transnational connections are retained (figure 8.7).

8.6. Scenes depicting lively gathering areas in and around the Ghubeiba bus stop, dominated by South Asian users.

8.7. Aerial view showing a main gathering area for low-income, predominantly South-Asian users, close to the Ghubeiba bus stop.

Further, highlighting this transnational connection is the ubiquitous presence of money changers, prominently displaying their presence with large signs. These stores tend to be the biggest in the area and the most attractive. In fact they convey the impression that they are the *raison d'être* for the presence of the workers. At weekends and at the end of each month it is a common sight to see large numbers of workers queuing to send their earnings home. Displays such as 'Send money back to Kerala for 10Dh' are quite common. Heavy investment by the UAE government in fibre optics allows for the instant transmission of money to home countries.[21] There are also numerous ethnic restaurants; some, being aware of the multicultural nature of potential clientele, entice customers by noting that the menu contains Indian, Chinese and Philippine specialties; others are limited to a certain ethnic group (e.g. Karachi) and this is made quite clear by means of decorative elements and other signs.

Karama : In comparison to the previous settings, which are anchored to a clearly identifiable space, Karama is a residential district lacking such intense nodes of activity. Furthermore, it has a more middle-class feel as its residents are better off than in Satwa or Ghubeiba. It was initially planned as a low-cost housing suburb for locals in the 1960s – interestingly, with the first running water supplied homes. In the late 1970s and early 1980s as locals moved out, the area was being developed into a residential district for expatriates with low-income public housing schemes developed in 1976 (Wilson, 1999). According to some long-time residents, when they first moved there in the 1970s there were 'no street lights and robberies were common'. One resident describes the scene as follows:[22]

It was very convenient living here; there were Indian restaurants nearby and you could get all the 'garam masalas'. We used to buy cardamoms and cloves and take them home to India as it was cheaper here.

Another description relates to the desolate character of the district at that time:

There were hardly any buildings 30 years ago. There were only sand dunes and people used to come and ride around on their quad bikes.

Because of the dominance of South Asian expatriates, the area is also known as 'Little India'. A walk down any of its streets will be dominated by speech in south Indian dialects and at weekends one would typically find long queues at its various vegetarian restaurants. But the area is increasingly acquiring a cosmopolitan character with a growing Filipino population and there is also a proliferation of Russian and Korean restaurants. Karama Center, in the middle of the district, acts as a community centre of sorts – in addition to selling saris it also holds cultural activities.

Thus, while the majority of Karama's population has traditionally been middle-class South Asian expatriates, other nationalities are represented as well. One notable national community is the Omani contingent, who originally settled in Karama in the early 1980s with the help of Dubai's ruler. About 8,000 Omanis, who were among the tens of thousands displaced from Zanzibar in the 1960s,

8.8. The desolate character of Karama's housing colonies.

later found themselves stateless and homeless until Sheikh Rashid offered them sanctuary with the construction of Hamdan Colony, a collection of apartment blocks which dominates the district's built environment (figure 8.8).

These colonies are for the most part large tracts of residential buildings without any visible sign of life, located in the district's interior areas. The external edges, as well as its main roadways contain a very vibrant and active street life, enhanced by the presence of commercial activities such as a variety of ethnic restaurants. Unlike the previous spaces, because there is no community square or central space, there are no crowded gathering points. Furthermore, the district is located at a crossroads to some of the wealthiest areas in the city. Simply crossing its outer edges and moving inside reveals another world.

Despite the lack of character of the buildings, their anonymity is overcome by a variety of displays signalling the ethnicity of occupants. These include for the most part lights celebrating the Indian Diwali festival, placed in balconies and other outdoor areas and visible even after the festivities. Another prominent feature, to be found in the district's streets, on walls and lampposts, are flyers written by residents, advertising rooms and apartments for compatriots (figure 8.9).

While the district lacks a communal square, there is a large public park, heavily used by a variety of residents, spanning all age groups, as well as the previously mentioned Karama Center, an indoor shopping mall. Teenagers were observed

8.9. Advertisements and signs posted in front of housing colonies are indicative of occupiers' ethnicity in Karama.

using some spaces for skating. A more interesting activity was cricket, a sport popular in the Indian sub-continent (and former British colonies in general), played in several parking lots distributed throughout the district. They become a replacement for settings back home and a way for children and teenagers to retain a distinct cultural identity through engaging in a highly ethnic-specific activity.

Satwa: Among these poor areas is the district of Satwa in the shadows of Dubai's skyscrapers on Sheikh Zayed Road, developed in the late 1960s by Sheikh Rashid to provide decent housing for the local population and consisting of identical 60 x 60 ft plots. The nationals eventually moved to outlying suburbs and turned the houses over to low-income workers. The area has one of the highest densities in the city and houses a variety of nationalities. It also has a high crime rate. One of the curious sights in the district is the presence of shacks built of corrugated iron whose residents are Arabs, without nationality – or *bidoon*; interestingly, I observed a yellow flag – sign of the Shiite Hezbollah group in Lebanon – on some of these dilapidated residences. The area has many narrow alleyways, and an active and vibrant street life. In addition, there are numerous graffiti signs on the walls of the hidden alleyways. A 1995 Dubai Municipality report describes the morphology of the district and outlines various steps that were taken to upgrade the area, such as paving the streets.[23] Walking through the district it is relatively well kept, all buildings have numbers, and there is a very clearly developed street system, all of which are a direct outcome of this report (figure 8.10).

The media occasionally document the plight of residents in this area. One report describes the conditions of a family living in a 'dilapidated shack in Satwa'.

8.10. Shabby housing conditions in Satwa. A flag connotes the religious orientation of one residence.

It notes that they do not have water supplies and occasionally no electricity as well. They are *bidoon*. There are depictions of extreme misery – an insane mother, a mentally challenged sister who was left abandoned and had to be rescued by a charity organization. The father is in jail and is described as alcoholic and abusive.[24] Another report is of a family of five and an unemployed father who have been asked to vacate their house – together with 300 other families – to make way for villa development. The area is occupied by low-income Emirati and *bidoon* families. The family in the article has no running water in the house but they get their supply from 'a well inside the house'.[25] Then there is the story of an Emirati woman – Zahra – who was forced to leave her home due to an eviction notice and resorted to living in a tent (her father's and brothers' homes were too crowded to accommodate her and her children). Her Iranian husband lived in a nearby mosque.[26] Or consider the story of Ayoub Khan, a Pakistani who climbs to the roof of his residence in Satwa to escape the crowdedness of the room which he shares with six others. On the roof he speaks into a cassette player, recording a tape for his family which he intends to send back home.[27] What makes these stories so striking is that they take place a few metres from the high-rises of Sheikh Zayed Road – among which are the Emirates Towers, a symbol of Dubai, and the seat of the government.

An interesting development concerns plans to redevelop the entire district, which has been allocated to a governmental agency, Meraas Holding, which will operate as a real estate agency, developing various sectors of old Dubai including Satwa. Detailed plans were kept under wraps until October 2008 when a model of the development was unveiled at the Cityscape exhibition under the name 'Jumeirah Gardens'. The cost of the project was estimated at Dh350 billion (US$95.28bn) envisioned as 'a fully integrated, mixed-use development project located in the old Satwa area west of Shaikh Zayed Road and flanked by Al Diyafa Street and Safa Park'. It was supposed to cater for a population of 50,000 to 60,000 residents. According to the developer 'The development will redefine living in one of the most popular neighborhoods of Dubai' which, it is casually observed, is 'currently undergoing demolition to pave the way for the new project'.[28]

The master plan includes three buildings by the Chicago architects Adrian Smith and Gordon Gill. The centrepiece is 1 Dubai, a building comprising three towers connected by sky bridges which will be more than 600 metres at its highest point. Other buildings would be spread throughout the gigantic development, along with smaller towers and a park 'half the size of Central Park'. Seven islands will be built just off the coast with mostly low-rise, residential buildings. A 14-kilometre boulevard with a tram system will snake through the project, while water taxis will be available on a network of canals. The company said that Sheikh Mohammed bin Rashid, Vice President of the UAE and Ruler of Dubai, created Meraas to help 'make Dubai a global city'. And the developer notes the significance of this project for Dubai by observing that 'Every great city has a great park. London has its Hyde Park, New York has its Central Park. This will be Dubai Park'.[29] In

2009, following the slowdown of the real estate market in Dubai, the development was put on hold, yet the announcement of the project and the various steps that have been taken reveal some interesting aspects of the city's strategy as well as residents' reactions to such schemes.

Various media reports have been lamenting the district's supposed demise – describing it in almost mythical terms as Dubai's version of New York's Greenwich village – a multicultural nirvana. Yet clearly this vision contradicted with how officials viewed the district – a blight on Dubai's urban landscape. Accordingly, the demolition is necessary because there are a large number of 'illegals' residing in the area. 'Around 60–70 per cent of people in Satwa don't have passports or UAE visas', according to the developer of Jumeirah Gardens, who also argues that 'They live, six to a room, in buildings completely unsuitable for habitation. When the Land Department come round to research how many people need rehousing, they have already scarpered'.[30] This view is also shared by many local residents who told me that they would never dream of setting foot in Satwa since it was a place infested with gangsters and illegals and should be avoided at all costs. No doubt such views were encouraged by media reports.

One report notes, for instance, that an abandoned post office building has become home to bachelors and labourers. Emphasizing the dilapidated conditions, it observes that 'there are stagnant pools of water in the dilapidated post office which is filled with garbage and buzzing with flies'. These men are forced to sleep on newspapers and place their personal belongings in municipal garbage bags. They live in constant fear of getting caught by the authorities but they do not have anywhere else to go. They obtain free food from cafeterias and small restaurants located close to the building and during Ramadan they save money on food as they join others at mosques during Iftar.[31] Of course the fact that this occurs next to some of the most exclusive areas of the city only heightens the sense of urgency for the developers. According to one official:

> These low-quality villas and the illegal inhabitants they house simply cannot continue to exist so close to Trade Center, Sheikh Zayed Road and the heart of the city. Not in such prime real estate.[32]

Given these viewpoints it was quite surprising that within the local – English language – media the demolition was portrayed as a loss to Dubai. Most based their accounts on expatriates who had come to regard the district as representing a sense of authenticity that could not be felt elsewhere in Dubai. A report in *Gulf News* describes the district as 'a tight-knit urban fabric, a dense conglomerate of houses shot through with narrow streets' and that it conceals 'an assortment of urban riches'.[33] It goes on to describe the feelings of the more than 200,000 residents who will lose their homes and businesses.

A film-maker[34] who while not living in the district nevertheless grew fond of it describes it as follows:

It is the quintessential pedestrian neighbourhood. You can walk from one shop to another for all your daily needs – from the tailor to the key cutter to Ravi's for dinner… It's a real community. All the shops are run by the people who own them. People talk to each other and know their neighbours – if they run out of change, they get it from the next shop. Satwa also has a high concentration of workers, who hang around the area after work… Every nationality has its own favourite hang-out spots, which makes this such a lively place in the evenings. Satwa has a unique dynamic which has not been modelled anymore in the newer neighbourhoods.[35]

Another report describes the character of the district in similar, nostalgic terms, noting that a stroll through Satwa 'greets visitors with the smell of roasting chicken, the hubbub of a busy suburb and the bright flashing signs of shops advertising their wares'. Furthermore 'a mechanic rolls a new tyre to a waiting motorist while another wipes the desert dust from a windscreen… Textile merchants throw swathes of multi-coloured fabric into the air, measuring it for their waiting customers'. And, with a great sense of loss, it is noted that Ravi's restaurant has been 'serving up Asian sub-continental food for the past 30 years'.[36] Another publication devoted its main coverage to the 'loss of Satwa' quoting some of its residents who are mostly poor South Asian workers, but also include merchants and traders as well as middle-class Europeans who were simply enchanted by the district's quirky character.[37]

While these media reports convey the sense of loss at Satwa's transformation a more pertinent question would be the degree to which this is felt by city residents – both locals and expatriates. How are they reacting to the destruction of Satwa? Is that sense of loss merely the musings of journalists, artists and others who are evoking a romantic scene that does not correspond to the reality of the area? Uncovering such reactions is difficult in the absence of any effective community organizations, public debates about such matters, or probing non-governmental organizations. Anecdotal evidence of viewpoints can be gleaned from conversations, but these are understandably limited. Increasingly, however, the Internet blogs have become an important source for understanding how such developments are received by the wider population. In one insightful comment a local citizen describes his reaction as follows:

How far Dubai will go? Demolishing lively places such as Satwa. We local people have no peace of mind anymore. Taking our lands and home with a minimal unrealistic compensation. Dubai is throwing its own people out to attract foreigners.[38]

Similar views are expressed in various blogs such as *Life in Dubai* under the title 'Goodbye to Satwa'.[39] Another resident comments on the efforts made by some residents of Satwa to resist eviction:

I know some of those poor residents repainted their houses and spent their scarce income on beautification of their otherwise old villas in order to convince the authorities not to demolish their homes but unfortunately they've lost all. No remedy on their attempts. Unbearable, to listen to the crying, desperate voices of homeless. And yet we have buried our heads under the comfortable blanket of ignorance. Is anybody there to listen?[40]

The same commentator goes on to describe the lively scene of the district and that it is essential to the character of the city as a whole. Its cosmopolitan population is the true 'Dubai identity' and thus its old villas need to be preserved.[41]

For me, perhaps the most memorable sight in Satwa was during Ramadan 2007. It is quite common to set up in various parts of the city what are known as *Iftar* tents, which is the designation of an area for the city's low-income Moslem population who would otherwise not be able to afford breaking their fast; it also serves as a communal gathering space where they can reinforce their sense of religious identity and belonging. While these are usually indoors, a large parking space adjacent to the Satwa bus stop was used for this purpose. The ground was covered with large pieces of cloth while volunteers were dispensing food to hundreds of people. In the background to this rather remarkable scene was the Sheikh Zayed Road skyline – representing a stark contrast to the more down-to-earth activity occurring in front of me. Also, on my way to the *Iftar* area I passed various street vendors selling traditional food typical of India or Pakistan. Here it seems were scenes that represented a counterpoint to the flashy image of Dubai. Poor and not so poor immigrants gathered together to celebrate a religious event, which in some way was an attempt to subvert the surrounding spectacle (figure 8.11).

The Other City

At present the gathering places of the city's low-income community are more or less integrated with the city fabric. They also form a strong part of the urban consciousness of residents, rich and poor. They are recognizable and there is, in

8.11(*a*). Ramadan 2007, a gathering of low-income people for a charity *Iftar* next to the Satwa bus stop.

8.11(b). On their way to the *Iftar* area.

some instances, a strong sense of attachment to them. Yet there is another part of the city – another Dubai even – which remains more or less entirely hidden. This 'other' city is home to the disenfranchised living in public housing projects slated for demolition; bachelors facing the threat of eviction; illegal labourers living in crowded conditions in houses under constant threat; and labour camps, which marginalize and stigmatize their occupants who are actively contributing to the city's development. I will uncover this 'other' city in the following sections.

Rashid Colony

'We won't leave.'

Graffiti writing on one of the apartment blocks in Rashid Colony, Spring 2008

Rashid Colony in Al Ghusais, a neighbourhood near Dubai International Airport, was built in the 1960s. It comprises a series of repetitive 4-storey residential blocks (figure 8.12). In 2006 eviction notices were issued to residents, comprising a mix of low-income expatriate families. They include: a travel consultant from India, who has lived in the UAE for 23 years, 18 of them in the colony; an Egyptian female; a female Pakistani who lives in an apartment rented by her father for 27 years and housing nine members of her family.[42]

My visit to the area in Spring 2008 showed a vibrant community alive with residents from many nationalities as I documented in the previous chapter. Yet, moving closer to the buildings, another picture emerged. Signs of deterioration and foreboding notices of eviction were plastered throughout the complex. There was also an eerie silence as I moved to the inner parts of the colony – as if the place

8.12. A residential block slated for demolition in Rashid Colony.

had been abandoned by its occupants. More telling were graffiti signs – always a sure sign of resistance – with one explicitly stating (in English): 'We won't leave' (see figure 7.21). The passageways within the buildings were dark and narrow, but there were smells of food, sounds of people, footsteps. Emerging from these passageways I observed residents moving from one block to another, seemingly oblivious to my presence. They were wearing 'house clothes' as if the spaces inside the colony constituted a semi-public area allowing them to wear less 'formal' clothing, the building blocks somehow protecting them from prying eyes. Around noon, schoolchildren accompanied by their mothers arrived; they engaged in various play activities at the colony's outer edges (figure 8.13). Moving further inside the colony, elderly women wearing elaborate saris accompanied by their husbands, perhaps parents visiting their children, were taking a walk across the rather inhospitable streets. Clearly, Rashid Colony served an important function in providing affordable accommodation, but the complex did stand in stark contrast to its luxurious surroundings – multi-million dirham villas and apartment blocks.

The decision to demolish the blocks was made because of the – supposedly – poor living conditions, as well as plans for redevelopment of the area (no details have been forthcoming so far). According to Hamui Mounzer, Director of the Properties Department of a Board set up to oversee the development: 'The blocks are over 35 years old. Lack of hygiene over the years has turned them into health hazards'. He said that the Board, in one of the inspections, had come across 20 to 25 people living in a single flat. 'There is no air circulation. Then we also have the problem of tenants sub-letting their flats to blue collar workers. They have turned it into mini labour accommodation. The key money asked by tenants for subletting goes up to Dh50,000'. He said that out of 384 tenants who stay in the three blocks only 180 are families and the rest are single men living together. 'We

8.13. Schoolchildren returning home.

have taken all this into consideration and decided to demolish the blocks. The Rashid Colony will be replaced by low cost residential blocks catering to the middle income group'.[43]

Following the eviction notices, residents protested to Dubai Municipality – and this was widely reported in the English language media. After intense negotiations, the authorities decided to provide them with alternative flats.[44] However, this was received with mixed reactions, mostly because of the high rents asked and the prospect of losing precious social ties and networks established over many years. For example, an Egyptian national, Hanan Mohammad notes: 'Sure, we're going to be provided with relatively cheap accommodation but we're still going to have to pay double the rent'. Another resident Farhana Naeemuddin, 27, from Pakistan, says that although she appreciates the Rent Committee's gesture, she will miss the two-bedroom apartment her father had rented for 27 years. 'We're so happy here. It's convenient, secure, and very close to all amenities. Our neighbours are like our family members'.[45]

While the issue seemed settled, more recently hundreds of residents of Shaikh Rashid Colony went to the Dubai Municipality's City Hall to seek reprieve from what they claim is a three-fold rise in rents. After an hour-long closed-door deliberation, the Municipality's Rent Committee handed down a compromise deal to break the standoff between the landlord, the state-owned Dubai Real Estate

Corporation (DREC), and the residents. According to media reports, the mostly Asian and Arab expatriate residents went home disappointed: the Rent Committee decided that they would now have to pay an annual rent of Dh36,000 for a one-bedroom unit and Dh45,000 for a two-bedroom unit. DREC, established in June 2007 in a merger of the Dubai Development Board and Dubai Real Estate Company, earlier wanted Dh42,000 and Dh55,000, respectively, for the brand-new units, according to residents.

In March 2008, at a meeting between the tenants, representatives of the Board and the Rent Committee, it was agreed that the replacement building will be given to existing tenants for Dh25,000 for one-bedroom units and Dh35,000 for two-bedroom units. The tenants agreed to this as the current market rate for a two-bedroom flat was between Dh60,000 and Dh90,000 in the Al Ghusais area. However, even with this decrease the price was still considered high. According to one resident: 'Shelter is a basic need. For that reason, if we want to seek this new flat, I need to reconsider whether to send my children to school in the UAE' – he currently pays Dh11,000 for a one-bedroom flat in the soon-to-be demolished colony. Another resident said: 'This would leave us with no choice but to send our families back home and work in Dubai as a bachelor'. Though the first batch of alternative accommodation in Muhaisna 1, comprising of 88 flats, was completed in March, most residents said they are unable to afford the alternative apartments.[46] Some said that they would become 'bachelors' – if one adds low-income to this seemingly benign distinction, a person is stigmatized and moves into a category almost comparable to the 'untouchables', as I detail in the following sections.

The Plight of Bachelors

'I work throughout the day and at night I come to this overcrowded small room. I feel like I have been transformed into a machine that works during the day and is put into this box at night.'

A Pakistani worker describing his 'room' in Deira[47]

Dubai's unique population structure discussed earlier is further skewed if one considers the ratio of males to females. Out of Dubai's total population of 1.422 million, around 1.07 million were males while just 349,000 were females. Furthermore, it is estimated that around 500,000 people in Dubai live as 'bachelors'. According to Dubai Municipality all single men and women are categorized as 'bachelors'. However, many so-called bachelors are married, but cannot afford or are not allowed to bring their families. They usually rent rooms in villas located in a variety of neighbourhoods in the city. The authorities are increasingly seeing them as a blight on the city's carefully maintained image and are issuing eviction notices to them. These measures are seen (along with increasing living costs, road tolls, etc.) as growing efforts by the city to remove low-income people.[48]

Thus, a very peculiar situation emerges – unprecedented anywhere in the world, at least in such a direct way. While there are measures to maintain homogeneity within given communities – tax laws, rents and house prices – no one is explicitly excluded. Indeed, if a high-income single executive is searching for an apartment or villa in Dubai, he or she would have no problem finding one. Perhaps, therefore, the word bachelor should be qualified 'low income'. These are some of their stories:

> Sara, a Filipina salesgirl, who lives in Jumeirah, said she along with 15 other women were evicted from a villa in Mankhool about six months ago. 'We were asked to leave after our water and electricity was cut… Five of us shared a flat and we ended up paying double the rent which we were paying in the villa', she said.

> Natasha, a 33-year-old secretary from Moscow, said it was an uphill task to find a flat. 'Every real estate agent demanded more money, especially because we were women. Despite giving assurances that I will not sublet the flat, they asked for more money to rent a flat,' she said.

> Tasleem Rana, a Pakistani banker, said he shares a room in a flat on Al Riqqa Street and pays Dh4,000 a month. 'It is very difficult to find a decent place for a bachelor. Most of the places, which the agents showed me, were like "labour camps" and in very bad shape.'

> … the landlords do not want bachelors in their buildings because they make them filthy… Also there have been complaints of drinking and other anti-social activities,' he said. The bachelors, he said, also sublet rooms which resulted in crowding in the flat as they keep as many as 20 to 30 people in a flat which is meant for only four to six people.[49]

As discussed in Chapter 2, similar situations can be observed all over the Gulf. Yet in Dubai, as can be seen from the quotes above, it has acquired much more acute and intense dimensions. This was further exacerbated by a fire which broke out in a traditional house in Naif, a neighbourhood in Deira, resulting in the death of eleven people and the injury of dozens of others. The house was a two-storey villa complex in which as many as 400 labourers may have been living illegally.[50] An Associated Press report observes that the house had been partitioned into at least thirty rooms, with as many as twenty workers living in some of them. Also, the second storey was a modification to accommodate the extra workers. The report notes that 'Foreign workers are officially supposed to live in labor camps or industrial zones that have been specifically designated for them'. Most of the people living in the house were unskilled labourers who earned up to 800 dirhams, or US$218, a month working as janitors or garbage collectors.[51]

The living conditions of these people are characterized by poverty and overcrowding – this is as close as one can get to a slum in Dubai (figure. 8.14). The fire took place in an area known locally as Satellite Street for its sale of television satellite equipment and other electronic products. The villa was an old Arab-style traditional home with two floors (one floor was added to the original to accommodate more people). Each room had just enough space for bunk beds, three or four beds high, and a radio or television set. Surviving workers told reporters that they took turns to sleep on the beds while the others slept on the floor. Yet, even within such misery there was a sense of community and attachment, what Suleyman Khalaf and Saad Alkobaisi (1999), in their examination of the lives of migrants in the UAE, have referred to as 'reinforcing a sense of identity' by being close together in such a crowded environment. Thus, there was a small kitchen area on all the floors which the workers used to make their meals. A palm tree growing in the middle of the villa, provided workers with a sense of comfort. The neighbourhood around the villa is a busy area populated largely by workers, but tucked behind the busy main road are several old villas that are home to some of the poorest residents of the city. According to one shopkeeper: 'This has become a sad fact of this part of the city. We wonder if anyone is safe here'.[52]

Because of this fire and the intense media attention, Dubai Municipality initiated a campaign called 'one villa, one family' – implementing a rule that would prevent landlords from renting villas or houses to more than one family. Many families in various 'poor areas' of the city, such as Rashidiya, Karama/Mankhool and Satwa, were thus served with eviction notices. To understand the extent of the problem, one landlord in Karama had converted three garages at a villa into accommodation for more than four families.[53] Eviction notices were followed with threats of cutting of utility supplies. In November 2008 more than 4,000 villas housing thousands of people were set to have power and water supplies disconnected as part of the 'one villa, one family policy'.[54]

Violations and illegal extensions are carefully and meticulously documented.

8.14. The back alleys of the district of Naif in Deira.

According to Dubai Municipality statistics for the third quarter of 2008, among the more than 120,000 buildings in Dubai about 1,096 were considered 'violating buildings'. Eighty per cent of these violations were illegal extensions. The district of Naif alone, where the fire took place, had 203 illegal buildings among more than 800 buildings in the area (representing a 25 per cent increase from 2007).[55]

Because of the increasing attention devoted to these 'illegals', the media began reporting on their living conditions, something which until then had been largely ignored. For instance, one report describes in graphic detail the spaces in which the workers live. In one example, it is observed that four men share a one-by-two metre windowless room in one of the many shared accommodations in Naif. Since the length of the room is only slightly more than the height of an adult male, the workers have to make vertical arrangements by having two sleep on a two-level bunk bed while the other two sleep on the tiles beneath. A fan is attached to a wall to keep them cool. These bed spaces are rented out to workers for Dh300 to Dh500 a month. Many of the houses have illegal extensions such as additional floors, bedrooms, bathrooms and kitchens. The extensions are often made with materials such as plywood, which pose a fire hazard. Some of the houses have makeshift kitchens consisting of mobile stoves and gas cylinders a few inches apart in corridors. And:

> A Pakistani worker … shares a room in Naif with seven people. The three-by-four metre room has four bunk beds, all occupied, while another two workers sleep on the floor… 'I work throughout the day and at night I come to this overcrowded small room. I feel like I have been transformed into a machine that works during the day and is put into this box at night'.[56]

These bed spaces are also rented out on a daily basis; in some instances workers resort to living in parks,[57] and in one case more than 200 were found living in cardboard boxes on a construction site.[58] While this is the situation of those residing within the city, the situation becomes increasingly more dramatic and intense if we begin to look at the conditions of construction workers in labour camps – the subject of discussion in the next section.

Labour Camps

'All around, a city of labour camps stretches out in the middle of the Arabian desert, a jumble of low, concrete barracks, corrugated iron, chicken-mesh walls, barbed wire, scrap metal, empty paint cans, rusted machinery and thousands of men with tired and gloomy faces.'
Ghaith Abdul-Ahad, *The Guardian*, 8 October 2008[59]

Closely related to the previous section is the much talked about issue of labour camps in Dubai. A Human Rights Watch report (HRW, 2006) titled 'Building ers, cheating workers' illustrated the extent to which workers live in sub- dard, slum-like conditions. According to the report Dubai, with its glittering new skyline of high-rise buildings and its profusion of luxury resorts and real estate, is the most globally emblematic evidence of the economic rise of the United Arab Emirates. As the UAE undergoes one of the largest construction booms in the world, at least half a million migrant construction workers are employed there. Behind '... the glitter and luxury, the experiences of these migrant workers present a much less attractive picture – of wage exploitation, indebtedness to unscrupulous recruiters, and working conditions that are hazardous to the point of being deadly'. UAE federal labour law offers a number of protections, but for migrant construction workers these are largely unenforced (HRW, 2006, p. 2). As of 2006, when the report was published, there were over 500,000 migrant construction workers in the country. With much of the construction activity concentrated in Dubai, in 2005 there were 304,983 workers employed in that Emirate's construction sector alone.

During visits to the two largest labour camps in Dubai, Al Quoz and Sonapur, Human Rights Watch researchers visited six establishments housing construction workers. A typical dwelling was a small room (12 feet by 9 feet [3.7 x 2.75 m]) in which as many as eight workers lived together. Three or four double bunk beds represented the only furniture in each room. The workers used communal bathrooms and showers outside their rooms.

Sonapur is the most notorious of these labour camps – the 'city of gold' in Hindi. It is a half-hour drive into the desert from Dubai and houses 50,000 workers. According to Jason de Perle, a *New York Times* journalist, the camp 'feels like an army base. Two- and three-story concrete-block buildings stretch across the horizon, throngs of South Asian laborers fill the streets and desert dust fills the air. Even at midnight the camp roars. Buses ferry workers to third-shift jobs. Earthmovers work the perimeter, breaking ground for more dorms'.[60] Another media report describes a typical workday of a worker which starts at 4.30 am and ends at 11 pm. Thirteen people live in one room. Their only day off is Friday which is spent in the camp as well.[61]

During a typical weekend in the labour camps of Sonapur vendors descend, selling vegetables and DVDs and there are also 'illegal taxis'. Labourers engage in activities that remind them of home – cooking local food, watching Bollywood movies, and playing cricket. Most stay in the camp and do not go into the city – citing traffic as the main reason. As such their lives are insulated, oscillating between their place of work and the labour camp. According to one observer: 'the city becomes a distant place, evoked through stories and glimpses caught on the bus ride'.[62]

While Sonapur is located at the city's outskirts, Al Quoz is in western Dubai, bordered to the north by Al Wasl and to the west by Umm Al Sheif, Al Manara and Al Safa (all upscale Western residential neighbourhoods) (figure 8.15). The area comprises four subcommunities which make up the Al Quoz Industrial District. These industrial areas, which occupy much of the south-western city limits, service development projects such as Dubai Marina and Emirates Hills as well as the freezone in Jebel Ali. Al Quoz is being developed by Dubai Municipality as an exclusive industrial area and thus contains labour accommodation units as well as factories and storage facilities. Some of the accommodation units – or camps – accommodate close to 2,000 labourers.[63]

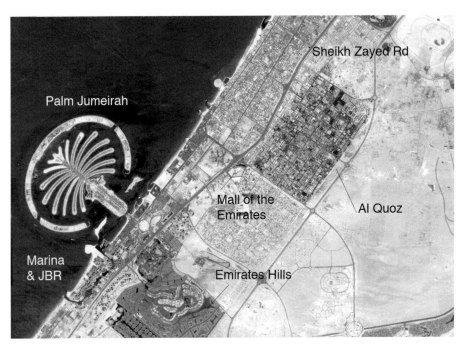

8.15. Location of Al Quoz Industrial Area in relation to some of the city's most exclusive areas. (*Source*: Based on an aerial image obtained by courtesy of Google Earth).

Similar to the sites which I described in the previous section, Al Quoz is not immediately accessible but needs to be penetrated from more well known areas of the city. One means of access is from behind the Mall of the Emirates (home of Ski Dubai). The area is characterized by a rigid street system which discourages any kind of pedestrian movement. In fact most activities observed were around these labour camps and the newly constructed Grand City Mall, which I discussed in the previous chapter. The camps are relatively well maintained although they have an almost 'military' character in the sense that they are surrounded by fences and walls, clothes are left out to dry in outdoor corridors, and many of these residences are marked by large numbers and letters (figure 8.16). Beyond toilets and showers, there are no facilities in the camp. Workers must find and pay for their own food. In one particular camp I observed Chinese paper lanterns hanging on a rope strung along the interior courtyard, indicating the ethnicity of labourers, which confirmed an official policy of segregation 'according to nationality to avoid disputes and fights breaking out'.[64]

There were some lively scenes around the entrances to the residences. In one instance I saw a labourer having a haircut; he was hidden from the main street

8.16. Labour camps housing hundreds of workers in military-style conditions.

behind a tree; other labourers were standing and sitting nearby. There were other areas which were gathering points such as a mosque, grocery and health clinic complex – outside the actual camps (figure 8.17). Overall, the entire district appeared lifeless, yet hidden behind these foreboding walls are stories of real people with aspirations and dreams. For instance, Kamali shares a room with six other men in a sprawling three-floor concrete complex. He describes his life as follows:

8.17. The areas outside some of the housing compounds are used for different activities such as receiving a haircut.

> I spend 200 dirhams [$55] a month on food, which I buy from a local restaurant. I have credit with them which I pay at the end of every month. So far, I have been paid on time by my company, but I worry about how I will live if they withhold payment for any amount of time, as other companies in Dubai have frequently done.

He uses most of the rest of his salary to pay off his debt and support his family in Bangladesh. He also notes that he has no medical insurance but instead his company reimburses him for invoices he brings from a local clinic providing they are below $50. If he does not have the money to pay the clinic up front, he again borrows from friends and incurs more debt.[65]

The spectacular city of Dubai with its rising skyscrapers is clearly visible from Al Quoz, yet for many labourers their lives are restricted to the labour camps and construction sites (figure 8.18). And for the well-off in the city the contrast could not be more striking. In close proximity are some of the most exclusive sites in the city. This is perhaps best expressed by the 'infamous' blogger of 'Secret Dubai':

> I find the degree of contrast in Dubai quite disorienting. In a matter of minutes you can drive from the Al Quoz labour camps to the Burj Al Arab, or Bur Dubai souq to Bur Juman Centre. It's like living in two different cities at the same time. I never cease to be humbled by it. But for an accident of birth.[66]

This notion of separation from the city, providing workers with a self-contained settlement and actively discouraging them from participating in the daily life of the luxurious city is an official policy. Further accentuating this is the government's response to the HRW report whereby they announced the construction of new labour camps, which would be built according to high standards.[67] A series of these

8.18. The spectacular city of Dubai appears at a great distance.

camps is planned for construction at Dubai Industrial City. The residential area is self-contained and will include 'restaurants; grocery stores; banks; medical centres; cinemas and other retail services'.[68] While commendable in a way – it nevertheless maintains a strict policy of segregation allowing for control as well as removing any images of poverty from the city proper. The notion of labourers spending their weekends or time off in the exclusive areas is not encouraged.

Transnational Cities – Transnational Spaces

My aim in this chapter was not just to provide an overview of Dubai's less spectacular spaces but to also create a typology of sorts. A taxonomy which would facilitate comparison with similar spaces elsewhere. As a first step it would be helpful to establish how these spaces relate to each other – are there any common features? And, taken together do they contribute to a new, and perhaps different, understanding of a globalizing city? In looking at these settings, a number of commonalities and interesting observations emerge:

◆   All – with the exception of Karama – are dominated by men (reflecting the city's demographic). In Karama, due to its middle-class residential structure, and being home to families, women are more visible, many of them working in various service sectors (commercial, hospitality, etc.).

◆   Locals are absent – except for those visiting commercial establishments (car repair shops; fashion/fabric stores; electronic appliance and repair shops, i.e. facilities which cannot be found in a modern shopping mall).

◆   Newspapers portray these areas – Baniyas, Sabkha, and Satwa – almost as exotic locales; places where one can find some sort of authentic living, which is contrasted with the high-style of Sheikh Zayed Road.[69] A particularly interesting feature relates to the use of public space. Looking at the gathering points of labourers showed that they occur at the edge of large spaces, empty lots, green lawns, parking lots and next to traffic lights. In other words, incidental spaces which were not planned for such use. Impromptu meetings also take place around non-fixed features such as lottery booths.

◆   These places are not isolated from the city – thus they are easily accessible and in some instances visible from the main roads. Being in them is not threatening, as there is still a sense of the main city being nearby. However informants have told me that some parts in Satwa and Naif become haunts for drug users, prostitutes, and other illegal activities in late hours. Crime rates are high and there are reports of murder and robbery.[70]

◆   Another level of unplanned, anti-social activity is graffiti, observed in the residential areas of Karama and Satwa. Usually written in Arabic, they contain obscenities, soccer proclamations, etc. In some instances they also express political views related to conflicts in the Indian sub-continent. These writings are not along the visible square or spaces, but are hidden and tucked away in alleyways. They offer an interesting counter point to the carefully groomed image of the city (figure 8.19).

The sites which I have analysed defy conventional modes of depiction. A key phrase enabling us to conceptualize them is 'transitory spaces'. These are spaces where by definition one stays only for a brief period of time. Similar to airport lounges, bus stops, railway stations, shopping malls and supermarkets, they are meant as spaces to be passed through, discouraging unnecessary lingering and hence attachment. The previous analysis revealed that there are a number of elements contributing to this transience such as anonymous building character thus minimizing their identity; districts have 'soft' boundaries making them easily permeable thus discouraging the formation of strong communities; and most significantly, the absence of any planned public space, a gathering point for a

8.19. Graffiti in various areas of the city.

community (with the exception of public parks). These spaces exist wherever there are migrants; they are places that, to quote Yeo (2003) who is describing Singapore, 'discourage … emotional attachment to the city as lived place'. This is seemingly a semi-official policy of planning-controlled settings where users interact according to a carefully crafted script dictated by the mandates of global capital. This sense of transience is further intensified by the legal status of expatriates. As noted earlier, there is no possibility of obtaining citizenship; also residency has to be renewed every three years in a lengthy and cumbersome process. Thus, according to one observer, 'foreign workers are perpetual visitors' (Nagy, 2006).

But, strategies are implemented allowing for the construction of 'in-group' identity through the sharing of space, time and food which, according to Suleyman Khalaf and Saad Alkobaisi (1999) in their analysis of the lives of migrants in Dubai, generates intensified forms of sociability. Through these conditions friendships are created which lead to social and moral support:

> These provide the migrants of specific ethnicities, nationalities and cultures with a sense of social balance in globalized multi-ethnic socio-economic structures in which they are not only exploited but also marginalized. The positive functioning of these kin and residence-related social forms of bonding help in the construction of in-group identities as well as maintaining shared inner personal symbols and meanings among the migrants. (Khalaf and Alklbaisi, 1999, p. 293)

Furthermore, these settings are not ghettos in any conventional sense. While relatively remote and not easily visible, they are nevertheless accessible. These areas retain a distinct character – a fact further highlighted by their close proximity to the wealthy areas of Dubai – but they are not excluded completely (not in the sense of Cabrini Green/Magnificent Mile in Chicago, for example; or Teresa Caldeira's (2001) depiction of São Paolo as a 'city of walls'). The local/global dichotomy is not present – both processes are played out – informal modes of communication vs. internet cafes; ethnic restaurants vs. remittance centres, and so on. A transnational trajectory where residents occupy both a local space (the city) and a remote, 'global' setting (home) – a form of polycentredness as noted by Michael Peter Smith (2001). The hybrid nature of global cities may also be questioned by examining such spaces. There is seemingly no mix, no emergence of new traditions. In fact there is a persistence of culturally specific activities: playing cricket; the presence of newspaper stands displaying Indian periodicals and newspapers; segregation of ethnic groups; announcing one's ethnicity through signs, etc. (figure 8.20).

Such spaces are not exclusively tied to Dubai. Anthropologist Marc Augé (1995) in *Non-Places* argues that they have become a distinct sign of *super-modern cities*. He writes:

> If a place can be defined as relational, historical and concerned with identity, then a space which cannot be defined as relational, or historical, or concerned with identity will be a non-place

8.20. Playing cricket in a parking lot in Karama.

> … supermodernity produces non-places, meaning spaces which do not integrate the earlier places … a world thus surrendered to solitary individuality, to the fleeting, the temporary and ephemeral, offers … a new object. (Augé, 1995, pp. 77–78)

Similarly in Dubai, its produced spaces are non-places, characterized by the ephemeral and the transient. But these settings are also places in which there is an 'intensification' of local processes. Residents are expressing themselves and do offer subtle forms of resistance to globalizing influences. One may speculate that these spaces have become characteristic of cities throughout the world, although in most instances they exist side-by-side with fixed settings – places with character and history. In Dubai, however, the notion of transience when applied to its urban environment is *the* defining character. There is no permanence anywhere. Interestingly, as I have tried to show, people are not passive, and even within these anonymous settings, and under adverse economic conditions, they are able to give meaning to these spaces – and perhaps for a brief period of time make them into places.

Notes

1.   He further writes that '… cosmopolitanism itself is always situated, always imbued with partiality and vulnerability … cosmopolitan liberal political philosophy, though inspiring in its universal ambitions, marginalizes other positions while failing to recognize its own limitations. In the same way, transnational capitalists, though posing as masters of space may end up as prisoners of geographical difference' (Ley, 2004, p. 162).

2.   This emphasis on the everyday goes back, of course, to Henry Lefebvre (1974, 1991) in *The*

Production of Space; and Michel de Certeau's (1984) *The Practice of Everyday life* among others. Even David Harvey elaborates on the notion of the 'web of life'. Within urban studies the work of Margaret Crawford (1999), *Everyday Urbanism* is particularly relevant.

3.   Tim Bunnell (1999), in an interesting article on the Petronas Twin Towers of Malaysia, argues that their '… role in national development is not merely aesthetic, envisioning a state conception of Malaysian urbanity; the building also promotes new "ways of seeing" among citizens' (p. 6). In an insightful analysis he presents both a view from above, the extent to which the state uses the tower to further modernization objectives and to establish a Malay identity, and a view from 'below' – how citizens' perception of, and reaction to, the towers plays a role in their representation.

4.   Gupte, Pranay (2009) 'An open season on Dubai', *Khaleej Times*, 19 April. http//www.khaleejti'mes.com/DisplayArticle.asp?xfile=data/opinion/2009/April/opinion_April90.xml&section=opinion&col=. Accessed 13 May 2009.

5.   Khaled and Aysha, personal communication. While locals are a minority, the notion of importing certain nationalities to conduct work is not unique in the world. A survey by *The Economist* on immigration notes: 'Many host countries "specialize" in importing people from particular areas: in Portugal, Brazilians account for 11% of foreigners settling there; in France, Moroccans and Algerians together make up 30% of incomers; and in Canada, the Chinese share of immigrants is more than 15%' (Economist Survey on Immigration, 31 October 2002).

6.   http://uaeinteract.com/docs/Dubai_population_makes_big_surge/24196.htm.

7.   Bowman, J. (2007) 'UAE flatly rejects citizenship for foreign workers', *Arabian Business*, 12 December.   http://www.arabianbusiness.com/506295-uae-flatly-rejects-citizenship-for-foreign-workers?ln=en. Accessed 14 January 2008.

8.   From the Dubai Comprehensive Statistical Survey, 2000. Dubai Municipality. http://www.dm.gov.ae/DMEGOV/OSI/dm-osi-dispatcher?Option=1&category_id=1010205&level_no=5.

9.   *Ibid*.

10.   Expatriates cannot receive a work visa after reaching the age of 65. Generally, this issue receives considerable debate. A senior editor for a local English daily for example observes: 'Regardless of how many years I will end up living in the UAE, of one thing I am certain. It is that I shall always look upon myself as a guest in this country… I learnt this lesson soon after arriving in the UAE about 30 years ago' (Coates, N. (2006) 'We came, we work, we go', *Gulf News*. http://archive.gulfnews.com/indepth/labour/Opinion/10049956.html. Or consider the following online comment in a business publication: 'I have worked in UAE since 1973. I constructed the first bridge in Al Ain in that year and the late Sheikh Zayed used to visit the site weekly. I used to shake his hands every week so don't I deserve to be a permanent UAE citizen? I love the UAE but I'll soon be 65 and I'll have to leave because by law you can't get a work permit if you are over 65' (http://www.arabianbusiness.com/506295-uae-flatly-rejects-citizenship-for-foreign-workers?ln=en).

11.   The statement deserves to be read in full (from an online comment on an article on immigration): 'My parents came to the UAE 31 years ago when the exchange rate to the rupee was 1:2, that's right – people were getting two rupees for every UAE dirham. They were brought to the UAE to work in appalling conditions, yet they stayed here and slowly their extended families moved here. Today, when our parents are crossing 65 and approaching retirement age they are conscious to go back. However, children are in a moral dilemma because their lives, jobs and friends are in the UAE. If you think they contributed nothing to the development of this country in 30 years, then really I don't know what more to say. Not everyone is a Choithram and a Jashanmal in UAE or are you saying that the benefit of citizenship is reserved purely for the ultra rich? The large majority of expatriates lead honest, straightforward middle class lives. Now, if people like us who may spend another 30 years of their lives here – our future is as uncertain as someone entering the UAE for the first time' (http://www.arabianbusiness.com/506295-uae-flatly-rejects-citizenship-for-foreign-workers?ln=en).

12.   Gale, I. (2006) 'Low-cost housing remains a distant dream in Dubai; most of the new residential projects are aimed at high-income earners', *Gulf News*, 10 June.

13.   This was pointed out in a letter published in *Khaleej Times*, 10 July 2007, p. 13. The writer describes the condition of buses to Sonapur and Alghusais areas which contain labour camps.

14.   See Egbert, C. (2007) 'Dubai to build $8m labour camp', *Arabian Business*, 28 March.

15.   The informants (identified by first name): Khaled, a former Dubai Municipality employee; Muna, (a former UAE University student); and Aysha (a Middle Eastern Studies scholar in the US). All are UAE citizens.

16.   Kutty, S. (2002) 'Meeting point, message circle', *Khaleej Times*, 29 May, p. 7.

17.   Hilotin, J. (2003) 'Baniyas Square – a testimony to early glory: while the other side of the city developed fast, the area north of Dubai creek retains its character as people flock to its perpetually busy streets' *Gulf News*, 29 March, p. 6.

18.   *Ibid*.

19.   *Ibid*.

20.   Menon, S. (2006) 'Heady illicit brew is on sale in Dubai suburbs: bootleggers masquerading as peanut sellers in Satwa and Mutheena serve drinks in plastic cups for Dh5', *Gulf News*, 4 February, p. 4.

21.   For an excellent analysis on the role of remittances and the extent to which they have revived local economies in India see Raymer, Steve (2005) 'Dubai's Kerala connection', *YaleGobal Online*. http://yaleglobal.yale.edu/display.article?id=5992. Accessed 8 March 2009.

22.   Saberi, Mahmood (2008) 'How 'Little India' took roots', *Gulf News*, 21 March, p. 11.

23.   Dubai Municipality (1995) *Planning Study for the Development of the Satwa Area*. Dubai: The Municipality.

24.   Issa, W. and Al Najami, S. (2007) 'A cry for help from a life of untold misery', *Gulf News*, 20 January, p. 3.

25.   Al Jandaly, Basma (2007) 'Emirati family has no place to live', *Gulf News*, 29 June, p. 3.

26.   Al Lawati, Abbas (2008) 'Evicted family make tent their new home', *Gulf News*, 20 May, p. 5; and Al Lawati, Abbas (2008) 'Evicted woman returns to her old house in Satwa', *Gulf News*, 23 May, p. 5.

27.   Sankar, Anjana (2008). 'Staying in touch using rusty cassette players', *Gulf News*, 22 November, p. 2.

28.   Fenton, Suzanne (2008) 'DH350b makeover for Dubai', *Gulf News*, 7 October, p. 1.

29.   Hope, Bradley (2008) 'Meraas takes wraps off Dh350bn development', *The National*, 7 October, p. 4.

30.   TimeOut (2008) 'The end of Satwa', *TimeOut Dubai*, 22–29 May.

31.   Menon, Sunita (2006) 'Homeless bachelors live amid garbage and flies in Satwa', *Gulf News*, 10 October. http://archive.gulfnews.com/articles/06/10/10/10073531.html. Accessed 24 November 2008.

32.   TimeOut (2008) 'The end of Satwa', *TimeOut Dubai*, 22–29 May.

33.   Paradkar, Shalaka (2008) 'Last goodbye to Satwa', *Gulf News* Tabloid Section, 25 June, p. 5.

34.   Mahmood Kaabour and Denise Halloway who recorded their impression in an art installation titled 'Satwa Stories'. Both are long-time residents of Dubai.

35.   *Ibid*.

36.   Johnson, Alice (2008) 'Soul of Satwa.' *Gulf News*, 3 October, p. 8.

37.   TimeOut (2008) 'The end of Satwa', *TimeOut Dubai*, 22–29 May. The following are some quotes from residents of Satwa:

> Mohammed Aslam Khan, 52, Pakistani, building maintenance company director: 'Around 32 bachelors live in this villa with me, mainly from Pakistan and India … I've lived here, in this villa, for 17 years, while my family have been back in Pakistan'.
>
> Davlath Khan, 47, Afghani, baker: I am from Afghanistan and have lived here for 25 years.

Ainah Duldulao,26, Filipino, coffee barista: 'I've been in Dubai for two years. I came over to work in Second Cup coffee shop because the salary was far better than at home. I live in the area near Rydges Plaza, behind Sheikh Zayed Road, in a villa with 12 rooms. Up to eight people live in each of them'.

Siobhán Hodge, 28, Irish, real estate agent: 'I've been living in Dubai for 22 years; in the same compound in Satwa with my husband for eight and a half. Why do I love it here so much? Because it's so unlike the rest of Dubai – the vibe, the smell, the hustle and bustle. There's a quirkiness to it that you don't really feel anywhere else'.

Ishwar, Indian, tailor: 'I've been here since 1981 – 27 years in total. I've always lived and worked right here in Satwa, along Satwa Road. The area has changed so much during my time here. It used to be just a single busy road, and there used to be an open-air theatre just across from us, showing movies after 8 pm. Now it's just another white building with shops'.

38. http://www.dubai-online.com/maps/jumeirah-garden-city.htm. Accessed 30 November 2008.

39. 'Apart from the nostalgia for an area I love walking around there's a practical problem and I wonder whether it's being addressed in the master plan. The press release makes me doubt it. Not only does Satwa provide much needed lower cost accommodation for poorly paid but vital members of our society, it also provides a huge variety of retail outlets where they (and we) can buy things we need at sensible prices. So it provides affordable living for many, many people')http://dubaithoughts.blogspot.com/2008/10/goodbye-to-satwa.html). Accessed 30 November 2008.

40. http://uaecommunity.blogspot.com/2008/05/say-goodbye-to-satwa.html. Accessed 30 November 2008.

41. 'Diversity and mixture of cultures, people of different color and various backgrounds living in harmony has always been an exceptional fact of Dubai life. What make Dubai a beautiful city are not only its clean green roads and tall buildings but also more essentially the imprint of daily scene of lively areas such as Satwa in random minds. The smell of freshly baked breads of old bakeries on their broken wooden tables, casual passing by of posh visitors through black Burke's of Arab women in Satwa, tinting of a three digit number plate brand new car in a tiny oily car repair shop, laughter of joyful Philippinas back from work, pleasure of an old lady in selling her twisted used bangle at a gold shop to buy a new design jewelry for her neighbor's wedding, crying of a bare footed young boy in search of his fake addidas ball, hot sale of saris and textile hung on the sticks besides shops … and you and me wondering among those as if we know each other for ages… This is called Dubai Identity. Nowhere else in the world you can experience it. Reproducing a replica of other completely different cities and forcing new identity on Dubai not only seems unfounded, but also will erase the unique identity of Dubai, which has evolved over years of history. Presence of old Satwa villas is not an obstacle in the way of the development of Dubai, rather the ability to see their uniqueness and be eager to refurbish and preserve them along with modern structures, is the barrier to overcome' (*Ibid.*).

42. Al Lawati, A. (2007) 'Tenants greet move with joy and anguish', *Gulf News*, 22 March, p. 4.

43. Menon, Sunita (2006) 'Move out, board tells Rashid colony tenants', *Gulf News*, 1 November. http://archive.gulfnews.com/articles/06/11/01/10079087.html. Accessed 29 November 2007.

44. Ahmed, A. (2007) 'Rashid colony residents get alternate flats; jubilant tenants break into applause after Dubai Rent Committee passes verdict on eviction', 21 March, p. 1.

45. Al Lawati, Abbas (2006) 'Tenants greet move with joy and anguish', *Gulf News*, 22 March. http://archive.gulfnews.com/articles/07/03/22/10112663.html. Accessed 29 November 2007.

46. Masudi, Faisal (2007) 'Residents protest rent hikes', *Xpress*, 22 October. http://www.xpress4me.com/news/uae/dubai/20003790.html. Accessed 30 November 2007.

47. Issa, Wafa (2008) 'Naif box spaces offer solace to workers', *Gulf News*, 9 November, p. 3.

48. Ahmed, Ashfaq (2007) 'Bachelors being evicted from villas'. *Gulf News*, 10 August, p. 6.

49. *Ibid*.

50. Menon, Praveen (2008) 'Early morning fire kills 11 men in overcrowded Deira housing', *The National*, 27 August, p. 1.

51. Associated Press (2008) 'Dubai owner warned of danger before deadly fire', *International Herald*

Tribune, 29 August. http://www.iht.com/articles/ap/2008/08/28/africa/ME-Dubai-Fire.php. Accessed 20 November 2008.

52.   Menon, Praveen (2008) 'We are all brothers here', *The National*, 27 August, p. 4.

53.   Johnson, Alice (2008) 'No place to call home …', *Gulf News*, 24 October, p. 8.

54.   Sambidge, Andy (2008) '4,000 villas in queue to have power supply cut', *Arabian Business*. http://www.arabianbusiness.com/537280-4000-villas-in-queue-to-have-power-supply-cut. Accessed 20 November 2008.

55.   The Naif area is a district in Deira that was the old commercial centre of Dubai. It is one of the oldest localities in Dubai and has more than 100 traditional townhouses. According to the 2005 census, 34,185 people live in the Naif district, out of which only 6,120 are female. There are more than 815 buildings in the district.

56.   Issa, Wafa (2008) 'Naif box spaces offer solace to workers', *Gulf News*, 9 November, p. 3.

57.   Dharmarajan, Subramani (2008) 'Labour villas or fire traps', *Xpress*, 8 September.

58.   Abu Baker, Rasha (2008) 'Workers made to live in boxes', *The National*, 23 July. http://www.thenational.ae/article/20080723/NATIONAL/311020688/1010/NEWS. Accessed 20 November 2008.

59.   http://www.guardian.co.uk/world/2008/oct/08/middleeast.construction. Accessed 30 November 2008.

60.   DePerle, Jason (2007) 'Fearful of Restive Foreign Labor, Dubai Eyes Reforms'. *The New York Times*, 6 August. http://www.nytimes.com/2007/08/06/world/middleeast/06dubai.html. Accessed 9 September 2007.

61.   *Construction Week* (2007) 'Site workers love their Fridays', *Construction Week*, 30 April, p. 5.

62.   Menon, Sunita (2007) 'Weekends far away from home; labour accommodation come alive on holidays', *Gulf News*, 31 March, p. 4.

63.   In March 2007, labourers from Al Quoz rioted, as part of a larger 8,000 strong protest against contracting companies, demanding better living conditions and a wage increase of Dh200 (US$55) and a food allowance of Dh150 (US$42) per month.

64.   http://www.alertnet.org/thenews/newsdesk/IRIN/2ca58fd1b898b3b6ebf5b617cd4f49b4.htm.

65.   *Ibid*.

66.   http://secretdubai.blogspot.com/2006/04/booming-bachelor-boys.html.

67.   Egbert, C. (2007) 'Dubai to build $8m labour camp', *Arabian Business*, 28 March.

68.   Egbert, C. (2007) 'First 'luxury' labour camp in Dubai', *Construction Week*, 3 March.

69.   For example, Bharadwaj, V. (2005) 'Beyond faces: Dubai's Sabkha is a different world', *Gulf News*, 23 August, pp. 6–9; and Landais, E. (2005) 'Almost anything is available here: Satwa is a place to pick up useful things at good prices', *Gulf News*, 2 September, p. 6.

70.   Al Jandaly. B. (2006) 'Body found at bus station near Satwa mosque', *Gulf News*, 15 June, p. 3.

Chapter 9

Global Dubai or *Dubaization*

'For decades it was the big, central Arab powers that set the tone for the Arab world and led innovation. But today the region is being led from the outer edges. It's the little guys that are doing the most interesting stuff, and it's the big guys that will be left behind if they don't wake up.'

Thomas Friedman, The fast eat the slow, *New York Times*, 2 February 2001[1]

It is appropriate to conclude the narrative which I have sketched in this book by looking at Dubai's place in the world or, more tellingly, how Dubai sees itself globally. This issue came to the fore in 2006 during what has become known as the Dubai Port episode. Dubai Port had acquired British port operator P&O which managed numerous ports worldwide including several in the US. A political upheaval ensued – mostly centred on Arabs and Moslems controlling ports of entry which might lead to terrorists entering unencumbered. Because of this controversy Dubai Port decided to forsake its control of US ports but retained the remainder of P&O's 'empire'. This incident exposed two significant points. First, from a local perspective, the notion that Dubai, because of its global integration, could somehow, miraculously, divorce itself from its regional (i.e. Arab/Moslem) context and secondly – and this is a critical point – that its global ambitions had began to attract the attention of lawmakers and decision-makers outside the region, who until then had viewed Dubai mostly as an amusing sideshow, not needing to be taken seriously. Clearly, this is not merely an Arabian fairytale – but a serious developmental model. Which takes us to the Friedman quote above.

The Dubai phenomenon is part of an upheaval in the Arab region whereby the centre of power has shifted to the Gulf states (GCC). And of course leading this 'revolution' is the city of Dubai. A variety of terms are beginning to describe this phenomenon: the Dubai model; Dubaization; Dubaification. The idea here is to show that the mode of development taking place in the city is so unique and different from what has been taking place throughout thousands of years of urbanization that a new term needs to be invented. But, is there such a thing as a 'Dubai model'? And if it exists, is it desirable to export elsewhere – in other words to what degree can this 'model' be replicated in other parts of the region? And how has the financial turmoil, which began as early as summer 2007 according to some reports,[2] affected the perceived attractiveness of this model?

Sheikh Mohamed bin Rashid al Maktoum, Dubai's ruler, in a 2008 *Wall Street Journal* article, observed that Dubai is 'A big city like no other'. And while acknowledging that Dubai's 'ethos' is commerce, he was keen to highlight its multicultural, and tolerant nature: 'the ethos of Dubai was, and is, all about building bridges to the outside world; it was, and is, about creating connections with different cultures'. He points out that Dubai has no political ambitions.[3] More recently, and within the context of the global financial crisis, he rightly notes the degree to which it has become integrated into the global financial system – that any blow to Dubai would have serious repercussions in the region, because we live in a 'global village'.[4]

But, there is a sense of difference, which is not just projected in official rhetoric but finds its way into the local media. Hardly a day passes without reports indicating the supremacy of Dubai over other Middle Eastern cities and its determination to join the ranks of leading world cities. But these do not just appear in the local media; international publications, such as *The Economist*, are filled with articles about the city, heralding the arrival of an Arabian tiger.[5] But beyond such anecdotal evidence is there hard empirical data supporting Dubai's projected supremacy and success?

My aim in this chapter is to investigate these issues. To that effect it is divided into three parts: first I look at the 'Dubai model' in detail, examining the rhetoric which has accompanied this term. My focus then shifts to a discussion of specific cases, to illustrate the degree to which this 'model' has been adopted both regionally in the Middle East as well as globally. A more detailed case study focusing on the city of Cairo follows this and concludes the chapter, where I question the focus on Dubai's megaprojects and suggest that potentially more useful lessons could be found by looking at the city's hidden spaces.

The Dubai Model?

I first introduced the term 'Dubaization' in 2004 during the International Association for the Study of Traditional Environments conference in Sharjah, in a paper discussing the influence of Dubai on Cairo, citing specific projects which I found to be inspired, directly or indirectly, by Dubai. I elaborated on this argument further during a workshop at the American University in Cairo and also during the International Union of Architects conference in Istanbul in 2005. These issues were further developed in two publications.[6] The dominance of Dubai during that time, and the proliferation of its megaprojects, made such a connection, however tenuous, very attractive. Yet since then the term itself – Dubaization – has been adapted and used in many discussions, papers and forums. For instance, a recent article discusses the 'Dubaification of Barbados' whereby the government is criticized for the development of offshore islands.[7] In a similar vein, an urban forum held in Panama defines Dubaization as 'the dense construction of high-rise buildings' in a discussion centring on the proliferation of these developments in Panama City.[8] Energy experts in India decry the 'Dubaization' of its cities – equated here with the construction of what they call 'glass towers'.[9]

While in these instances the term refers to locally initiated developments, on other occasions there is direct intervention from Dubai-based developers. In Istanbul, locals refer to the construction of luxury towers in the financial district of Levent (one is called Dubai Towers) as 'the Dubaification of Istanbul'.[10] The tower is supposed to be the highest in the district (construction is yet to commence) (figure 9.1). In a similar vein Asad Yawar discusses the extent to which Dubai-based entities are buying UK football stadia and sponsoring British teams. He observes that '… the economic vibrancy of Dubai has made such a strong impression globally that some are beginning to talk of a "Dubai model" that poor countries can leverage to catapult themselves into first-world levels of affluence'.[11]

9.1. The Levent district of Istanbul in January 2009, supposed site of the Dubai Tower. Its construction has not yet begun and is awaiting approval from Istanbul Municipality.

In some instances the term goes beyond the incursion of real estate companies and mega-developments to denote certain qualities – and it is here that it acquires a negative dimension. For many the word connotes fakedness and artificiality. For example, the demolition of an old playhouse building in New York is derided by preservationist groups because it only preserves the façade. One commentator argued that: 'They want the Dubaization and aggrandizement of NYU and nothing else'.[12] An *Economist* article, titled 'Fake Parks: Dubai in America', discusses the construction of fake parks (developing activities which mimic nature in an artificial setting): 'Is America catching up with Dubai, home of desert skiing, the world's only seven-star hotel and other outlandish attractions?'[13] Given these discursive representations of the Dubai phenomenon, how does Dubai see itself in all of this? How does it project its power, and are such depictions heralding the emergence of a hegemonic, empire-like status? In the following two sections, I discuss this in some detail. My focus begins by looking at the rhetoric itself, the degree to which the city's intelligentsia views itself and its place in the world and this is followed by an examination of the visible manifestation of *Dubai Hegemonic*.

Rhetoric: Debating the Dubai Moment

Is there such a thing as a Dubai model? One commentator expresses his views as follows:

> Welcome to the ultimate sociopolitical model for the 21st century: a Blade Runner-esque melting pot of neoliberalism and 'subterranean' economy, Sunni Arab Islam and low taxes, souks and artificial islands, a giant warehouse and a tourist paradise, life in the fast lane and post-modern slavery. The model spells out an apolitical, consumer-mad, citizenship-free society.[14]

He ties this to similar developments in Asia: 'Deng Xiaoping's dictum – "to get rich is glorious" – ultimately prevails. Lee Kwan Yew applied it in Singapore – and it worked marvels'.[15] These are expressions of popular sentiments, but has this model actually been studied by researchers and academics?

The notion of a Dubai model has been raised by local commentators and researchers. Chief among them is Abdul Khaleq Abdullah, a Dubai based political scientist who has written extensively about the virtue of this model – to the extent of noting that we are witnessing a 'Dubai moment'. He elaborated on this argument in a 2006 article – written in Arabic – comparing Dubai to Tokyo, Shanghai, Singapore, Frankfurt, London and New York. He then observes:

> At this moment Dubai is the Arab city rushing forward to emphasize its global presence… Dubai has transformed into a model (Arabic: *qudwa*) city in the Arab region and has become a developmental, urban and population phenomenon, raising debate. (Abdullah, 2006a, p. 58)

And because of this 'This is Dubai's moment in history … which she has waited for, for a long time' (*Ibid.*, p. 61). His argument is centred on the notion that Dubai is the most globally integrated city in the region and because of its success there will be some sort of Arab renaissance. That sense of supremacy, particularly with regard to its neighbours, is expressed as follows:

> The Dubai moment is the moment for all Arabs. Its success is also a success for these cities who could use its experience in rapid development. And as Baghdad, Damascus, and Cairo and after them Beirut had their moment, so is Dubai now. Its star is shining in the Arabian sky. Dubai is the emerging Arab city, all eyes are on it, and lights from the Arab history are shining on this city which is completing the Arab city journey… (*Ibid.*, p. 63)

In aggressive and provocative language, he notes that whatever Dubai does or initiates becomes a source for emulation among its neighbours. He then applies the model theory to everything: Dubai has the model airport, model hotels, etc. Because of this 'Dubai moment' there is deep resentment among Arabs. He recognizes that the city is not a model in some aspects such as the population imbalance, loss of identity, exaggeration of its accomplishments, absence of transparency and proliferation of prostitution. In an insightful depiction, he notes the fleeting nature of this model:

> Dubai is building a new Arabian dream and no one knows for how long this will last. Especially since it is not supported by a solid foundation – through public participation, institutional development and social debates. Instead the city is administered through individuals, more as a company than a government. (*Ibid.*, p. 70)

He elaborates on these arguments further in his other writings. For instance, the notion that Dubai is the subject of study by foreign researchers.[16] Or that it has become a truly global city because of the relocation of companies such as US based Halliburton to Dubai.[17] And that one of its unique characteristics is its 'political neutrality' which everyone is 'trying to emulate but in vain'.[18]

Samir Amin, noted economist, in a robust rebuttal refutes the existence of such a model. Writing from a neo-Marxist perspective, essentially viewing the entire planet engulfed in what he has called elsewhere 'Americanization', he argues that regional powers, which would include Dubai, 'will not be allowed to have a margin of movement allowing them to become a center combining between financial and political power' (Amin, 2006, p. 159). This became evident when the 'Washington regime' refused to allow the UAE to use its money to buy companies administering some US ports. What is acceptable, according to Amin, is for these monies to be put under US control, which in turn entails ownership rights: 'This is the limit that colonialists will not allow to be transgressed'.

On the notion of Dubai being another Singapore, he argues that there are some similarities, for instance acting as a mediator for giant transnational firms. But Singapore contains productive activities which are conducted by these firms, whereas this is not the case in Dubai. And since this mediator – Dubai or Singapore – benefits financially from the situation, this does not give it the chance to be promoted to a 'new centre', thus having the benefits of the real centre, that is controlling decisions, and having complete control over capitalist ownership. And while Dubai is seeking to become a financial centre, going beyond the 'oil economy' to become a 'local post-oil company', there are, according to Amin, limitations for such a system.

> In Dubai's post-oil economy there is not a single element characterizing the economic situation of capitalist centers. And there is nothing that would indicate that there has been any progress in this regard. Economic systems of centers are based on certain privileges, which are absent

outside the triad of (USA, Europe and Japan). And these are: technological innovation which is accompanied by true control over systems of production through intellectual and industrial copyright laws; controlling financing patterns through the accumulation of money to the desired extent and controlling spending; monopolizing extraction of natural resources (such as oil) without limitations; controlling the decision on how they will be used; and monopolizing military means guaranteeing control over international affairs. (Amin, 2006, p. 160)

Amin thus argues that while there are certain aspects of global centres that exist in Dubai, political and economic limitations pertaining to 'American' hegemony more or less prevent the city from becoming a real centre – which is only 'allowed' to happen in the financial capitals of the world – the triad: London, New York and Tokyo. Yet clearly such a view could be disputed by many economists and political scientists. For instance, the emergence of BRIC economies (Brazil, Russia, Ireland, and China) as well as the recent global financial meltdown indicate that the centres of power are shifting. This argument is also made by Abdul Khaleq Abdullah in responding to this rebuttal. He disputes Amin's notion of true centres, arguing that in the current globalizing conditions there are no more absolute centres vs. those at the margin. New centres emerge all the time, and Dubai will become a centre for a new region.[19] Moreover, he refutes Amin's example of the Dubai Port episode, which he suggests was a minor episode in Dubai World's global acquisitions and that in the case of the US the blockage of the deal was racially motivated.

Of course this whole debate about the supremacy or existence of a 'Dubai model' has not addressed its viability or sustainability. According to some critics the 'model' is neither sustainable nor should it be emulated as it is based on certain conditions which do not exist elsewhere. For instance, Asad Yawar (2006) discusses the limitations of the Dubai 'model'. He disputes the officially perpetrated vision/megaprojects version of the city and asks if 'Dubai [is] a realistic, or even a desirable, model for emulation'.[20] He then enumerates a set of factors which show its unique situation: unique location as a port city; location in an oil-rich region; and proximity to the lucrative markets of Asia. The global economic condition prior to 2008 is an additional factor: 'Dubai is now awash with literally hundreds of billions of dollars in surplus funds from nearby Arabic- and Persian-speaking states that would in other times have found a home in New York or Zurich'.

Furthermore, he argues that there is a series of problems with the Dubai model that 'render it not just hard to copy, but potentially unmanageable'. There is no transfer of skills from expatriates to locals; business arrangements do not boost the indigenous skills base; the 'model' is 'contingent to an important degree on almost fantastical levels of exploitation of foreign labor at the lower levels of the economy' (he cites as an example the Burj Dubai project which he suggests is put together by labourers earning $4/day); lack of the possibility of citizenship (even for those born in the UAE) leads to lack of attachment – in times of financial hardship this could potentially lead to 'societal tumult'. Further, environmental feasibility is another problem – 'the modern city has been designed as if global warming did not exist'.

Also, the city's developmental strategy based on cheap mass international transport could be thrown into disarray if there are rises in jet fuel prices.

Yet, in spite of all these criticisms directed at this particular mode of development, looking not just at the region but also globally, we can see that Dubai's developers have been active in perpetuating their urban development vision. In many instances, though, such incursions are encouraged by local governments and investors who are in the end motivated by profit. In the following sections, I review some examples pertaining to the 'hegemonic' qualities of the Dubai project and the extent to which it is attempting to become a regional centre.

Competitive Dubai

Going beyond the rhetoric – either for or against the model – reports and studies do in fact suggest that Dubai has surpassed its Middle Eastern neighbours. For example, the Arab World Competitiveness Report commissioned by the United Nations places the UAE (and other Gulf cities) squarely ahead of Egypt, Algeria and Lebanon, among others.[21] Another study, developed by the consulting firm Ernst & Young, compares Dubai with Cairo and other cities, using various criteria that track favourable business environments. No surprise here, either: Dubai supersedes Cairo on all counts (e.g. infrastructure, telecommunications, regulatory environment, etc.).[22] One particular organization, the Globalization and World Cities Study Group (GaWC), based in the UK, is interested in establishing objective measures for world city status. Using data from studies of over 150 cities in which each city was assigned a score based on the number of headquarters or regional offices of multinational corporations located within that particular city, it was found that London and New York are at the top. Dubai is in the lower part, followed closely by Cairo and Beirut (figure 9.2).[23] These are data from 2000, however, when Dubai was still in 'relative' infancy. Since then it has embarked on its aforementioned massive construction effort, with megaprojects announced almost daily. Based on such a general picture, I would speculate that recent data would confirm that Dubai, along with other Gulf cities, has moved further ahead.[24]

In fact a recent Global City Index report released in 2008 by the Urban Land Institute (ULI) shows that London and New York still rank among the world's most successful cities, but face increasing competition from other global cities, according to an analysis of thirty major global indices and other data. Both cities – according to the report – face formidable challenges from global cities such as Tokyo, Hong Kong, Paris, Shanghai, Dubai and Mumbai.[25] And there are, of course, many other indicators which seem to show that Dubai's distinctive status, particularly in the Middle East, finds some affirmation. For instance, the 2008 Global Cities Index developed by Foreign Policy, with A.T. Kearney and the Chicago Council on Global Affairs, using a broad range of indicators, and relying on such experts as Saskia Sassen, Janet Abu Lughod and Peter Taylor, has shown

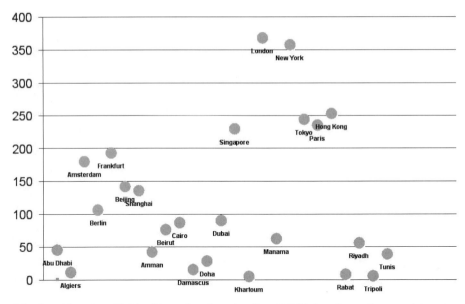

9.2. A ranking of world cities (*Source*: Based on data from GaWC, http://www.lboro.ac.uk/gawc)

that Dubai ranks 27th among 60 cities included in the survey – the only other Middle Eastern city to come close is Cairo at 38.[26]

Dubaization in the Middle East

The phenomenon of spectacular developments based on the construction of megaprojects has engulfed the entire Middle East; it is not just relegated to Dubai anymore. In Saudi Arabia for example, Prince Fahd bin Sultan has begun construction of what is intended as a showcase for a new Saudi Arabia: a $300 billion multicultural metropolis designed to lure 700,000 inhabitants from around the globe. The construction of this and five other megacities scheduled for completion by 2020 will be funded by oil revenue. One of the partners in this venture is Lebanese, Bahaa Hariri (son of the late prime minister Rafiq Hariri). Every economic city is planned as a multipurpose hub featuring housing complexes, educational facilities, entertainment areas, agriculture, logistics, food processing, mining and a variety of industries. This will create an astounding number of new jobs, estimated at 1.3 million. The six cities are intended to turn Saudi Arabia into one of the world's 10 most competitive nations by 2020.[27]

Damascus is another example of a city reconfigured to cater for global capital and various investment interests. For instance, reports indicate that there are plans to bulldoze two ancient districts just outside the city's northern gates to build an eight-lane motorway flanked by high-rise blocks skirting the city. This has prompted some to argue that 'While Baghdad is being destroyed by war … are we to see Damascus destroyed by vested interests?'[28] Another report examines the recent boom in consumption in Syria due to the policies of Bashar Al-Assad's government which has 'pushed economic development and private enterprise in an effort to make up for the loss of oil export'. This rush to consume is extending to almost all types of goods and services. New clothing shops, shopping centres, cafés and restaurants are opening daily. New hotels are being planned, especially in Damascus, which has only about five four- and five-star hotels compared with dozens in Beirut. Various Gulf conglomerates and development companies have allocated hundreds of millions of dollars to build shopping malls, hotels and residential complexes.[29]

In Khartoum, investors are coming from the Gulf, China, India and Malaysia. To cater for this growing business, the government of Sudan approved a project to provide 'state-of-the-art' facilities for business executives. Called the Al Mogran Development Project, it is next to the Hilton Hotel and the Ministry of Investment, at the confluence of the White and Blue Niles, and is developed by Al Sunut Development Company, Sudan's leading real estate firm. At an estimated cost of over $4 billion, it is spread over several thousand acres.[30] Described by some as an effort *'to build a new Dubai'*, it consists of a vast complex of gleaming offices, duplexes and golf courses. The first tower of the development will be the headquarters of the Greater Nile Petroleum Operating Company. Close behind, in a building shaped like a sail (locals note that it reminds them of the Burj Al Arab), will rise the headquarters of Petrodar. A Sudanese company, DAL Group, is investing about $700m in the infrastructure for the project, but the buildings themselves are being put up by their new owners. These include all the Gulf states which are buying plots. Opposite Al Mogran, on the Omdurman side, Saudi and Kuwaiti investors have bought a large plot of land on which they intend to build a huge financial centre. Interestingly, Al Mogran is not the only huge construction site in Khartoum. About 15 km (9 miles) across the city the largest American embassy in Africa is going up, which will supposedly house the biggest CIA listening post outside America.[31]

In Istanbul, Sama Dubai, the real-estate arm of the state-owned Dubai Holding, is to develop a site in the city's business district, previously used as a bus stop, to build the previously mentioned Dubai Towers complex.[32] And in Iraq, the President of the American Chamber of Commerce said that Dubai's economic model could be applied for every region in the country. This would include the building of an international airport and a $200 billion investment arm in the Kurdish region.[33]

Dubai's Emaar is developing the Zowara-Abou Kemash area on the Mediterranean coast near Tripoli, Libya. It is considered to be one of the largest projects in Emaar's portfolio (380 million square metres).[34] However, the North African region in particular has not been as receptive as the rest of the Middle East. Some commentators have pointed out the difficult business climate in some countries. For example, Morocco ranks 115 out of 175 in a World Bank ranking for business-friendly countries, Algeria is 120, and Libya does not have a ranking. In Algiers, reports indicated a multibillion dollar project to modernize part of its antiquated waterfront – but there are no concrete proposals yet. In Morocco, rules are streamlined and projects fast-tracked for 'the benefit of Gulf developers'. According to a recent report: 'Dubai Holding is working round the clock in the sleepy capital Rabat, rapidly transforming the Bouregreg estuary in a $2.7 billion project to add walkways, hotels, shops and a marina under the impressed, if bemused, gaze of locals'. These projects are not just restricted to Dubai-based investors. There is, for instance, the $350 million Mazagan Resort under construction south of Casablanca developed by Dubai World and an assortment of local and international investors[35] and Qatar investors have launched a $600 million coastal complex of hotels, holiday homes and a golf course near Tangier in the north.[36] In Tunisia, Emaar is developing Marina Al Qussor, a US$1.88 billion, 4.5 million square metre development of the country's eastern coastline.[37] The deal was endorsed in 2007 by Tunisian legislators with particular emphasis placed on the jobs that would be created by the development, an interesting observation given the high unemployment rate in the country. Another project in Tunisia, called 'Century City', and described as a 'luxury real estate development', is proposed by Sama Dubai at a value estimated around US$14 billion.[38]

Direct Intervention: The Case of Morocco

As I noted above, Dubai has been particularly active in Morocco. Among the various projects initiated by Dubai based developers are Amelkis II, a US$327 million luxury residential golfing complex, and Bahia Bay, a US$1.2 billion residential golfing community. Another series of projects is planned as part of a US$5.34 billion agreement between the Moroccan government and Emaar: Oukalmeden, a project for a 'four season mountain destination for recreation, entertainment and relaxation, as well as … the Middle East and Africa's only golf and ski resort'; Saphira, a development located on Rabat's western side and set 'to become the leisure and tourism hub of Rabat city', while next to Tangiers the so-called Tinja will be a marina and luxurious seaside development.

According to a World Bank report, Morocco has been among the economies in the region benefiting from an inflow of petrodollars recycled from the Arabian Gulf. Such Gulf investment has flowed into real-estate and infrastructure developments, agro-industry and the country's small bourse. The picturesque estuary on the outskirts of the capital, Rabat, for example, is the site of a $2bn tourist development by Sama Dubai, the real-estate arm of the state-owned Dubai Holding, along with Morocco's state-controlled CDG investment fund. King Mohamed enjoys cordial relations with the Gulf rulers, but Gulf investment has also been encouraged by tax breaks and the availability of cheap, formerly state-held, land.[39]

Pockets of extreme deprivation are being targeted by a palace-led 'human development' initiative – as frequently shown in the news bulletins on state-controlled television. However, Jamila Bargach (2008), an anthropologist, provides an interesting account of how Sama Dubai is playing a major role in transforming the cityscape of Rabat to cater primarily for global capital and in the process is alienating the city's citizens. She writes about Rabat and her sister city Salé, which she suggests has the largest concentration of shantytowns or *bidonvilles*. One particular event which transformed the way the government dealt with public housing and slums was the Casablanca bombings in 2003, whose perpetrators came from one of the poorest slums in the city. This led to a 're-orientation' in housing policy whereby private firms were invited to participate in reconstruction and demolition.

Bargach argues that citizens' needs are not taken into account in these projects; they primarily serve global capital. In fact they have resulted in the displacement and relocation of people living along the river. In an interview with a government official she was told that the government is dealing with the poor by providing a low-income housing project called Tamesna, located far from the city. Because of the separation she writes that 'each city will move in its own orbit'. This occurs all through the Middle East to varying degrees. There are cases, however, where Dubai's mode of urbanism is more inspirational in the sense that local actors aim to emulate Dubai without directly benefiting from the clout and 'expertise' of its developers. One such case is the Abdali project in Amman which I discuss in the following section.

Inspired by Dubai: The Case of Amman

In Amman, the real estate industry is expanding significantly due to an influx of Iraqis as well as developments across a range of industries. Leading this growth is Mawared, a state owned development and investment company. One of their key projects is Abdali carried out in partnership with the Hariri family and the Kuwaiti investment group Kipco. Abdali will eventually become a fully functioning city centre for Amman. The project is viewed as an anchor that will attract global business to Jordan (figure 9.3).[40] The case of this development in Amman is interesting here because it is modelled after the Solidere development in Beirut. In an interview about the city's masterplan, Amman's mayor made some poignant comments about the new form of governance which is responsible for projects like Abdali:

> We also contracted a specialist company, The Bearing Point, from the US and Canada, to help us in the technicalities of drafting of our master plan... Eventually, after we fully understand what the city wants, we will bring in international companies that deal with national, city and country branding and come out with a focused message about the city that will help us market the city and promote it not just as a tourism spot but to give it the right definition and true identity.[41]

Rami Daher, an architectural scholar and practitioner in Amman, observes that the Abdali project is part of wider phenomenon in Amman, which includes a

9.3. The Abdali development in downtown Amman. A model display during the 2007 Cityscape exhibition in Dubai.

proliferation of malls and gated communities in addition to luxurious towers which represent a form of 'living above the city'. He notes that these transformations are part of what he calls neoliberal urban restructuring – a privatization of public space. Beirut and Dubai serve as models in this regard. Al-Abdali, for example, is modelled after Solidere in Beirut. He writes that both in its orientation and design it is turning their backs to Amman's original downtown. Mawared in collaboration with Saudi Oger (the developer responsible for Solidere) formed a partnership, the Abdali Investment Company, but according to Daher 'the state is not absent but heavily involved'. The project has led to a displacement of a major transportation terminal, as well as the removal of informal vendors. It will, in its current form, compete with the existing downtown (Daher, 2008).

It is interesting to place this project in a wider context involving the city of Amman which is increasingly being demarcated along economic lines – a rich eastern area, site of the Abdali project and various upscale malls, and a poorer western part containing slums and refugee camps. Development efforts are increasingly geared towards the former. Daher makes an interesting point related to urban governance, namely the notion of resistance.

Resisting the Model: Beyond the Middle East

In the previous two sections I looked at the extent to which Dubai is either directly influencing or inspiring developments throughout the Middle East. But elsewhere in the world one can see a similar 'Dubaization' process. For instance in the UK, Dubai Ports World acquired a deal to develop a new port east of London which will help 'the UK compete with Rotterdam as a vital European distribution hub'.[42] In India, Sama Dubai is planning to construct 'Smart City', envisioned as the largest business park in India and based on the Internet & Media City model in Dubai. There was strong local opposition to the project and as a result terms of the deal were revised: Smart City is leasing the land for 99 years, as opposed to outright ownership.[43] Such forms of resistance are rare and may offer a lesson for the Middle East. Similar objections have also accompanied the planning of a luxury resort in South Africa, on the grounds that it will displace local farmers.

The South African case is particularly interesting as it highlights the degree to which some of these proposals are clashing with local interests and raising issues that are not applicable in Dubai's *tabula rasa* like landscape. The project in question is called Amazulu World and is developed by Dubai based Ruwaad – a private developer, initially specializing in signage and branding. The project is described as being the largest leisure and shopping centre in Africa and will include, among other things, a 106-metre high statue of a Zulu warrior king. The project was unveiled in 2008, but faced fierce opposition from local residents and farmers because of their planned relocation. Having occupied this land for generations, the area has cultural and religious qualities which would not exist elsewhere. Some critics liken the way in which the project has been portrayed to policies of forced settlements under the apartheid government. Ruwaad's CEO in a manner befitting a colonialist rather than a developer argues:

> We have left the social engagement process to the government. A few members of the community are misconstruing this project. There is a long history of these people opposing economic development initiatives… This project will improve the whole region.

These objections are, however, not raised by a 'few people' – they number, according to some reports, more than 10,000 families.[44] Such insensitivities to local conditions occur elsewhere. For example, at the level of retail, Emaar is planning to build 'India's largest mall' basing its development on the Dubai Mall.[45] There is no consideration at all for the appropriateness of constructing such provocative projects. But one cannot blame Emaar in this case: India has what is perhaps the only shopping mall in the world, in New Delhi, which charges its customers for entry to preserve its elite status!

These endeavours can thus be criticized on social grounds (intensifying existing social divisions; social inequity; displacement), but they also seem to commodify cultural symbols and as such are also a threat to the local culture. This is not the fault of Dubai of course, because local players are more than happy to appropriate their cultural heritage to maximize profit. Some of the projects which I have reviewed use regional elements (the gates of Damascus), apply them to unexpected contexts (entry to a gated community), and add other stylistic elements (arches, decorations, etc.), thus reworking the symbolism or imagery of the original and creating a new image. This new image, in turn, becomes in itself a point of reference, a Debordian spectacle.

While Dubai claims that it is nonpolitical in its outlook, the mere fact that all these interventions are taking place and the degree to which they create economic and cultural situations that many would construe as problematic seems to undermine the political neutrality claim. According to some observers (see my discussion of Abdul Khaleq Abdullah), this is the main tenet of the Dubai model. But, to quote the well known Indonesian writer Pramoedya Ananta Toer:

> Just as politics cannot be separated from life, life cannot be separated from politics. People who consider themselves to be non-political are no different; they've already been assimilated by the dominant political culture – they just don't feel it any more.[46]

The mere act of intervention and development is political. To understand this phenomenon better, I shift my focus to the city of Cairo – the traditional centre of the Arab world – and the extent of the influence which is exerted there by Dubai.[47]

The Case of Cairo

*'Al Qahirah laysat Duba*i.' (Cairo is not Dubai)
Egyptian newspaper headline describing the failure of Cairo in emulating the
Dubai Shopping Festival (*Al-Ahram*, 2006)

The whole notion of Egypt and Cairo being influenced by the Gulf is not a recent phenomenon. Raymond Williams observes that Egypt is presently experiencing a second wave of influences from Arabia. The first came as *Saudization* in the 1960s and 1970s and left the imprint of a conservative Islam on the masses, who brought back from their work in Saudi Arabia narrow and restrictive Wahhabi habits of 'mind and heart'. Today, according to Williams, it is the rich who feel the influence from the Gulf, this time of – and he uses this term – 'Dubaization'. In this context it would mean artificiality – a view shared by many Egyptians. Symptoms of this would include malls, high-rise office buildings, hotels, and 'tasteless villas convey the sense of an absence of authentic culture and identity; everything, just like in Dubai, seems borrowed and rootless'.[48] Such views are not necessarily accurate, but they play into the sense of 'cultural superiority' experienced by the Egyptian intellectual elite in particular. But aside from this, is there any truth to this notion that Dubai is influencing Cairo?

To understand the extent of Dubai's influence we may look at just one Dubai-based company, Emaar.[49] Emaar currently has planned projects in Egypt which include Cairo Heights, an exclusive US$4 billion residential development in Cairo; Smart Village, an integrated community located next to the Cairo's IT centre; and Bibliotheca Alexandrina, a waterfront development project in Alexandria. Most recently, the company was awarded a lucrative development located on Egypt's Mediterranean coast, an area which encompasses 6 million square metres. Other developers such as Damac and Al Futaim have also begun to develop projects in Cairo. Thus, there is a Dubai presence on the Cairene landscape, but the construct of influence needs to be defined further as it seems to suggest a one-way directionality.

In looking at the 'directionality' of influence in Cairo, two possible areas of investigation exist: 1. state-sponsored projects, which more or less adopt an 'idea' without copying its 'form' directly; such projects are modelled on similar ventures throughout the world; 2. investment from Dubai-based companies, directly installing a successful Dubai formula. The first tends to follow a diversity of influences emanating from different parts of the world; the second usually involves direct copying, both the main idea and actual physical forms.

The first category in Cairo includes the 'Smart Village' project, modelled after Dubai's Internet City; the second category includes the City Center shopping mall concept introduced by Dubai's Al-Futtaim group. Both of these are apparently distinctive Dubai-based ideas. But they are also not unique to the city, and occur in other centres throughout the world in different forms. Internet City, for example, is modelled after Silicon Valley, California and the technology parks in Southeast Asia. The concept of the hypermarket is not a Dubai invention, but one which occurs throughout the developed world. However, the singularity of these projects within an Egyptian context, occurring after their success in Dubai, does suggest a strong influence, particularly with regard to the City Center project. In the following two sections I explore the extent to which these two projects deviate from, and approximate to, the Dubai model.

The IT Link

In 1999 Sheikh Muhammad bin Rashid announced the creation of an IT centre called Dubai Internet City (DIC). A year later, with landscaping and high rises as its finishing touches, the project was complete, and has since then become an unqualified success. Occupied by big names in the IT industry, it has made Dubai the IT hub of the region. Comprised of a series of office buildings overlooking an artificial lake and lush gardens, the centre is located adjacent to Sheikh Zayed Road. One is led through a gate designed to reflect a traditional wind tower, on to a series of screens with 'Islamic' motifs, and then to a sequence of glass buildings such as one might find in any high-tech park in Malaysia or Silicon Valley. Although entry is free to anyone (provided they have a car), a protective fence surrounds the development. Located nearby is Media City, a project similar to Internet City, although in this case the occupants are from the media industry. This 'city' also comprises office blocks set in an artificial landscape. It houses studios and newsrooms and has become a regional centre for media companies such as Reuters, CNN, MBC and others. The anonymity of the office blocks in both these 'cities', which are distinguished only by the logo of their respective inhabitants, seems to highlight the fact that they operate primarily on a regional and global level, in some way disconnected from the surrounding reality (figure 9.4).

9.4. The lush gardens of Dubai Internet City.

The Smart Village Project in Cairo is Egypt's attempt to claim the mantle of the region's IT hub. Officials say that it is modelled on similar projects in Ireland and India, countries, they argue, that have successfully integrated into the global IT service sector. Located along the Cairo-Alexandria desert highway, the 300-acre (1,214,000 square metres) park will eventually house more than fifty office

9.5. Entrance to Cairo's Smart Village as it appeared in 2004.

buildings accommodating, in total, 20,000–30,000 employees (figure 9.5). Plots of land are offered to potential companies, who can then build their own office space.[50]

Although Egyptian officials highlight the similarities to the aforementioned IT and media enclaves in Dubai, in reality the differences – when this project was still in its initial stages – were striking. With regard to location, Dubai Internet City is outside the traditional city on a highway leading to Abu Dhabi. Nevertheless, it is located on a growth corridor and has become a centre of the new Dubai. Nearby projects include luxury resorts, the ruler's palace, various gated communities and the Palm Island. Driving to DIC, one does not have the feeling of 'leaving' Dubai, whereas with Cairo's Smart Village, which is located along the Cairo-Alexandria highway next to a toll station, the sense of leaving the city and embarking on a long journey is strong. Although attempts are made to develop the area as a new centre – similar to Dubai. Nearby is a mega-mall (called Dandy Mall) and Emaar is creating a mixed-use development there as well.

Another difference relates to accessibility. In Dubai anyone with a car can enter and walk within the project without interference. The food court is a common meeting place containing a variety of shops and restaurants. It thus integrates well, relative to the Cairo project, with the city. The situation in Cairo is quite different. Here entry is through a guarded gate and subsequent movement within the grounds is closely observed. In both the Dubai and Cairo projects, photography is only allowed after securing permission from the authorities, but DIC has a more flexible and relaxed attitude.[51] Numbers also show the striking difference between these two centres. While DIC started with over 200 multinational companies, the numbers have reached 716; Smart Village in Cairo has about fifty-eight companies, most of them locally based (2006 data).[52]

To understand more fully the link between the two projects, they need to be set in their regional and global contexts. The notion of dedicating an entire zone for IT development may of course be traced back to Silicon Valley in California. Within the Asian region Malaysia's Multimedia Supercorridor was introduced in 1998. At that time the Egyptian government proposed the creation of a similar zone in Sinai, Sinai Technology Valley (STV).[53] In 1999 Dubai announced the creation of its Internet City project, whereupon the Egyptian STV project was relocated to Cairo and renamed Smart Village. In 2000, DIC was inaugurated while Smart Village was officially opened in 2003 (figure 9.6). Thus the history of these two projects is both closely intertwined and influenced by global developments, with Cairo playing 'catch up' to Dubai.[54]

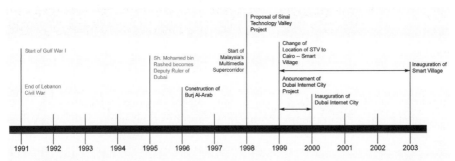

9.6. Timeline illustrating the development of Dubai Internet City and Cairo's Smart Village.

Mega-Malls in Cairo

The retail sector is one segment where the 'Dubai Idea' is directly transplanted into an Egyptian context, as evidenced in the Maadi City Center. The Majid Al Futtaim Group of Companies (MAF Group) of Dubai broke ground in mid-November 2001 in the desert outside Cairo for a 22,500 square metre shopping mall to be anchored by the French food retailer Carrefour. The project, Egypt's first 'hypermarket', is one of a series of developments planned to be opened by the MAF Group and Carrefour. The partners started the concept in Dubai in 1995 with the Deira City Center (see Chapter 7).[55] In addition to the French hypermarket, Cairo's mall initially included more than forty shops, several restaurants and a family entertainment centre. A recent extension increased the number of shops and included a Starbucks, one of ten operating in Egypt (as of 2008) (figure 9.7).[56]

The centre is located in an area of Cairo known as Qattamiy'ya, at the foot of the Moqatam mountain, near the suburb of Maadi and along a highway leading to a new development named New Cairo. The site is surrounded by empty tracts of land, undeveloped areas; and a large public housing project (figure 9.8). The

9.7. Maadi City Center in Cairo.

location was chosen specifically to 'develop new residential zones' according to the developer. An 'example of the type of undeveloped area targeted by the group's development scheme', it thus ties in with what is termed 'Carrefour's vision' for Egypt.[57] This vision entails, in addition to location, a provision of a land area large enough to accommodate such a complex and extensive parking. Thus the Maadi City Center occupies a 69,000 square metre parcel of land of which 3,500 square metres is Carrefour.[58]

9.8. The grim surroundings of Maadi City Center.

It is interesting to observe that the Egyptian local press largely downplays the Dubai connection and the fact that the entire centre is based on a Dubai model. More emphasis is placed on the French connection, in a sense suggesting that Egypt will become Western by constructing centres such as these. According to some observers: 'From a shopper's point of view, the shopping center in Qattamiy'ya is perfect. Once you walk inside, you could be anywhere in the world'.[59] This is in contrast to accounts in the local Gulf press which gleefully point out that Dubai-based businesses are making inroads into Cairo (and other cities as well). The similarities between Maadi City Center and Deira City Center, on which it is modelled, are striking; entering the mall one is struck by the neat detailing of the parking lot with traffic signs pointing out that traffic rules 'still' apply in the area. The atmosphere stands in stark contrast to the modest, and somewhat shabby, surroundings (figure 9.9).

9.9. Advertisement for the City Center Mall, anchored by the French supermarket chain of Carrefour, on a main highway surrounded by middle-class housing projects.

The same applies to the interior which, as in Dubai, has extremely high design and construction standards and a level of cleanliness not found in other Egyptian malls. The Dubai connection becomes even more apparent due to the presence of a UAE-based bank branch. There are, however, differences. The most obvious one is size. Deira City Center is a large centre comprised of multiple levels and several buildings. It occupies the equivalent of several city blocks. In Cairo, the Maadi City Center is spread out on one level and is dominated by Carrefour. Another difference pertains to location. Maadi City Center is located at the edge of the city, making it difficult to reach, unlike in Dubai where Deira City Center is located in the heart of Deira, a commercial and business hub. Deira City Center, moreover, is a major meeting place for city residents, again differentiating it from its younger Cairene cousin. Deira City Center is also notorious for always being crowded and catering for a cash-rich, multinational clientele in addition to locals from Dubai and other emirates.

In Egypt the target population is the nearby Maadi suburb, but there are other segments targeted as well. Among them are returnees from the Gulf region who feel 'at home' in such a space. Its location, however, precludes the centre from becoming a major meeting place. It has more the feel of a curiosity. However, recent visits to the centre show that it has become increasingly attractive for a certain segment of Egyptian society: upper middle-class visitors, Egyptians returning from the Gulf, foreigners, and Arab visitors. At weekends and evenings the mall is packed with shoppers.[60] Thus, recent developments have shown the success of this venture. For instance there has been an expansion of Maadi City Center and the addition of a multi-level parking structure. The developer, Al Futaim, announced plans in 2007 for the construction of five new malls.[61] In a similar manner Emaar is planning the construction of the largest mall in Egypt (part of the Cairo Gate project, located next to the Smart Village).[62]

Gated Communities

Gated communities are a relatively recent phenomenon in Egypt, although it does follow worldwide trends where such compounds are increasingly dominating cities.[63] A drive through New Cairo would show the sheer extravagance of these compounds which are heavily secured. But they are located at the fringes of the city and are not (yet) part of people's perception of Cairo's urban landscape. Of much more interest are some of the projects that are being planned within the city, where they are part of its urban fabric. One of these is a major development by Emaar.

The project was initially called Cairo Heights because of its location on Cairo's Muqattam mountain – immediately overlooking the notorious Manshiet Nasser slum. Dubai officials claimed, in what has become a familiar refrain, that the project will 'reshape the face and lifestyle of the historic Egyptian capital' and that the project will 'recreate the luxury and style that are features of Emaar's world class Dubai developments'. Its CEO places the project within its historical context: 'Cairo has been described as the Jewel of the Orient, the city of the thousand minarets, and the melting pot of ancient and modern Egyptian civilizations. It is undoubtedly one of the greatest cities in the world and it is a rare privilege to be able to contribute to its evolution'.[64]

The development was initially set up with an Egyptian partner, ARTOC, whereby Emaar had a 40 per cent share and ARTOC 60 per cent. As the project reached the implementation stage in 2007, Emaar decided it wished to increase its share, which led to a conflict. They eventually managed to acquire the remaining 60 per cent and have full ownership – apparently with the government's blessing. According to their Chairman: 'We thank the Egyptian government and all parties who played a key role in making this deal to acquire Emaar Misr a reality'.[65]

Basically a mixed-use development, it is located at the highest point in the city – about 200 metres above sea level – from where there are dramatic views of Cairo. A journalist observes, with a hint of sarcasm, that the area has significant historical interest – its stones were used to build the pyramids; in addition it contains an old Christian monastery and cathedral and is adjacent to the oldest surviving Fatimid mosque in Cairo, the Giyushi Mosque. Hence, 'That history is about to take a back seat to Emaar's Uptown Cairo development' (figure 9.10).[66]

Understandably the project met with opposition from various conservation groups, and urban planning experts on the grounds that it would create traffic

9.10(a). Entrance to the Uptown Cairo project in Muqattam.

9.10(b). The Mubarak housing project overlooking the future site of Uptown Cairo.

congestion on one of the city's main arteries, Salah Salem Road; its environmental impact; and a social issue, namely that it overlooks two low-income areas – a public housing project sponsored by Mrs Mubarak (the President's wife), and the aforementioned Manshiet Nasser. Rumours were circulating that due to the close proximity to the Mubarak Housing project, a dense forest of trees would be placed between them so as not to spoil the view for the Uptown Cairo residents. However, these objections did not amount to an organized campaign that hindered approval.

In the summer of 2007, residential units went on sale. A large advertisement in local newspapers informed people that the sale would start the following day at 10 am – required papers were an ID and a chequebook. No unit prices were given (which is Emaar custom in Dubai). Interestingly, in spite of the high-price, apparently all the units were sold. One particular attraction promoted by the developer is that all roads leading to the project would be built by Emaar.

This last point is of particular significance since it shows the extent to which the developer is trying to maintain a distance from the Cairene context. The closeness to one of the most notorious *ashwai'yat* (slums) in Cairo may lead to social trouble, primarily because it makes visible in a most direct way the social polarization of Cairene society. Marcuse and van Kempen's (2000) metaphor of the slum/citadel acquires poignant irony. In a more recent development Emaar has expanded its portfolio significantly in the Egyptian market, promising more of the same: upscale residential communities located next to the new American University of Cairo campus in New Cairo and another one next to Cairo's Smart City.[67]

One must wonder whether this Gulf-based onslaught on Cairo's urban landscape – spearheaded by Dubai – has received any local opposition. In a 2007 article, well known journalist Salama Ahmed Salama expressed a view shared by some in Egypt about the relevancy and sustainability of these developments as well as questioning the ability of Egypt to compete with the Gulf.[68] Such inclinations serve to widen the divide between 'the super rich and a majority of the super poor'. In harsh words, he notes that luxury real estate will 'heighten the sense of social injustice and political exclusion' and, coupled with political extremism and oppression, may threaten the very 'social fabric of our country'.[69] Looking at such developments elsewhere in the world (e.g. Rio de Janeiro, Mumbai) such prophecies may actually come true. The Egyptian poet Farouq Guweida has expressed similar sentiments, criticizing the government's policies that favour the rich.[70] Yet only few dare to express such viewpoints; recent events such as the global credit crisis may offer a wake-up call.

Reverse Influence: Copying Egypt

The discussion would be incomplete if it did not include an examination of Egypt's and Cairo's influence on Dubai. In the 1960s and 1970s architects and urban planners from Egypt practised in the Gulf and many of their designs found their way into the urban landscape of cities such as Abu Dhabi, Dubai and Al Ain. Such buildings are still to be found today although dilapidated, and their outdated aesthetics are making them candidates for demolition. Of more interest is the adoption of Egyptian historical symbols, which is particularly evident in Dubai. For instance, the Wafi Mall adopts Pharaonic motives which are evident throughout the complex, even using the shape of the pyramid for some of the buildings (one houses the luxurious Raffles hotel). Symbols of Islamic Cairo, exemplified by the use of *mashrabiy'yas* (wooden screens), are to be found in various shopping centres, for example in the extension of the Burjuman Mall.

The Madinat Jumeirah complex is a curious case because it adopts symbols from different cultures in the region – as well as plagiarizing Dubai's own heritage (which in turn is adopted from Iran) (figure. 9.11). Yet the Egyptian connection is quite strong. The complex, in its advertising campaign, even uses orientalist imagery – paintings depicting traditional motifs (reclining, turbaned men; horsemen at the gates, etc.) – and situates them within the context of the Dubai project. It is here that the adoption of these symbols acquires an almost subversive quality – undermining the very cultures from which they are taken, recasting them in a new context and thus suggesting that Dubai has become the 'new' centre for the 'new' Middle East. I discussed the degree to which this rhetoric is actually used in academic circles in the beginning of this chapter, exemplified by the writings of Abdulkhaleq Abdullah, but such language is also used by local developers. For instance, a Dubai Municipality official claimed in all seriousness that Egypt has the pyramids but 'does not know what to do with them'.[71] Dubai's answer is to construct them again and set them within a giant theme park.

9.11. The Madinat Jumeirah project. The Burj Al-Arab looms in the background.

Illustrating this *cultural plagiarism* is the Jumeirah Mosque. Built in the 1980s, it is part of Dubai's official tourist trail. Visitors being shown the sites in the city stop at this mosque. Yet curiously it is not based on any Gulf model, but is a copy of a mosque in Egypt (the Mursi Al Abbas in Alexandria, and other Mameluk style mosques). Tourists can be observed taking photographs alongside the building, which is portrayed as an authentic Dubai monument without any nod to its origins (figure 9.12). While irking some Egyptian officials who were actually seriously thinking about calling for copyright fees,[72] such adaptations do perhaps show the true ingenuity of the Dubai model. Copying symbols from other cultures is not a new phenomenon, it has been occurring throughout history. But perhaps the commercialization of this is what sets Dubai apart – for better or worse.

9.12. Tourists stopping for photographs alongside Dubai's Jumeirah mosque.

Conclusion: The *True* Dubai Model

'The flight from Cairo or Beirut to the Gulf states takes only a couple of hours, and in that time the traveler is transported to what might as well be a different planet. He leaves behind a world of decay and dulled tones and steps into one of glitter and dazzle.'

D. Lamb (2002) *The Arabs: Journeys Beyond the Mirage*, p. 34

The above is reflective of a popular viewpoint propagated by journalists and casual observers. Thomas Friedman, for example, proclaims in all seriousness that '... Dubai is precisely the sort of decent, modernizing model we should be trying to nurture in the Arab-Muslim world'.[73] Lee Smith, another journalist, compares Dubai to Baghdad during its Abbasid heyday, since the city has reincarnated the ideals of this ancient capital – openness, tolerance and curiosity. Furthermore, he declares that the 'Dubai model suggests how the Arab world might revive its historical role as a trade and communications center'. In that way 'the Arab world itself becomes a free zone, embracing not only liberal economic policies and new media technologies but eventually political and social reforms'. Finally, 'what's good for Dubai may in turn be good for the Arab world'.[74] The city, according to these viewpoints, should thus be groomed to become the centre for a new Middle East, moulded in the image of neoliberal agenda makers.

Along similar lines Ashfin Molavi argues in a 2007 article that 'Key "caravan posts" on the new Silk Road are regional economic "winners" or rising stars: Dubai, Beijing, Mumbai, Chennai, Tokyo, Doha, Kuala Lumpur, Singapore, Hong Kong, Riyadh, Shanghai, Abu Dhabi. The old Silk Road civilization centers such as Persia (Iran), the Levant (Lebanon, Syria, Jordan) and Mesopotamia (Iraq) lag behind'. Thus *'Dubai, it might be argued, is the unofficial Middle East capital of the new Silk Road* – a gathering place of capital, ideas and traders fueling the growth – and Iran, once a central force, is the sick man, albeit with enormous potential' (my emphasis).[75]

Dubai is seemingly becoming a centre of, and model for, urbanism in the Arab world. Furthermore, a number of events suggest that Dubai is becoming the centre of a 'new' Middle East.[76] Other cities are influenced as well. Some observers have noted that Beirut has been overshadowed by Dubai, which has in effect assumed the Lebanese capital's previous mantle as a 'gateway to the East'. Thus 'the legend of the Lebanese gateway to the Middle East, if it were ever based on anything solid, has now attained the status of myth. Economically, at least, the gateway is lying in ruins'.[77] The recent wars in Lebanon, particularly the Israeli offensive of 2006, only strengthen Dubai's position. The influence is not, however, restricted to traditional Middle Eastern centres, as I have argued in this chapter, but extends to Gulf cities as well. Qatar is at the present constructing an island named 'the Pearl,' which is modelled on the Palm Islands in Dubai. Similar developments are occurring in Kuwait (City of Silk) and in Muscat (The Blue City).

As Friedman and others argue, Dubai has thus become, for better or worse, a model for cities throughout the Arab world. But, and this is a critical question, is there any harm in this? It could be argued that such intensification of social divisions, caused by adapting Gulf-based modes of urbanism may lead to a sense of injustice and hence may drive some residents towards acts of resistance (see Chapter 2 where I discuss this notion of inequality in the Arab world in more detail).

I am not suggesting that there is a direct correlation between terrorism and Emaar constructing megaprojects in Cairo and other cities. But places like Dubai lend themselves to this kind of *tabula rasa* development – and thus are quite successful for (almost) everyone. 'Everyone' here would refer primarily to the city's high-income population, investors, an assortment of tourists and world millionaires. The global financial crisis has, however, questioned even this degree of success (see Chapter 1). Of more concern is the juxtaposition of slums with luxury developments which is not yet as characteristic of Dubai as it is of Amman and, especially, of Cairo. Megaprojects and enclaves of the 'new Dubai'-type are, nevertheless, inherently rife with *explosive* socio-political issues.

But does Dubai's 'mode of development' offer anything positive, any potential lessons? It may be more useful to argue that Dubai is a model for the Arab world not through its megaprojects, but because it accommodates multiple nationalities, a fact that may contribute to its unique response to globalizing conditions. I have shown this in the previous two chapters where I discussed the city's 'forgotten urban public spaces', which I have also termed 'transient sites'. These are the sites of the Hindu Temple and the Iranian Special Ustadi as well as the Karachi Darbar and Bombay fast food restaurants. Or its various gathering spaces located in the midst of its old *souqs* or along the Creek. The discourse on Dubai typically ignores these spaces by focusing instead on the megaprojects. However, as I noted, a form of informal urbanity is emerging which caters for a largely migrant and transient community. These new citizens of the global economy – one might call them 'the foot soldiers of globalization' – appropriate such public settings by connecting to the local while at the same time maintaining ties to their homelands. In that way vibrant settings are created in which one finds an intermingling of different nationalities supported by the structure of the built environment. This is – in my view – the true 'Dubai model' where the rest of the 'dysfunctional' and 'crumbling' Middle East may find some useful lessons.

Notes

1. http://www.udel.edu/communication/COMM418/begleite/globalagenda/readings/NYTFriedman020201.html. Accessed 5 January 2009.

2. See for example: Elliott, Larry (2008) 'Credit crisis: how it all began', *The Guardian*, 5 August. http://www.guardian.co.uk/business/2008/aug/05/northernrock.banking. Accessed 24 February 2009.

3. 'I am also often asked, "What are Dubai's political ambitions?" Well, here's my answer: We don't have political ambitions. We don't want to be a superpower or any other kind of political power. The whole region is over-politicized as it is. We don't see politics as our thing, we don't want it, we don't think this is the right thing to do.' (Al Maktoum, Mohamed bin Rashid (2008) 'Our Ambitions for the Middle East', *Wall Street Journal*, 12 January, p. A9)

4. Brooks, Rosa (2008) 'If Dubai sneezes, who gets a cold?', *Los Angeles Times*, 13 November. http://www.latimes.com/news/opinion/commentary/la-oe-brooks13-2008nov13,0,5513249.column. Accessed 2 December 2008.

5. *The Economist*, 27 May 2004. http://www.economist.com/business/displaystory.cfm?story_id=E1_NSDJNRN. Accessed 11 March 2009.

6. Elsheshtawy (2004, 2005, 2006 and forthcoming).

7. Barbados Travel Advisor (2008) 'The Dubaification of Barbados: Roads to riches or Faustian bargain', Barbados Travel Advisor (Blog). July 23. http://barbadostraveladvisor.blogspot.com/2008/07/dubaification-of-barbados-road-to.html. Accessed 2 December 2008.

8.   http://www.proventionconsortium.org/themes/default/pdfs/ProVention_News/ProVention News_Jul08.pdf. Accessed 2 December 2008.

9.   'Say no to "Dubaisation" of Indian cities, say experts', 5 February 2007. http://news.boloji.com/200702/01535.htm. Accessed 26 January 2009.

10.   Athanasiadis, Iason (2007) 'Istanbul's breakdancing gypsies', *World Politics Review*, 25 July. http://www.worldpoliticsreview.com/blog/blog.aspx?id=955. Accessed 2 December 2008.

11.   Yawar, Asad (2006) 'Viva Las Dubai? Does the UAE metropolis show the path to economic development', *Ohmynews*, 22 December. http://english.ohmynews.com/articleview/article_view.asp?no=336227&rel_no=1. Accessed 2 December 2008.

12.   Chan, Sewell (2008) 'Dispute fester over village playhouse's fate', *The New York Times*, 20 October. http://cityroom.blogs.nytimes.com/2008/10/20/dispute-festers-over-village-playhouses-fate/. Accessed 2 December 2008.

13.   *The Economist* (2006) 'Fake Parks: Dubai in America', *The Economist*, 13 July. http://www.economist.com/displaystory.cfm?story_id=E1_STGJVTD. Accessed 2 December 2008.

14.   Escobar, Pepe (2006) 'Dubai lives the post-oil Arab Dream', *Asia Times*, 7 June. http://www.atimes.com/atimes/Middle_East/HF07Ak01.html. Accessed 2 December 2008.

15.   *Ibid*.

16.   Abdullah, Abdul Khaleq (2007) 'Dubai model is a subject of study: the emirates development has sparked the curiosity of foreign researchers', *Gulf News*, 15 March, p. 10.

17.   Abdullah, Abdul Khaleq (2007) 'Halliburton's move is linked to oil', *Gulf News*, 22 March, p. 10.

18.   Abdullah, Abdul Khaleq (2008) 'A politically neutral city', *Gulf News*, 13 February, p. 13.

19.   'The city (Dubai) has a historical and cultural project which comes from an assumption of the emergence of a new economic center in the world within the next 50 years. This is the "world central" area. This area is currently being formed. Dubai is ahead of these developments and will not accept less than being the capital of this new financial region. This region consists of approximately 30 nations and holds more than a quarter of the world's population. It is located in the middle between western Europe and the US and eastern Japan. This geographic region is spread between Pakistan in the east and Morocco to the west. And from Turkey and the independent republics to the north, till middle and east Africa to the south. This is the vibrant region for Dubai's investment. Dubai has determined for itself this region and its investments have reached US$100bn in 2006. Leading these are five of its biggest companies: Dubai Holding; Emaar; Dubai Port; and Emirates Airlines and a telecommunications company. These are the companies that will lead Dubai from localism to globalism' (Abdullah, 2006b, p. 106).

20.   Yawar, Asad (2006) 'Viva Las Dubai? Does the UAE metropolis show the path to economic development?'. http://english.ohmynews.com/articleview/article_view.asp?no=336227&rel_no=1. Accessed 11 March 2009.

21.   Lopez-Claros, A. and Schwab, K. (2005) *The Arab World Competitiveness Report 2005* (World Economic Forum). Basingstoke: Palgrave Macmillan.

22.   Madar Research Special (2003) *Dubai Knowledge Economy: 2003–2008*. Dubai: Madar Research Group.

23.   http://www.lboro.ac.uk/gawc. Accessed 6 September 2006.

24.   This whole notion of ranking according to a set of criteria has received quite considerable criticism due to its Western bias. For a more detailed analysis see e.g. Benton-Short *et al*. (2005); Robinson (2002). Also Peter-Smith (2001). And of particular importance is Ley (2004) writing about transnationalism.

25.   Urban Land Institute (2008) 'ULI Launches Global City Index Report: London, New York Still Rank As World Leaders, But Face Competition from Other Global Cities'. Press release 18 November.   http://www.uli.org/sitecore/content/ULI2Home/News/MediaCenter/PressReleases/2008/London%20NY%20Dialogue%202008.aspx. Accessed 2 December 2008.

26. The Global Cities Index, 2008. http://www.foreignpolicy.com/story/cms.php?story_id=4509 &page=1. Accessed 24 February 2009.

27. Walid Tamara (2007) 'The giant is awake ... and moving ahead', *Arabian Business*, 8 July. http:/ /www.arabianbusiness.com/index.php?option=com_content&view=article&id=495808. Accessed 18 July 2007.

28. *The Economist* (2007) 'A road that is not straight', *The Economist*, 4 August, p. 35.

29. Oweis, Khaled Yacoub (2007) 'Syria's opening up for investment', *Gulf News*, 28 April, p. 48.

30. Marques, Joseph (2007) 'Prosperity awaits', *Gulf News*, Weekend Supplement, 11 May, p. 9.

31. El-Fasher, Juba (2006) 'Glittering towers in a war zone', *The Economist*, 7 December. http: //www.economist.com/world/displaystory.cfm?story_id=8380843. Accessed 19 September 2007.

32. Reuters (2007) 'Dubai to invest $5 billion in Istanbul', *Arabian Business*, 21 March. http: //www.arabianbusiness.com. Accessed 23 March 2007.

33. Aris, G. (2007) 'Provinces should look to Dubai for inspiration; economic miracle can be mirrored in Iraq', *Gulf News*, 11 January, p. 43.

34. Gulf News (2007) 'Emaar studies proposals for massive Libyan project', *Gulf News*, 18 June, p. 42.

35. The project is developed by Dubai World subsidiary Istithmar PJSC, Kerzner International Holdings Limited, and a cluster of Moroccan Government and private investors. Zawya.com (2007) 'Work begins on Dubai World's new US$ 350 Million resort project in Morocco'. http: //zawya.com/printstory.cfm?storyid=ZAWYA20070625131920&l=131900070625. Accessed 24 February 2009.

36. Pfeiffer, Tom (2007) 'Uphill struggle for Gulf investors in N. Africa.', Reuters, 3 July. http: //africa.reuters.com. Accessed 6 July 2007.

37. Arabian Business (2006) 'The rise and rise of Emaar Properties', *Arabian Business*, 23–29 July, pp. 34–39

38. Reuters (2007) 'Sama Dubai set for $14bn Tunisia deal', *Arabian Business*, 18 July. http: //www.arabianbusiness.com. Accessed 18 July 2007; and Bowman, Daniel (2007) 'Century City to create more than 100,000 jobs', *Arabian Business*, 8 August. http://www.arabianbusiness.com. Accessed 13 August 2007.

39. Byrne, Eileen (2007) 'Morocco open for business', *Gulf News*, 10 August, p. 37.

40. Mernin, Andrew (2007) 'Amman on a mission', *Arabian Business*, 18 February. http://www. arabianbusiness.com. Accessed 19 February 2007.

41. Thekepat, Shiva Kumar (2007) 'Recreating the future', *Friday* (Gulf News Supplement), 22 June, pp. 44–47.

42. Mathiason, Nick (2006) 'Dubai clinches deal to build new port on Thames', *Observer*, 13 August. http://observer.guardian.co.uk. Accessed 24 August 2006.

43. Branton, Peter (2007) 'Dubai finally signs SmartCity Kochi deal', *Arabian Business*, 14 May. http://www.arabianbusiness.com. Accessed 15 May 2007.

44. For more on this see: Hope, Bradley (2008) 'Ruwaad project comes under protest', *The National*, 7 December, p. 13. Also, in a major one-page article: Hope, Bradley (2008) 'Memories of forced settlements', *The National*, 21 December, p. 6.

45. Roberts, Lynne (2007) 'Emaar MGF to build India's largest mall', *Arabian Business*, 25 June. http://www.arabianbusiness.com. Accessed 21 June 2007.

46. Quoted in Ali, Tariq (2006) 'Pramoedya Ananta Toer: Obituary', *The Independent*, 2 May. http://www.independent.co.uk/news/obituaries/pramoedya-ananta-toer-476426.html. Accessed 24 February 2009.

47. This argument is developed in more detail in Elsheshtawy (2006).

48. Williams, Raymond (undated) 'Egypt'. *International Affairs Forum-Response*. http://www.ia-forum. org/Popup/ResponseReadMore.cfm?ResponseID=34. Accessed 4 April 2007.

49. For a more detailed discussion of the term 'Dubaization' see Elsheshtawy (2005).

50. http://www.smart-villages.com/default.asp?action=article&ID=27. Accessed 6 September 2006.

51. In Cairo I was stopped by security officials and taken to the head of security. After a series of questions and after I told him that I am working in the UAE as a University Professor he agreed to my picture taking – mostly because his son is an architect working in Dubai and he wanted him to pursue graduate studies. As a result I was able to continue my pursuit in Cairo's Smart City.

52. Information supplied by the respective centres' websites. Dubai Internet City: http://www.dubaiinternetcity.com/partner_directory/. Smart Village: http://www.smart-villages.com/default.asp?action=article&ID=31. Accessed 1 September 2006.

53. Information obtained from the American Chamber of Commerce in Egypt. http://www.amcham.org.eg/operation/committees/Committees98Brief.asp. Accessed 6 September 2006.

54. For a celebratory and uncritical account of DIC's success story see Sampler and Eigner (2003).

55. Postlewaite, S. (2001) 'FDI still apparent: Gulf investors stay despite capital flight', *Business Monthly Online*, November. http://www.amcham.org.eg/Publications/BusinessMonthly/December%2001/Followup(InvestmentGoesOn).asp}. Accessed 23 September 2005.

56. 'Starbucks made its debut into the Egyptian market end of December 2006, when it opened its first outlet in City Center, Nasr City. It later opened 10 more venues across Egypt in Cairo Airport, CityStars, Heliopolis, Maadi, Nile City Mall, Carrefour Alexandria, San Stefano Grand Plaza, and Sharm El-Sheikh', *Daily News Egypt*, 22 April 2008. http://www.thedailynewsegypt.com/article.aspx?ArticleID=13364. Accessed 4 January 2009.

57. Rashdan, H. (2003) 'Egypt Gets Hyper', *Al-Ahram Weekly Online*, 30 January–5 February.

58. Hinde, T. (2003) 'Interview', *Business Today Online*, February.

59. *Ibid*.

60. For an interesting analysis of shopping mall culture in Cairo see, Abaza (2006).

61. Malik, Talal (2007) 'City Centre malls planned for Egypt', *Arabian Business*, 9 August. http://www.arabianbusiness.com. Accessed 13 August 2007.

62. Khaleej Times (2007) 'Emaar Misr launches largest mall in Egypt', *Khaleej Times*, 12 July. http://www.khaleejtimes.com. Accessed 12 July 2007.

63. See Adham (2004) for a thorough discussion of this as well as an elaboration on one particular case – Dreamland.

64. Press release by Emaar, August 2005. http://www.emaar.com/index.aspx?page=press-release-details&id=647. Accessed 14 February 2009.

65. Ditcham, R. (2007) 'Emaar to buy out Egyptian firm', *Gulf News*, 14 March, p. 37.

66. Corder, Roy (2007) 'Emaar Misr redevelops birthplace of Pyramids', *Arabian Business*, 3 July. http://www.arabianbusiness.com. Accessed 18 July 2007.

67. *Gulf News* (2007) 'Emaar expands portfolio in Egyptian market', *Gulf News*, 19 April, p. 42.

68. Salama, Salama (2007) 'Gated Communities', *Al Ahram Weekly*, 9–15 August, no. 857. http://weekly.ahram.org.eg, Accessed 17 August 2007.

69. In another article written in the daily *Al Ahram*, he offers a searing indictment of these neoliberal economic policies. Salama, Salama A. (2007) 'Thaqafet Al Fashkhara (The culture of showing off)', *Al-Ahram*, 29 July.

70. Guweida writes: 'I have attempted to understand this contradiction … between an amazing success in establishing a basic infrastructure in Sharm Al-Shaikh and an utter failure in combating the problem of informal settlements where more than 15 million Egyptians live; between luxurious and beautiful resorts in Qatamiy'ya, and poverty ridden disasters in Qala'at Al-Kabash… Egypt is divided into two parts with no third party in between. A few whom the government has provided with all necessary richness, wealth, consumption and opportunities and an impoverished majority

looking amidst this darkness for a guiding light'. Goweda, Farouq (2007). *Tanqudat Masriy'ya (Egyptian contradictions)*, *Al-Ahram*, 10 July, p. 40.

71.   Here is the full quote: 'In 2002, the Egyptians got 5.3 million tourists and we got 4.7 million. They have the pyramids, and they do nothing with them. Can you imagine what we'd do with the pyramids?'. (Cited in Lee, S. (2004) 'The Road to Tech Mecca', *Wired Magazine*. http://www.wired.com/wired/archive/12.07/dubai.html. Accessed 6 September 2006).

72.   McCarthy, Rory (2007) 'Egypt to copyright the pyramids and antiquities', *The Guardian*, 27 December. http://www.guardian.co.uk/world/2007/dec/27/egypt.artnews. Accessed 21 January 2009.

73.   Friedman, T. (2006) 'Dubai and dunces', *New York Times*, 15 March. http://select.nytimes.com/2006/03/15/opinion/15friedman.html. Accessed 6 September 2006.

74.   Smith, L. (2006) 'The Road to Tech Mecca', *Wired Magazine*. http://www.wired.com/wired/12.07/dubai_pr.html. Accessed 6 September 2006.

75.   Molavi, Ashfin (2007) The new Silk Road. *Washington Post*, 9 April.

76.   See, for example, the following articles: *The Economist* (2004) 'Arabia's field of dreams', 27 May, pp. 61–63; *Gulf News*, 2 April 2004, p. 40; *Gulf News*, 4 January 2004, p. 38. In addition, the last few years have witnessed a plethora of newspaper articles, attempting to describe and analyse this newly emerging city. For example, the well-known German newsmagazine *Der Spiegel* included an article titled 'The Gold of the new Pharaohs' in which it was noted – with alarm – that Dubai would like to become the most modern city in the world, a metropolis which will merge East with West – Dubai as a mixture of Singapore, Seattle, and Saint Tropez (*Spiegel Special*, 2003, pp. 126–129).

77.   Champion, D. (2004) 'Does the gateway to the Middle East lie in ruins? Golden days seem far away', *The Daily Star Online* 10 February. http://www.dailystar.com.lb. Accessed 21 September 2005.

Bibliography

Abaza, Mona (2006) *The Changing Consumer of Modern Egypt. Cairo's Urban Reshaping*. Cairo: AUC Press.

Abdullah, Abdulkhaleq (2006*a*) Dubai: Rihlat Madina Arabiya min Al Mahaliya ila Al Alamia (Dubai: an Arab city journey from localism to globalism). *Al-Mustaqbal Al-Arabi (The Arab Future)*, January, No. 323, pp. 57–84.

Abdullah, Abdulkhaleq (2006*b*) Dubai Rihlat Madina Arabiya min Al Mahaliya ila Al Alamia – Munaqashit Ta'aliq Samir Amin (Dubai: an Arab city journey from localism to globalism – discussing Samir Amin's commentary). *Al-Mustaqbal Al-Arabi (The Arab Future)*, August, No. 330, pp. 100–106.

Abu-Lughod, Janet (1995) Comparing Chicago, New York and Los Angeles: testing some world cities hypotheses, in Knox, P. and Taylor, P. (eds.) *World Cities in a World System*. Cambridge: Cambridge University Press.

Adorno, Theodor (1991) *The Culture Industry*. London: Routledge.

Adham, Khaled (2004) Cairo's urban déjà vu: globalization and urban fantasies, in Elsheshtawy, Yasser (ed.) *Planning Middle Eastern Cities*. London: Routledge, pp. 134–168.

Adham, Khaled (2008) Rediscovering the island: Doha's urbanity from pearls to spectacle, in Elsheshtawy, Yasser (ed.) *The Evolving Arab City*. London: Routledge, 218–257.

Al-Maktoum, Mohammed bin Rashid (2006) *My Vision – Challenges in the Race for the Excellence* (in Arabic). Dubai: Motivate.

Al-Rasheed, Madawi (ed.) (2005) Transnational Connections and the Arab Gulf. London: Routledge.

Al-Sayegh, Fatma (1998) Merchants' role in a changing society: the case of Dubai, 1900–90. *Middle Eastern Studies*, **34**(1), pp. 87–102.

Ali, Mir M. and Moon, Kyoung Sun (2007) Structural developments in tall buildings: current trends and future prospects. *Architectural Science Review*, **50**(3), pp. 205–223.

AlSayyad, Nezar (2001) *Hybrid Urbanism: On the Identity Discourse and the Built Environment*. New York: Praeger.

AlShafeei, Salem (1997) The Spatial Implications of Urban Land Policies in Dubai City. Unpublished Report, Dubai Municipality.

Amin, Samir (2006) Munaqashit maqalit Abdulkhaleq Abdullah: Dubai Rihlat Madina Arabiya min Al Mahaliya ila Al Alamia. (Discussion of Abdul Khaleq Abdullah's article – Dubai: an Arab city's journey from localism to globalism.) *Al-Mustaqbal Al-Arabi (The Arab Future)*, June, No. 328, pp. 157–160.

Amin, Ash and Graham, Stephen (1997) The ordinary city. *Transactions of the Institute of British Geographers*, **22**(4), pp. 411–429.

Anderson, Benedict (1998) *The Spectre of Comparisons: Nationalism, Southeast Asia, and the World*. London: Verso.

Appadurai, Arjun (1996) *Modernity at Large: Cultural Dimensions of Globalization*. Minneapolis, MN: University of Minnesota Press.

Augé, Marc (1995) *Non-Places: An Introduction to the Anthropology of Supermodernity*. London: Verso.

Bargach, Jamila (2008) Rabat: from capital to global metropolis, in Elsheshtawy, Yasser (ed.) *The Evolving Arab City*. London: Routledge, pp. 99–117.

Baudrillard, Jean (1972) *For a Critique of the Political Economy of the Sign* (Translated and introduced by Charles Levin). St. Louis, MO: Telos Press.

Baudrillard, Jean (1995) *Simulacrum and Simulation* (translated by Sheila Glaser). Ann Arbor, MI: University of Michigan Press.

Beaverstock, Jonathan V., Smith, Richard G. and Taylor, Peter J. (2000) World city network: a new meta-geography? *Annals of Association of American Geographers*, **90**(1), pp. 123–134.

Benjamin, Walter (1999) *The Arcades Project*. Cambridge, MA: The Belknap Press of Harvard University.

Benton-Short, Lisa, Price, Marie D. and Friedman, Samantha (2005) Globalization from below: the ranking of global immigrant cities. *International Journal of Urban and Regional Research*, **29**(4), pp. 945–959.

Berner, E. and Korff, R. (1995) Globalization and local resistance: the creation of localities in Manila and Bangkok. *International Journal of Urban and Regional Research*, **19**(2), pp. 208–222.

Bhabha, Homi (2004) *The Location of Culture*. London: Routledge.

Borges, Jorge Luis and Casares, Adolfo Bioy (1935, 1975) 'Of Exactitude in Science', from *Travels of Praiseworthy Men* (1658) by J.A. Suarez Miranda, in Borges, J.L. *A Universal History of Infamy*. London: Penguin.

Brenner, Neil and Kiel, Roger (2006) Editors' introduction: global city theory in retrospect and prospect, in Brenner, Neil and Kiel, Roger (eds.)*The Global Cities Reader*. London: Routledge.

Buck, Ian, Gordon, Ian, Hall, Peter, Harloe, Michael and Kleinman, Mark (2002) *Working Capital: Life and Labour in Contemporary London*. London: Routledge.

Bunnell, Tim G. (1999) Views from above and below: the Petronas Twin Towers and/in contesting visions of development in contemporary Malaysia. *Singapore Journal of Tropical Geography*, **20**(1), pp. 1–23.

Burdett, Anita L.O. (ed.) (2000) *Records of Dubai, 1761–1960*. Slough: Cambridge Archive Editions.

Caldeira, Teresa (2001) *City of Walls: Crime, Segregation, and Citizenship in São Paulo*. Berkeley, CA: University of California Press.

Calhoun, Craig J. (2002) The class consciousness of frequent travelers: toward a critique of actually existing cosmopolitanism. *South Atlantic Quarterly*, **101**(4), pp. 869–897.

Calvino, Italo (1974, 1997) *Invisible Cities* (translated by William Weaver). London: Vintage.

Castells, Manuel (2000) *The Rise of the Network Society*, 2nd ed. Oxford: Wiley Blackwell.

Charney, Igal (2005) The politics of design: architecture, tall buildings and the skyline of central London. *Area*, **39**(2), pp. 195–205.

Chase, John, Kaliski, John and Crawford, Margaret (eds.) (1999) *Everyday Urbanism*. New York: Monacelli.

Cheah, Pheng (1998) Given culture: rethinking cosmopolitan freedom in trans-nationalism, Cheah, Pheng and Robbins, Bruce (eds.) *Cosmopolitics: Thinking and Feeling Beyond the Nation*. Minneapolis, MN: University of Minnesota, pp. 290–328.

Cheah, Pheng and Robbins, Bruce (eds.) (1998**)** *Cosmopolitics: Thinking and Feeling Beyond the Nation*. Minneapolis, MN: University of Minnesota Press.

Chew, Khuan and Schmitt, Uschi (2000) *1001 Nights at the Burj al Arab*. Dubai: ABC Millennium.

Codrai, Ronald (1956) Desert Sheikdoms of Arabia's Pirate Coast: in Trucial Oman's Principalities, cradled by seas of sand and salt, camels, dates and pearls support a fiercely independent people. *National Geographic*, July, pp. 65–104.

Coles, Anne and Jackson, Peter (2007) *Windtower: Houses of the Bastak*. London: Stacey International.

Conrad, Joseph (1900) *Lord Jim*. London.

Crawford, Margaret (1992, 2002) The world in a shopping mall, in Borden, Iain, Hall, Tim and Miles, Malcolm (eds.) *The City Cultures Reader*, 2nd ed. London. New York: Routledge, pp. 124–140.

Crawford, Margaret (1999) Introduction, in Chase, John, Kaliski, John and Crawford, Margaret (eds.) *Everyday Urbanism*. New York: Monacelli.

Cross, T. (2006) There gores the neighbourhood: how London has changed in the past 108 years – and how it hasn't. *The Economist*, 6 May, pp. 35–36.

Daher, Rami Farouk (2008) Amman: disguised genealogy and recent urban restructuring and neoliberal threats, in Elsheshtawy, Yasser (ed.) *The Evolving Arab City*. London: Routledge, pp. 37–68.

Davidson, Christopher M. (2005) *The United Arab Emirates: A Study in Survival*. Boulder, CO: Lynne Reiner.

Davidson, Christopher M. (2008) *Dubai: The Vulnerability of Success*. New York: Columbia University Press.

Davis, Mike (2005) Dubai: sinister paradise: does the road to the future end at Dubai? http://www.tomdispatch.com/post/5807/mike_davis_on_a_paradise_built_on_oil. Accessed 27 February 2009.

Davis, Mike and Monk, Daniel (2008) *Evil Paradises: Dreamworlds of Neoliberalism*. New York: The New Press.

de Certeau, Michel (1984) *The Practice of Everyday Life*. Berkeley, CA: University of California Press.

Debord, Guy (1967, 1995) *The Society of Spectacle*. Brooklyn, NY: Zone Books.

Debord, Guy (1988, 1998) *Comments on the Society of Spectacle*. London: Verso.

Didion, Joan (1979) *The White Album*. New York: Farrer, Straus and Giroux.

Dubai Municipality (1995) *Structure Plan for the Dubai Urban Area (1993–2012)*. Report prepared by Parsons Harland Bartholomew & Associates, Inc.

Edensor, Tim (1998) The culture of the Indian street, in Fyfe, N. (ed.) *The Image of the Street*. London: Routledge with Uma Kothari.

Ehrenreich, Barbara and Hochschild, Arlie R. (2002) *Global Woman: Nannies, Maids and Sex Workers in the New Economy*. New York: Henry Holt.

Elsheshtawy, Yasser (2004) Redrawing boundaries: Dubai, an emerging global city, in Elsheshtawy, Yasser (ed.) *Planning Middle Eastern Cities*. London: Routledge, pp. 169–199.

Elsheshtawy, Yasser (2005) Reversing Influences: The Dubaization of Cairo. Paper presented at the XXII World Congress of Architecture of the UIA, 'Cities: Grand Bazaar of Architects', Istanbul.

Elsheshtawy, Yasser (2006) From Dubai to Cairo: competing global cities, models and shifting centers of influence, in Singerman, Diane and Amar, Paul (eds.) *Cairo Cosmopolitan: Politics, Culture and Urban Space in the New Middle East*. Cairo: AUC Press.

Elsheshtawy, Yasser (2008a) Cities of sand and fog: Abu Dhabi's global ambitions, in Elsheshtawy, Yasser (ed.) *The Evolving Arab City* London: Routledge, pp. 258–304.

Elsheshtawy, Yasser (2008b) The great divide: struggling and emerging cities in the Arab world, in Elsheshtawy, Yasser (ed.) *The Evolving Arab City*. London: Routledge, pp. 1–26.

Elsheshtawy, Yasser (forthcoming, 2009) The global and the everyday: situating the Dubai spectacle. in Kanna, Ahmed (ed.) *The Superlative City Dubai and the Urban Condition in the Early Twenty-First Century*. Cambridge, MA: Harvard University Press.

Fainstein, Susan (2001) *The City Builders: Property, Politics and Planning in New York and London*, 2nd ed. Kansas City, KS: University of Kansas Press.

Frampton, Kenneth and Khan, Hassan Uddin (2000) *World Architecture 1900–2000: A Critical Mosaic. The Middle East*. Vienna: Springer.

Friedmann, John (1986) The world city hypothesis. *Development and Change*, **17**(1), pp. 69–83.

Friedmann, John and Wolff, Gerald (1982) World city formation: an agenda for research and action. *International Journal of Urban and Regional Research*, **6**(3), pp. 309–344.

Fuccaro, Nelida (2001) Urban studies of the Gulf: visions of the city. *Bulletin of the Middle East Studies Association of North America*, **35**(2), pp. 175–188.

Gabriel, Erhard F. (1987) *The Dubai Handbook*. Ahrensburg: Institute for Applied Economic Geography.

Galassi, Peter *et al.* (2006) *Henri Cartier-Bresson: The Man, The Image & The World: A Retrospective*. London: Thames & Hudson.

Gardner, Andrew (2008) Strategic transnationalism: the Indian diasporic elite in contemporary Bahrain. *City & Society*, **20**(1), pp. 54–78.

Gehl, Jan (1987) *Life between Buildings: Using Public Spaces*. New York: Van Nostrand Reinhold.

Graham, Stephen and Marvin, Simon (2001) *Splintering Urbanism: Networked Infrastructures, Technological Mobilities and the Urban Condition*. London: Routledge.

Gugler, Josef (2004) *World Cities beyond the West: Globalization, Development and Inequality*. Cambridge: Cambridge University Press.

Haila, Anne (1997) The neglected builder of global cities, in Källtorp, O., Elander, I., Ericsson, O. and Franzén, M. (eds.) *Cities in Transformation: Transformation in Cities*. Aldershot: Avebury.

Hannerz, Ulf (1991) *Cultural Complexity*. New York: Columbia University Press.

Harvey, David (1989) *The Condition of Postmodernity*. Oxford: Blackwell.

Harvey, David (2006) *Spaces of Global Capitalism*. London: Verso.

Haughton, Graham (1999) Environmental justice and the sustainable city. *Journal of Planning Education and Research*, **18**(3), pp. 233–243.

Hazbun, Waleed (2008) *Beaches, Ruins, Resorts: The Politics of Tourism in the Arab World*. Minneapolis, MN: University of Minnesota Press.

Headley, Lela (1958) *Give Me the World*. New York: Simon and Schuster.

Heards-Bey, Frauke (1982) *From Trucial States to United Arab Emirates*. London: Longman.

Held, David, McGrew, Anthony, Goldblatt, David and Perraton, Jonathan (1999) *Global Transformations*. Cambridge: Polity Press.

Hirst, Paul and Thompson, Grahame (1996) Globalization: a necessary myth? in Hirst, P. and Thompson, G. (eds.) *Globalization in Question*. Cambridge: Polity Press, pp. 1–17.

Human Rights Watch (2006) *Building Towers, Cheating Workers: Exploitation of Migrant Construction Workers in the United Arab Emirates*. New York: Human Rights Watch.

Jackson, Peter, Crang, Philip and Dwyer, Claire (eds.) (2004) *Transnational Spaces*. London: Routledge.

Jacobs, Jane M. (1996) *Edge of Empire: Postcolonialism and the City*. London: Routledge.

Jumeno, Mattias (2004) Let's build a palm island: playfulness in complex times, in Sheller, M. and Urry, J. (eds.) *Tourism Mobilities: Places to Play, Places in Play*. London: Routledge.

Kanna, Ahmed (2005) The 'state philosophical' in the 'land without philosophy': shopping malls, interior cities, and the image of utopia in Dubai. *Traditional Dwellings and Settlements Review*, **16**(2), pp. 59–73.

Kazim, Aqil (2000) *The United Arab Emirates AD600 to the Present*. Dubai: Gulf Book Center.

Kelley, Kevin Ervin (2005) Architecture for sale(s): an unabashed apologia, in Saunders William S. (ed.) *Commodification and Spectacle in Architecture*. Minneapolis, MN: University of Minnesota Press.

Khalaf, Suleyman and Alkobaisi, Saad (1999) Migrants' strategies of coping and patterns of accommodation in the oil-rich Gulf societies: evidence from the UAE. *British Journal of Middle Eastern Studies*, **26**(2), pp. 271–298.

King, Anthony D. (1990*a*) *Global Cities*. London: Routledge.

King, Anthony D. (1990*b*) *Urbanism, Colonialism and the World Economy*. London: Routledge.

King, Anthony D. (2004) *Spaces of Global Cultures*. London: Routledge.

Lamb, David (2002) *The Arabs: Journeys Beyond the Mirage*, revised edition. London: Vintage.

Lamb, Sarah (2002) Intimacy in a transnational era: the remaking of aging among Indian Americans. *Diaspora*, **11**(3), pp. 299–330.

Lawrence, Andrew (1999) *The Skyscraper Index: Faulty Towers*. Property Report. London/Frankfurt: Dresdner Kleinwort Wasserstein Research.

Lee, Leo Ou-fan (1999) *Shanghai Modern: The Flowering of a New Urban Culture in China*. Cambridge, MA: Harvard University Press.

Lefebvre, Henri (1971) *Everyday Life in the Modern World*. New York: Harper and Row.

Lefebvre, Henri (1972) *Die Revolution der Städte*. Munich: Munich Syndicat.

Lefebvre, Henri (1974, 1991) *The Production of Space* (translated by Donald Nicholson-Smith). Oxford: Blackwell.

Lehrer, Ute (2006) Willing the global city: Berlin's cultural strategies of interurban competition after 1989, in Brenner, N. and Keil, R. (eds.) *The Global City Reader*. London: Routledge.

Leonard, Karen (2007) *Locating Home*. Stanford, CA: Stanford University Press.

Ley, David (2004) Transnational spaces and everyday lives. *Transactions of the Institute of British Geographers*, **29**(2), pp. 151–164.

Lienhardt, Peter (2001) *Sheikhdoms of Eastern Arabia* (edited by Al-Shahi, Ahmed). Basingstoke: Palgrave Macmillan.

Lopez-Claros, Augusto and Schwab, Klaus (2005) *The Arab World Competitiveness Report 2005* (World Economic Forum). Basingstoke: Palgrave Macmillan.

Madanipour, Ali (1998) *Tehran: The Making of a Metropolis*. Chicester: Wiley.

Magnusson, Warren (1996) *The Search for Political Space: Globalization, Social Movements, and the Urban Political Experience*. Toronto: University of Toronto Press.

Mahgoub, Yasser (2008) Kuwait: learning from a globalized city, in Elsheshtawy, Yasser (ed.) *The Evolving Arab City*. London: Routledge, pp. 152–183.

Marchal, Roland (2005) Dubai: Global city and transnational hub, in Al-Rasheed, Madawi (ed.) *Transnational Connections and the Arab Gulf*. London: Routledge.

Marcuse, Peter (2006) Space in the globalizing city, in Brenner, N. and Keil, R. (eds.) *The Global City Reader*. London: Routledge.

Marcuse, Peter and van Kempen, Ronald (2000) *Globalizing Cities: A New Spatial Order*. Oxford: Blackwell.

McBride, Edward (2000) Burj Al Arab. *Architecture*, **89**(8), pp. 116–127.

Miles, Malcolm, Hall, Tim and Borden, Iain (2004) Introduction to Part 6, in Miles *et al.* (eds.) *The City Cultures Reader*, 2nd ed. London: Routledge.

Mitchell, Katharyne (1997) Different diasporas and the hype of hybridity. *Environment and Planning D: Society and Space*, **15**(5) pp. 533–553.

Munif, Abd al-Rahman (1988) *Cities of Salt* (translated by Peter Theroux). London: Vintage.

Nagy, Sharon (2006) Making room for migrants, making sense of difference: spatial and ideological expressions of social diversity in urban Qatar. *Urban Studies*, **43**(1), pp. 119–137.

Newman, Peter and Thornley, Andrew (2005) *Planning World Cities: Globalisation and Urban Politics*. Basingstoke: Palgrave Macmillan.

Oldenburg, Ray (1999) *Celebrating the Third Place: Inspiring Stories about the 'Great Good Places' at the Heart of Our Communities*. New York: Marlowe & Co.

Oxford Business Group (2006) Construction and Real Estate. *Dubai Report*. Dubai: OBG.

Packard, Vance (1957) *The Hidden Persuaders*. New York: Pocket Books.

Pandey, Vishai (2008) How sustainable is Dubai? *Urban Land, Special Report: Building Green*. Washington DC: Urban Land Institute.

Peter Smith, Michael (2001) *Transnational Urbanism: Locating Globalization*. Oxford: Blackwell.

Peter Smith, Michael (2005) Transnational urbanism revisited. *Journal of Ethnic and Migration Studies*, **31**(2), pp. 235–244.

Poynor, Rick (2005) Hyphenation nation: blurred forms for a blurred world, in Saunders, William (ed.) (2005) *Commodification and Spectacle in Architecture*. Minneapolis, MN: University of Minnesota Press.

Raban, Jonathan (1979) *Arabia: Journey through the Labyrinth*. New York: Simon and Schuster.

Rapoport, Amos (1990) *Meaning of the Built Environment. A Nonverbal Communications Approach*. Tucson, AZ: Arizona University Press.

Rees, William (1990) *Sustainable Development and the Biosphere: Concepts and Principles*. Woodbridge. CT: Teilhard Studies Papers.

Robinson, Jennifer (2002) Global and world cities. A view from off the map. *International Journal of Urban and Regional Research*, **26**(3), pp. 531–554.

Rushdie, Salman (1991) *Imaginary Homelands: Essays and Criticism 1981–1991*. Cambridge: Granta.

Sachs, Wolfgang *et al.* (1998) *Greening the North: A Post-Industrial Blueprint for Ecology and Equity*. London: Zed Books.

Sampler, Jeffery and Eigner, Saeb (2003) *Sand to Silicon: Achieving Rapid Growth Lessons from Dubai*. London: Profile.

Sassen, Saskia (2001) *The Global City: London, New York, Tokyo*. Princeton, NJ: Princeton University Press.

Saunders, William (ed.) (2005) *Commodification and Spectacle in Architecture*. Minneapolis, MN: University of Minnesota Press.

Sennett, Richard (1977) *The Fall of Public Man*. New York: Knopf.

Sennett, Richard (2007) The open city, in Burdett, Ricky and Sudjic, Deyan (eds.) *The Endless City*. London: Phaidon, pp. 290–297.

Sennett, Richard (2008) *The Uses of Disorder: Personal Identity and City Life*. London: Yale University Press.

Smith, Alan (1991) *Creating a World Economy: Merchant Capital, Colonialism, and World Trade, 1400–1852*. Boulder, CO: Westview Press.

Soja, Edward W. (2000) *Postmetropolis: Critical Studies of Cities and Regions*. Oxford: Blackwell.

The Economist (2007) A Special Report on Cities: The World Goes to Town. *The Economist*, 5 May.

Thesiger, Wilfred (1959) *Arabian Sands*. London: Dutton.

Thornton, Mark (2005) Skyscrapers and business cycles. *Quarterly Journal of Austrian Economics*, **8**(1), pp. 51–74.

Traub, James (2004) *The Devil's Playground: A Century of Pleasure and Profit in Times Square*. New York: Random House.

UN- ESCWA (United Nations Economic and Social Commission for Western Asia) (2000) *Health and Millennium Development Goals in the ESCWA Region*. http://www.escwa.un.org/information/publications/edit/upload/scu-07-tp2-e.pdf.

UN-Habitat (2001) *Cities in A Globalizing World – Global Report on Human Settlements 2001*. http://www.unhsp.org/pmss/getPage.asp?page=bookView&book=1618. Accessed 3 January 2008.

UN-Habitat (2007) *The State of the World's Cities Report 2006/2007*. London: Earthscan.

United Nations Human Development Programme (1999) *United Nations Human Development Report 1999*. New York: United Nations.

United Nations Population Division (2002) *International Migration Report, 2002*. New York: United Nations.

United Nations Population Fund (2007) *State of the Word Population, 2007*. New York: UNFPA.

Urban Land Institute (2008) *Global City Index Report*. Washington DC: Urban Land Institute.

van Leeuwen, Thomas A.P. (1988) *The Skyward Trend of Thought: The Metaphysics of the American Skyscraper*. Cambridge, MA: MIT Press.

Vertovec, Steven (2005) Transnationalism, in Al-Rasheed, M. (ed.)*Transnational Connections and the Arab Gulf*. London: Routledge

Walsh, Katie (2006) 'Dad says I'm tied to a shooting star!' Grounding (research on) British expatriate belonging. *Area*, **38**(3), pp. 268–278.

Weiss, William (1976) *The Limits to Satisfaction*. Toronto: University of Toronto Press.

Wheeler, Julia and Thuysbaert, Paul (2005) *Telling Tales: An Oral History of Dubai*. Dubai: Explorer Publishing.

Whyte, William (1980) *The Social Life of Small Urban Spaces*. New York: Project for Public Spaces.

Willis, Carol (1995) *Form Follows Finance: Skyscrapers and Skylines in New York and Chicago*. New York: Princeton Architectural Press.

Wilson, Graeme (1999) *Father of Dubai: Sheikh Rashid bin Saeed Al-Maktoum*. Dubai: Media Prima.

World Commission on the Social Dimensions of Globalization (2004) *A Fair Globalization: Creating Opportunities for All*. Geneva: ILO.

Yeo, W. (2003) City as theatre. Singapore, state of distraction, in Bishop, R., Philips, J. and Yeo, W. (eds.) *Postcolonial Urbanismin South Asia Cities and Global Processes*. London: Routledge, pp. 245–262.

Yeoh, Brenda (1999) Global/globalizing cities. *Progress in Human Geography*, **23**(4), pp. 607–616.

Zachariah, K.C,. Prakash, B.A. and Irudaya Rajan, S. (2004) Indian workers in UAE: employment, wages and working conditions. *Economic and Political Weekly*, **36**(22), pp. 2227–2234.

Zukin, Sharon (2001) *Landscapes of Power: From Detroit to Disney World*. Berkeley, CA: University of California Press.

Index

Note: Figures are indicated by *italic page numbers*, notes by suffix 'n[ ]'